Colonel Thomas L. Kane

and the Mormons, 1846–1883

Edited by David J. Whittaker

BYU Studies
Provo, Utah

Prepared for publication by BYU Studies
Cover Image: Steel engraving of Thomas L. Kane in his Civil War uniform, by Atlantic Publishing & Engraving Co., N.Y., 9.5" x 12", L. Tom Perry Special Collections, Harold B. Lee Library Brigham Young University.

Distributed to the academic trade and libraries by
University of Utah Press, www.UofUpress.com.
© 2010 Brigham Young University. All rights reserved.

Opinions expressed in this publication are the opinions of the editors, and their views should not necessarily be attributed to The Church of Jesus Christ of Latter-day Saints, Brigham Young University, BYU Studies, or the University of Utah. No part of this book may be reprinted or reproduced or utilized in any form or by any electronic, digital, mechanical or other means, now known or hereafter invented, including photocopying and recording or in an information storage or retrieval system, without permission in writing from the publisher. To contact BYU Studies, write to 403 CB, Brigham Young University, PO Box 24098, Provo, Utah 84602, or visit http://byustudies.byu.edu.

Library of Congress Cataloging-in-Publication Data

Colonel Thomas L. Kane and the Mormons, 1846-1883 /
edited by David J. Whittaker.
    p. cm.
 Includes bibliographical references.
 ISBN 978-0-8425-2756-9 (paper back : alk. paper)
1. Kane, Thomas Leiper, 1822-1883. 2. Kane, Thomas Leiper, 1822-1883—Relations with Mormons. 3. Mormon Church—United States—History--19th century. 4. Mormons—West (U.S.)—History—19th century. 5. Utah Expedition (1857-1858) 6. Church of Jesus Christ of Latter-day Saints—History—19th century. I. Whittaker, David J. II. Title.

F826.K27C65 2010
289.3092--dc22

2009053512

Printed in the United States of America
10 9 8 7 6 5 4 3 2 1

CONTENTS

PREFACE 6

ARTICLES

Thomas L. Kane and Nineteenth-Century American Culture **12**
    Matthew J. Grow

"He Is Our Friend":
Thomas L. Kane and the Mormons in Exodus, 1846–1850 **36**
    Richard E. Bennett

Thomas L. Kane and
the Mormon Problem in National Politics **57**
    Thomas G. Alexander 39 pp

"Full of Courage": Thomas L. Kane,
The Utah War, and BYU's Kane Collection as Lodestone **89**
    William P. MacKinnon 26 pp

Tom and Bessie Kane and the Mormons **120**
    Edward A. Geary

Touring Polygamous Utah with Elizabeth W. Kane,
Winter 1872–1873 **158**
    Lowell C. (Ben) Bennion and Thomas Carter

"My Dear Friend": The Friendship and Correspondence of
Brigham Young and Thomas L. Kane **193**
    David J. Whittaker

REVIEW

"Liberty to the Downtrodden": Thomas L. Kane, Romantic Reformer
by Matthew J. Grow
    Reviewed by Charles S. Peterson **226**

BIBLIOGRAPHY **230**

INDEX **236**

List of Figures

Thomas L. Kane	10
Patriarch John Smith	12
Orson Hyde	12
Eleanor McComb Pratt	13
Thomas L. Kane Memorial Chapel	15
Ralph Waldo Emerson	16
Elisha Kent Kane	17
Horace Greeley	20
C. C. A. Christensen painting of Winter Quarters	34
Mormon Camps, 1846	36
Brigham Young, c. 1853	37
James K. Polk	40
Jesse Carter Little	41
Letter of introduction from Jessee C. Little	44
Letter from Indian Subagent R. B. Mitchell	46
Enlisting camp sketch, July 14, 1846	47
Another sketch from Thomas Kane's papers	47
Josiah Quincy	49
John M. Bernhisel	57
Almon Whiting Babbitt	57
Wilford Woodruff	58
Zachary Taylor	58
Millard Fillmore	58
George M. Dallas	58
Stephen A. Douglas	59
Truman Smith	60
Willard Richards	62
Zerubbabel Snow	62
Seth M. Blair	62
Joseph L. Heywood	62
Daniel Webster	63
Heber C. Kimball	64
Newel K. Whitney	64
Perry E. Brocchus	65
Jedediah M. Grant	71
James B. McKean	74
Robert N. Baskin	75
John Fitch Kinney	75
Ann Eliza Young	79
James Buchanan	89

Proclamation by the Governor	90
Albert Sidney Johnston	91
John B. Floyd	92
Winfield Scott	95
Letter from Brigham Young to Thomas L. Kane, May 8, 1858	100
Alfred Cumming	105
"To Col. Thomas L. Kane," by Eliza R. Snow	108–9
Elizabeth Dennistoun Wood Kane	116
Thomas L. Kane, photograph taken by Elizabeth W. Kane	116
John Kintzing Kane	118
William Wood	120
George Q. Cannon	124
Elizabeth Wood Kane at various ages	130
Elizabeth Wood Kane, May 1858	131
Female Medical College of Pennsylvania seal	133
Elizabeth W. Kane with son	136
William C. Staines	138
Brigham Young's Beehive and Lion houses, Salt Lake City	145
Elizabeth W. Kane, 1872–73	154
Thirteen Mormon towns visited by the Kanes	156
Brigham Young's touring party	157
House in Fillmore, c. 1900–4	160
Jacob and Mary Ware Gates's I-house in Bellevue, Utah	161
Samuel Pitchforth's Nephi, c. 1870	163
Pitchforth family house	164
East side of Main Street, Nephi	164
Samuel Pitchforth	166
Mary M. Pitchforth	166
Reconstructed drawing of the Pitchforth family house	167
Diagrammatic representation of the three main phases of nineteenth-century Mormon architecture	169
Conjectural floor plans of the Pitchforth family house	171
John Kienke	173
Sarah B. Kienke	173
Goldsbrough Inn	174
Mount Nebo from the southwest	175
Utah age structure, 1870	176
Properties of Nephi's plural families, c. 1870	178
Thomas L. Kane, c. 1861–64	191
Bucktail reunion	192
Kane mansion	193
Detail of Thomas L. Kane's patriarchal blessing	196
Thomas L. Kane, postmortem	199
Thomas L. Kane's tombstone	200
Title page from *The Mormons*	202
William I. Appleby to Thomas L. Kane, October 9, 1848	203
Title page from *Three Letters from the New York Herald*	207
Brigham Young, 1876	211

Preface

The L. Tom Perry Special Collections in the Harold B. Lee Library at Brigham Young University has been acquiring manuscripts relating to the life of Thomas Leiper Kane for many years. The focus of searching out and collecting these manuscripts has been to discover more about Kane's relationship with the Mormons from 1846 until his death in 1883. Over the years, items of significance have been catalogued in the Perry Special Collections' Mormon Americana collection. In 1996, the Lee Library was able to obtain a significant Kane family archive consisting of journals, scrapbooks, letters, and other manuscripts and photographs that, when combined with the university's existing Kane materials, for the first time allowed scholars an in-depth look at the life and work of this influential friend to the Latter-day Saints. These documents reveal important information about his family life, his service in the American Civil War, his business interests, and his political dealings. The documents also include an extensive collection of journals, scrapbooks, and correspondence belonging to Thomas's wife, Elizabeth Wood Kane.[1]

During the 2008–9 school years, staff at Perry Special Collections prepared a public exhibition of significant manuscripts focusing on Thomas Kane and his relationship with the Mormons. During the exhibition, the library sponsored a lecture series by prominent scholars on various aspects of Kane's interactions with the Latter-day Saints. These public lectures have been transformed into the essays that appear in this volume.

Thomas Kane (January 27, 1822–December 26, 1883) was born in Philadelphia, Pennsylvania, the second-oldest son of John K. Kane and Jane Duval Leiper. Thomas's father was well connected to the political and aristocratic powers of east coast America. He was a personal friend of U.S. presidents Andrew Jackson and James K. Polk, and these connections served his son Thomas well in his later attempts to defend the Latter-day Saints.

From 1840 to 1844, Thomas lived in England and France, where he caught the spirit of social reform and a broad religion of humanity. He was influenced by Auguste Comté, who seems to have encouraged his life's work of assisting those who were downtrodden. After returning to America in 1844, Thomas studied law. He was admitted to the Pennsylvania Bar in 1846 but was not interested in practicing as a lawyer. His early interest in politics led him to associate with his father's friends; it also taught him the value of newspapers and other publications in shaping popular opinion. After James K. Polk became president, John Kane was appointed attorney general of Pennsylvania and later a federal judge; for several years, Thomas worked as his father's law clerk.

Although he favored peace, Thomas Kane came to see the need for the United States to engage in a war with Mexico. He enlisted in the Pennsylvania militia as a private, and in 1846 the governor commissioned Kane as a lieutenant colonel in the state militia; thereafter he carried the title of Colonel Kane. Working for a variety of causes, he made friends with people like Horace Greeley and George Dallas, with whom he worked in the American Society for Promoting the Abolition of Capital Punishment in 1845.

In January and February 1846, Kane read accounts in the Philadelphia newspapers of the forced exile of the Mormons from their homes in western Illinois. Shortly after the declaration of war against Mexico in May, Kane sought out Mormon leaders in Philadelphia. He first met Jesse C. Little, who gave Kane the latest information on the Mormons and their plight. He then obtained letters of introduction to Mormon leaders from Little, met with President Polk to obtain his assurances and assistance, and headed west, where he eventually assisted with the call of the Mormon Battalion and began his lifelong friendship with Brigham Young and other prominent Latter-day Saints.

In addition to his involvement with the Mormons, Kane was active in the antislavery movement and worked with the Underground Railroad. He also fought in the American Civil War for the Union Army (leading a group of western Pennsylvania sharpshooters called the Bucktails), fighting at Gettysburg and in other battles. After the war, he became involved in land development and was a developer of Kane, a small town in northwestern Pennsylvania. He also involved himself in prison and educational reform, helped to establish a medical school, served as the first president of the Pennsylvania Board of State Charities, and helped organize the New York, Lake Erie, and Western Railroad and Coal Company along with other such social and economic institutions. But it was the Mormon connection that was the major thread that ran through his life—and his friendship with Brigham Young remained a significant part of that tapestry.[2]

The Kane lecture series was presented chronologically according to specific themes of Kane's relationship with the Mormons. In this volume, we have altered the original order of presentation but have generally maintained a chronological sequence. Although there is some necessary overlap in a few places, each essay can be read separately for insight into the various aspects of Kane's defense of his Mormon friends.

In the first essay, Matthew J. Grow introduces readers to the rich life of Thomas Kane by providing the larger context of Kane's America. As the major scholar of Kane, Grow offers new insights into the life and times of the man who did so much for the Saints. The second essay, by Mormon trails historian Richard E. Bennett, probes the earliest meetings of Kane and the Mormons, meetings that took place as the Mormons were beginning their exodus to the American West. Here, Kane assisted with the call of the Mormon Battalion, conveyed the interests and concerns of President James K. Polk, and began his friendship with Brigham Young and other Mormon leaders. In the third essay, Utah historian Thomas G. Alexander takes a closer look at Kane's ongoing role as a mediator in various episodes that continued to plague Utah's efforts to obtain statehood through the nineteenth century. The fourth essay, by William P. MacKinnon, an authority on the Utah Expedition, focuses on the events surrounding the Utah War of 1857–58, in which Kane proved his skills as an unofficial peacemaker. In the fifth essay, Edward A. Geary provides a vivid portrait of Thomas and Elizabeth themselves, their marriage as a partnership, and the challenges that came to them both as Thomas developed his relationship with the Mormons. The sixth essay, by Lowell C. (Ben) Bennion and Thomas R. Carter, examines the important trip the Kanes made to Utah in 1872–73 and invites readers to view the social world of polygamous Mormonism through the eyewitness accounts and pen of Elizabeth Wood Kane; the authors provide fuller identification of the various homes where the Kanes stayed during their trip from Salt Lake City to St. George with Brigham Young, homes that Elizabeth had disguised in her book, *Twelve Mormon Homes* (1874). The authors provide a closer look at the Kanes' stay with the Pitchforths in Nephi, a stay that Elizabeth devoted significant space to in her published account. In the final essay, David J. Whittaker provides a more personal view of the friendship of Brigham Young and Thomas Kane. Using excerpts from their extensive correspondence, this essay invites readers into the powerful friendship that existed between these two men, revealing the deep feelings each had for the other and some of the consequences of that friendship. Finally, this volume includes a bibliography of published material on Kane that will lead serious readers to the literature on this interesting individual and his family.

All the essays work together to further illuminate the interesting and complex life of one of the major friends of the Latter-day Saints in the nineteenth century. In a time when Mormons found few supporters outside their faith, Kane's friendship provides insights for the twenty-first century, an era in which tolerance and friendship could offer solutions in a world of violence and intolerance.

The following individuals deserve special thanks for their contributions to and support for this volume: Randy Olsen, university librarian, Harold B. Lee Library, BYU, for his constant support and for providing funding for the Kane Exhibit Lectures; Gerald Bradford, executive director of the Neal A. Maxwell Institute for Religious Scholarship at BYU, for providing funds for some of the costs associated with editing and source checking; John W. Welch, editor in chief of BYU Studies, for cosponsoring the Kane lecture series and for his encouragement throughout the project of bringing the oral presentations into print; Tom Wells, curator of photographs in the L. Tom Perry Special Collections in the Lee Library, for providing significant assistance in the preparation and scanning of the photographs used in this issue; Heather M. Seferovich, senior executive editor of BYU Studies, an editor extraordinaire, for carefully shepherding these essays from early drafts to their final versions; Marny K. Parkin for compiling the index on a very tight schedule; and Elizabeth Pew and Holly Mueller, editing interns at BYU Studies, for their work of editing and source checking.

David J. Whittaker

---

1. For an overview, see David J. Whittaker, "New Sources on Old Friends: The Thomas L. Kane and Elizabeth W. Kane Collection," *Journal of Mormon History* 27 (Spring 2001): 67–94.

2. For more on the life of Thomas L. Kane, see Matthew J. Grow, *"Liberty to the Downtrodden": Thomas L. Kane, Romantic Reformer* (New Haven, Conn.: Yale University Press, 2009).

FIG. 1. Thomas L. Kane, steel engraving. Albert L. Zobell Jr. was the first biographer of Kane, beginning with a master's thesis in 1944 and then with *Sentinel in the East* in 1965. *Sentinel*, frontispiece.

Thomas L. Kane and Nineteenth-Century American Culture

Matthew J. Grow

From nearly the moment Thomas L. Kane (fig. 1) walked into Mormon history in 1846, Latter-day Saint leaders promised that his name would long be honored by the Mormons. In part they wanted to bolster Kane's determination to take the deeply controversial stance of defending the Saints. When Kane announced his decision to travel to the Mormon refugee camps in Iowa in 1846, his family responded with panic. His father, John, saw only potential ruin in involvement with such a disreputable cause. "The case has no bright side," he lamented, as Tom "is about to deal a blow to his own character as a right minded man, which he will feel through life." He considered it the "veriest hallucination that ever afflicted an educated mind. It bows me in sorrow. All but this I could bear."[1]

The Mormons, however, immediately recognized the value of such a well-connected individual, and they treated Kane as royalty when he arrived. When he spoke in public, the applause was "positively deafening." Kane told his parents, "I am idolized by my good friends."[2] In September 1846, as Kane prepared to leave the camps, Patriarch John Smith (fig. 2), an uncle of Joseph Smith, promised him in a patriarchal blessing, "Thy name shall be had in honorable remembrance among the Saints to all generations."[3]

As Kane defended the Mormons for nearly the next four decades, Latter-day Saint leaders often reiterated this promise. In 1847, Elder Willard Richards rejoiced "that there is one Master Spirit, one noble soul inspired by heaven, in the nineteenth century, who wills that truth shall flow forth, . . . concerning an opprest and a suffering people."[4] Mormons renamed their principal town in Iowa, Council Bluffs, to Kanesville. Following the publication of Kane's influential 1850 pamphlet, *The Mormons*, Elder Orson

Hyde (fig. 3) told Kane this work "will forever immortalize your name in the records, and in the memory of the Saints."[5] And when Kane arrived in Salt Lake City in 1857 to mediate the Utah War, Brigham Young promised, "Brother Thomas the Lord sent you here and he will not let you die.... I want to have your name live with the Saints to all Eternity. You have done a great work and you will do a greater work still."[6]

The Saints had little doubt of Kane's divinely appointed role as their defender. After the Utah War, Eleanor McComb Pratt (fig. 4), widow of the slain Elder Parley P. Pratt, wrote to Kane that he was "inspired by God to stand in the defence of oppressed innocence, and inasmuch as you continue to act obedient to this inspiration I know the God of Israel will bless you and millions will rise up and call you blessed."[7] In 1864, as a symbol of their gratitude, the Saints named a county in southern Utah after Kane.

Nineteenth-century Mormons saw the world in dichotomies: good and evil, pure and corrupt, Saint and Gentile. Their historical narratives emphasized their persecution at the hands of a wicked nation. However, Kane was a reminder that not everyone could be placed into these simple categories; to the nineteenth-century Mormon mind, he was proof that God occasionally used outsiders (or "Gentiles," as they would have said) to protect Zion and further his work.

Nineteenth-century Americans also thought in dichotomies when they noted the growth of Mormonism, which they considered fraudulent and dangerous to American democracy and to the sanctity of the monogamous family. They had no category

FIG. 2. Patriarch John Smith. Uncle to the Prophet Joseph Smith, John Smith served as Church Patriarch from 1849 until his death in 1854. He gave a patriarchal blessing to Thomas L. Kane in 1846. Church History Library.

FIG. 3. Orson Hyde, steel engraving, c. 1853. Hyde recognized and appreciated Thomas L. Kane's work on behalf of the Mormons. Church History Library.

in which to place an individual like Kane, who, though not a Mormon, worked on their behalf. This suspicious attitude contributed to the rumors that swirled for decades that Kane had been baptized secretly and worked not as a humanitarian but as a covert Mormon.[8]

Since Kane's death in 1883, Mormon leaders have frequently returned to their promise to remember their nineteenth-century champion. In 1939, E. Kent Kane, a grandson of Kane, visited Utah and, along with Church President Heber J. Grant, recreated his grandparents' 1872 journey from Salt Lake City to St. George with Brigham Young, which Thomas's wife, Elizabeth, memorialized in her classic book *Twelve Mormon Homes*.[9] In the 1940s, Church President George Albert Smith encouraged E. Kent Kane to write a biography of his grandfather with Church official Frank Evans. Smith instructed, "I feel that the Church should rise to its duty and its opportunity" to recognize "the sacrifices, the devotion, and the great achievements of our distinguished friend who so valiantly served us in our times of greatest need."[10] Although the book was worked on intermittently for decades, it was never finished. Smith also invited E. Kent Kane to be a rare non-Mormon speaker at a session of the Church's semiannual general conference.[11] In the 1950s, Utah philanthropist and history booster Nicholas Morgan commissioned a statue of Kane, which identified him as a "Friend of the Mormons," for the Utah State Capitol. Morgan also funded the publication of a biography of Kane, Albert Zobell's *Sentinel in the East*, which focused on Kane's involvement with the Latter-day Saints.[12]

In the early 1970s, the Church purchased a Presbyterian chapel in Kane, Pennsylvania, which Kane had constructed in the late 1870s and where he is buried. In support of the Church's action, two of Kane's grandchildren (E. Kent Kane and Sybil Kent Kane) wrote in the local newspaper, the *Kane Republican*, that Kane "is a man far better known and honored in Utah today than here in Kane, Pa." Church leader Norman Bowen stated,

FIG. 4. Eleanor McComb Pratt, wife of Parley P. Pratt. Following Parley's death in 1857, Eleanor wrote a letter to Thomas L. Kane praising his defense of the Mormons. Church History Library.

"It is the desire of the Church to protect and preserve the final resting place of this great man . . . as well as to collect for posterity his papers and effects, for the edification of the public and future generations."[13] The chapel (fig. 5) has since been used as a Mormon meetinghouse and as a historical site commemorating Kane's assistance to the Saints. The Thomas L. Kane Memorial Chapel, however, has drawn relatively few visitors as a result of its location and is no longer open on a regular basis.

Beginning in 1998, the Mormon History Association has bestowed a Thomas L. Kane Award each year at its annual meeting on "a person outside of the Mormon community who made a significant contribution to Mormon history."[14]

Thus, Kane's legacy has been passed down in memory primarily as a "friend of the Mormons" and as their "sentinel in the East." Viewing Kane exculsively through a Mormon lens, however, has obscured the rest of his life as well as his motivations for embracing the Mormon cause. Immersing Kane into his own social and cultural contexts, particularly nineteenth-century social reform, illuminates both his life and the lives of other reformers of his era.

Anti-Evangelical, Democratic, Romantic Reform

The sheer volume of documents by and about Kane and the broad range of his interests make the search for thematic unity in his life difficult. Among his many humanitarian causes, Kane championed the end of the death penalty, peace, women's rights, the establishment of inner-city schools for young children, the abolition of slavery, and liberty for religious minorities. Besides being a reformer, Kane worked as a law clerk, a lawyer, a Civil War general, and a large-scale land developer. In addition, he was a man of both apparent and real paradoxes: a peacemaker who became a general; an antislavery crusader who longed for the chivalrous world of the southern gentry; a cosmopolitan gentleman who spent his last twenty-five years in the rustic Alleghenies; a Jacksonian Democrat who became a Free Soiler and then a Republican; a Presbyterian attracted to Auguste Comté's "Religion of Humanity" and atheism before settling on an antidenominational Christianity; an abolitionist who feared racial mixing; a diminutive, fragile, often depressed, and feminine-looking man with a pattern of aggressively masculine actions.[15]

Notwithstanding these contrasts, Kane's choices have an underlying unity that sheds light on like-minded social reformers who were historically important but who have been largely dismissed by the past generation of historians. In the decades before the Civil War, as the

FIG. 5. Thomas L. Kane Memorial Chapel, October 1877. This church, in the Gothic Revival architectural style, was built from locally quarried sandstone. This image shows the scaffolding and the workers. L. Tom Perry Special Collections, Harold B. Lee Library, Brigham Young University.

United States embraced a market economy and democratic politics, reform movements swept across the country, aiming to improve nearly every aspect of American society. In 1841, Kane's friend Ralph Waldo Emerson (fig. 6) captured the spirit of the times: "In the history of the world the doctrine of Reform had never such scope as at the present hour," as reformers sought to change "Christianity, the laws, commerce, schools, the farm, the laboratory." In Emerson's estimation, a reformer "cast aside all evil customs, timidities, and limitations" to fight injustices and to "find or cut a straight road to everything excellent in the earth, and not only go honorably himself, but make it easier for all who follow him."[16]

FIG. 6. Ralph Waldo Emerson. Transcendentalist philosopher, poet, and essayist, Emerson was a friend of Thomas L. Kane and expressed interest in the Mormon's plight after the publication of Kane's 1850 pamphlet *The Mormons*. Library of Congress.

Historians have generally located the roots of nineteenth-century reform in the religious fervor of the Second Great Awakening. Emphasizing the duty of Christians to engage actively in society through revivalism and social reform, Evangelical Protestants became the religious and cultural mainstream of American life in the early and mid-1800s. Hoping to perfect individuals and to create a Christian America, they established interdenominational reform societies, which historians have dubbed the "Benevolent Empire." Evangelical reformers found further motivation in Whig Party politics and in the Whig philosophy of orderly economic growth, moral and religious reform, deference to elites, and suspicion of cultural and religious diversity. The religious, economic, and intellectual center of this type of reform remained in New England and among Yankee migrants in New York and the Old Northwest even as its influence spread across the nation.[17]

In contrast, Kane represents reformers driven by Democratic Party ideology, romanticism, and anti-Evangelicalism. The antebellum Democratic Party has often been seen as the party of slaveholders and interpreted as being intensely hostile to reform. However, the party spurred a reform vision inspired by its egalitarian impulses and more inclusive views of religious, cultural, and ethnic diversity.[18] Romanticism, with its emphasis on the individual and its belief in human perfectibility, also profoundly shaped the ethos of Kane and similar reformers. He, like other romantics, was suspicious of traditional religion, though many retained a deep religious sensibility. Furthermore, romanticism prompted such reformers to defend those on society's margins and to declare war against human suffering.[19] An obituary insightfully labeled Kane's philosophy as "liberty to the down-trodden."[20] Kane and other reformers positioned themselves against mainstream Evangelicalism and Evangelical reformers. In these reformers' views, the Benevolent Empire encouraged clerical meddling in politics and blurred the separation of church and state. Thus, Kane's reform roots were far from unique; rather, they are emblematic of a larger community of reformers who contributed as much to nineteenth-century reform as did their Whig, Evangelical counterparts.

Raised in a wealthy and socially prominent Philadelphia family, Thomas Kane wrote that he had been "born with the gold spoon in [his] mouth, to station and influence and responsibility," which required him to be "an earnest missionary of Truth and Progress and Reform."[21] His mother, Jane Duval Leiper, came from a politically powerful and aristocratic Philadelphia family, and his father, John Kintzing Kane, became a nationally known Democratic Party insider and a prominent federal judge. John's connections with Democratic Presidents James Polk and James Buchanan opened the White House doors to Thomas, enabling him to raise the Mormon Battalion and mediate the Utah War. Thomas's talented older brother and close confidant, Elisha (fig. 7), with whom he shared a sickly disposition and a voracious ambition, overshadowed him during his life and became an international hero as an Arctic explorer before dying at a tragically young age. Thomas described Elisha as one who "spends his life doing the fine things that ladies love and men envy."[22]

As with many of his counterparts, Thomas viewed reform in a transatlantic context. As a young man in the early 1840s, he took two journeys to England and France. During his Parisian adventures,

FIG. 7. Elisha Kent Kane, older brother to Thomas. The two maintained a close relationship until Elisha's death in 1857. L. Tom Perry Special Collections, Harold B. Lee Library, Brigham Young University.

Thomas met (and became a sometime disciple of) the philosopher Auguste Comté, the father of positivism, whose vision of a "Religion of Humanity" fueled Thomas's humanitarian drive and religious unorthodoxy.[23] Thomas's parents hoped his European journeys would improve his perpetually fragile health. While in Europe, he stated that he had overcome his former "deficiency of vitality," which had led to "blind fatalism" and to "laziness." "Such as I am, you will find me active—a doing person," he pledged to his father.[24] He tried to assure his mother that his time in France had converted him to a "wholesome conservatism of ideas" and that he would not come "back to you a destructive, a radical" but rather a "lover of the respectabilities, an abhorrer of social changes."[25] Elizabeth, his future wife, more correctly diagnosed his attitude, suggesting he had told his mother what she had undoubtedly wished to hear. Upon his return, Elizabeth wrote, "he threw himself with youthful heat into numerous reform movements of which the general drift was an introduction of advanced French politics into American."[26]

Anti-Evangelicalism and a Religious Quest

Events shortly after his return, as well as family influences, solidified Thomas's reform trajectory. John Kane, a staunch Presbyterian, supported the Old School faction during the denominational split of the late 1830s and shared with other Old Schoolers a deep suspicion of the Evangelical reform embraced by their New School coreligionists. Furthermore, he was a Mason and a committed Democrat, whereas most Evangelicals voted Whig and Anti-Mason.[27] Following Thomas's 1844 return from Paris, John expressed his exasperation with the "fanaticism" of Evangelical reform, which "has run itself nearly out of breath on Abolition and Temperance: and now it has taken hold of the Bible."[28] Catholic complaints about the use of the Protestant Bible in Philadelphia public schools led to the formation of a nativist party and riots in the streets of Philadelphia between nativists and Catholics. As a member of a local militia, Thomas "stood sentinel with a musket for four nights" to help end the riots. John Kane, who helped organize the citizens' response to end the riots, wrote that the events gave Thomas—who had come home with "good resolves to mingle with the World around him and be a part of it"—a "fair opportunity of testing the strength both of these resolves and of his bodily frame."[29]

Significantly, the Kanes blamed the riots on the clergy. After a visit from the Reverend Cornelius C. Cuyler, the Kanes' pastor who had been active in the nativist campaign, Thomas mocked him as "St. Cornelius" and lambasted the "profound Theologian" for his criticism of a religiously diverse society: "'No Church ought to exist contrary to the wishes of the great part of the population of a Country, or to the sense of a Community opposed to its tenets.'" Kane snickered that Cuyler, "a man active in sending Missionaries among all manner of Heathen Majorities," failed to see the irony.[30] The riots deepened Thomas's distrust of Evangelical reformers and illustrated for him the necessity of religious liberty for minority groups.

Thomas Kane's own religious unorthodoxy further enabled his commitment to radical reform. As a young man, Kane even had designs to create a "religion suited to the 19th century—a religion containing in itself women—slaves—industrial classes . . . finally a religion of movement." He, however, "lost [his] noble aspirations" and burned his religious writings.[31] In France, he admired Catholicism, saying, "perhaps if I were a Christian I might become a Catholic."[32] To his mother he mocked the long list of frequently condemned Evangelical vices, pledging, "I'll not drink juleps or cocktails, nor cobblers, nor go to horse races, cockfights or theatres, nor keep a setter dog, sulky & trotter, or mistress, nor chew tobacco, smoke, or snuff, nor play taro cards or billiards, nor marry a chambermaid." Rising to his own rhetoric, Kane wrote, "I will try to be a good child, a comfort & not a torment to you and Papa and possibly even go to church every Sunday, and say the Sermon was good by pious falsehood, and the long prayer was not long." He would further pay his "Pew Rents" and support the "diverse respective Bible Tract, Missionary and other Societies, and persecute the Papist Malignants, Jesuits included."[33]

Through most of the 1840s and 1850s, Kane's personal religion blended Comté's Religion of Humanity with Christian asceticism. As Kane told his fiancée in 1852, he hoped her religion would not be confined within "four walls, but . . . [within] the mighty congregation of Humanity, the one and only Holy Catholic Church which Christ had founded."[34] Kane also continually derided both Evangelical religion and Evangelical reform. One Sunday he heard a "dreadful" noise, which turned out to be "one of the Methodist Meeting Houses where the law permits wicked people to make lunatics nearly as fast as the Hospitals can cure them."[35]

Career as a Reformer

Amid this personal religious journey, Kane looked for ways to transform society. In 1845, he engaged in his first organized reform activity, becoming a secretary for the American Society for the Abolition of Capital Punishment. By the mid-1840s, a national movement against capital punishment had led to the formation of this group, headed by James

Polk's vice president George M. Dallas, a close friend of the Kane family.[36] Joining the crusade against the death penalty gave Kane an important entrée into the wider reform community. Horace Greeley (fig. 8), for instance, who became Kane's friend and ally, was a vice president of the society. Kane also became involved in the allied projects of peace and prison reform.[37]

For Thomas Kane, genuine humanitarianism and personal ambition were not mutually exclusive. During his 1846 visit to the Mormon camps, he wrote his parents, "If you haven't resigned my place with the Anti-Capital P. men, keep it for me, as my life whether of one kind or another must begin when I get into Philadelphia this time."[38] Nor was Thomas a purist who refused to alter his beliefs. In December 1846, as Thomas jockeyed for an army commission in the Mexican-American War, John Kane wrote Elisha, "Would you ever believe it, your philanthropist—philosopher—anti war—anti capital punishment brother, who denies the right of man to take life even for crime, Tom, even Tom Kane, is rabid for a chance of shooting Mexicans."[39]

FIG. 8. Horace Greeley, c. 1855–65. Founder and editor of the highly influential *New York Tribune*, Greeley was a friend of Thomas L. Kane and supported his work on behalf of the Mormons. Library of Congress.

As with many reformers, Thomas extensively used newspapers and pamphlets to promote his causes. In the early 1840s, he organized a "club of young men, to influence the Public Press." Elizabeth explained, "He wrote much, though anonymously for several years, both in French and English, in newspapers and periodicals." Along with his associates, Thomas agitated "against all unnecessary Laws, against Capital Punishment, Against Wars, against all unnecessary Imprisonment—for the Rights of Man but Woman first—and the Abolition of Slavery."[40] Thomas was particularly savvy at using his writing to "manufacture public opinion."[41] For instance, he planted in newspapers anonymous or pseudonymous letters, articles (some of which even quoted himself), and editorials; wrote public letters to leading politicians that were widely reprinted; and held well-publicized fundraising meetings.

In the late 1840s, Thomas Kane became enthralled with a new reform—the restriction of slavery. In 1848, he became chairman of the Pennsylvania Free Soil Committee. The Free Soilers arose during the 1848 presidential campaign, dedicated to restricting slavery from the territories acquired in the Mexican-American War. Although the Free Soil Party attracted support from members of the Whig and Liberty Parties, the bulk of its membership comprised Democrats disaffected by their party's increasingly proslavery stance.[42] As the Free Soil movement fizzled in the early 1850s, Kane returned to the Democratic Party but continued his antislavery agitation, affiliating himself with a wing of the party known as the Radical Democracy. These Democratic antislavery activists, most of whom later joined the Republican Party, were motivated by the Jacksonian rhetoric of freedom, the desire to protect the racial purity of the American West, and the romantic hope that abolition would contribute to the global spread of liberty.[43] Similar to most abolitionists, Kane was no racial egalitarian; rather, he worried intensely about racial intermarriage.[44]

Kane directed his antislavery energies in the 1850s against the Fugitive Slave Act. Passed as part of the Compromise of 1850, this legislation denied traditional rights (such as a jury trial) to escaped slaves and forced Northerners, particularly U.S. Commissioners, to participate actively in returning escaped slaves to the South.[45] In October 1850, Kane, a twenty-eight-year-old law clerk and U.S. Commissioner, entered his father's federal courtroom in Philadelphia's Independence Hall to resign his position as a commissioner in a sharply worded letter. Kane's resignation struck a raw national nerve, earning him the ire of Southerners and the respect of abolitionists. He wrote to his sister, "I have received another complimentary newspaper from the South, in which, with reference to our Fathers pro-slavery Democracy [the Democratic Party]—I am called <u>a renegade to my parents Faith</u>."[46] The *Pennsylvania Freeman*, an abolitionist paper, praised Kane's resignation and predicted it would be "honored by every man who can appreciate a noble deed."[47]

That apparently did not include Judge Kane, who sentenced Thomas to prison for contempt of court.[48] Fortunately for Thomas, an associate justice of the U.S. Supreme Court, Robert C. Grier, overruled Judge Kane's conviction. This clash with his father fed Thomas's sense of himself as a defender of the downtrodden and as a romantic martyr for conscience sake. Thomas continued to work as his father's clerk even as Judge Kane's courtroom became a hotly contested arena in the national debate over fugitive slaves.[49] In a series of highly publicized trials, Thomas subverted his father's strict interpretation of the law by publicly supporting those on trial for assisting fugitives and by privately participating in the Underground Railroad.[50] The abolitionist press made public the familial rift: "Who will stand the best with posterity—the father who prostitutes his powers as a Judge to procure the conviction of peaceable citizens . . . or the son who ministered to the wants of those citizens while incarcerated in a loathsome prison?"[51]

Thomas's 1853 marriage to his talented sixteen-year-old second cousin Elizabeth Dennistoun Wood also influenced his reform career. They jointly envisioned a society based on gender equality, sought to advance women's education, and wished to reform the institution of marriage. Shortly after their marriage, Thomas encouraged Elizabeth to enroll in the pioneering Philadelphia-based Female Medical College of Pennsylvania (for which he served as a corporator, the equivalent of a member of the board of trustees) to "help the college by the influence of her social position."[52] He also hoped Elizabeth would become an author to press women's rights issues through her writing.[53] In their early years of marriage, Elizabeth assisted Thomas in his battles against Philadelphia's urban poverty as he founded and financed a school for Philadelphia's poor children modeled on the French *salles d'asiles* (infant schools) and served as a local leader for the House of Refuge movement, which sought to reform juvenile delinquents. The influence of Elizabeth and her Evangelical father, William Wood, also brought Thomas closer to orthodox Christianity, which ultimately led to his conversion to nondenominational Christianity in the late 1850s and early 1860s.[54]

Kane and the Mormons

Throughout this period, Thomas Kane engaged in a more unusual type of reform—defense of the Latter-day Saints. As amply demonstrated by the other articles in this volume, Kane helped raise the Mormon Battalion, lobbied for the Saints in the halls of Congress, shaped the public image of Mormonism, mediated the Utah War, and advised Brigham Young and other leaders. Kane had a range of motivations for his involvement with the Saints, including a desire for adventure and fame (in part, a sibling rivalry with Elisha), genuine friendship with Young and other Mormons, and a commitment to defend his own honor as well as that of the Saints. Reform, however, was paramount in Kane's motivation.

While Kane passed in and out of several other reforms, his devotion to the Mormons continued from 1846 until his death in 1883. His Democratic ideology of liberty and his own religious heterodoxy enabled his commitment to religious minorities. In addition, Kane's antipathy toward Evangelicalism inspired his crusade for the Mormons' religious liberty. During the second half of the nineteenth century, Evangelical reformers emerged as the leaders of the anti-Mormon political and cultural crusade. In their vision of reform they hoped to protect the nation from Mormon political subversion, shield the monogamous family from Mormon polygamy, and save individuals from the lure of the Latter-day Saints. Even though Kane strongly disagreed with some Latter-day Saint practices (especially plural marriage), he worked to preserve the religious liberty of the Latter-day Saints from the Evangelical reformers.[55]

According to Elizabeth Kane, Thomas also saw the Mormons as a laboratory for his reform ideas. She wrote that her husband believed the Mormons could create a "new Puritan commonwealth" through "the principle of cooperation carried out on a great scale—by a simple pastoral people." In this vision, Thomas joined various religious and secular reformers who believed that communal living and economics could create a more just and united society in the nineteenth century. However, Elizabeth continued, her husband's Mormon pupils "constantly disappointed" him with their implementation of his ideas. Nevertheless, "much of the Mormons' prosperity, such as their Z.C.M.I. Co-op. Stores, Order of Enoch, and communal ranches, sprang from Kane's ideas transmuted by Brigham Young's brain."[56] Indeed, during the 1870s, Thomas strongly supported the Mormon leader's attempts to establish communal United Orders.[57] While Elizabeth overestimated Thomas's influences on Mormon initiatives, her statement indicated that her husband saw his relationship with the Saints in terms of reform.

Thomas Kane's connection of reform to the defense of the Saints explains issues in both Mormon history and in reform more broadly. For example, Kane's immersion in reform circles helps explain the success of his efforts to remake the Mormon image in the late 1840s and early 1850s. After returning from the Mormon camps to Philadelphia in 1846, Kane sought to alter national opinions of Mormonism so Americans could view members of this faith as worthy objects of sympathy and charity rather than as deluded and dangerous fanatics. To create an image of the suffering Saints, he borrowed the tactics of abolitionists and other reformers in graphically depicting Mormons' woes in published letters, articles, and pamphlets. Kane's strategy struck a cultural chord, particularly among fellow reformers, because they reflected shifting philosophical notions about the nature of pain. In Western culture, pain had long been viewed as inevitable and redemptive; during the eighteenth and nineteenth centuries, however, suffering was seen increasingly as unacceptable and even eradicable.[58]

As a result of Kane's campaign, it became temporarily fashionable to sympathize with the suffering Saints. After Kane published his signature statement on Mormon suffering in an 1850 pamphlet, *The Mormons*, he distributed it widely to other reformers. Massachusetts senator and abolitionist Charles Sumner lauded Kane's "good & glorious work."[59] Wendell Phillips, another leading abolitionist, "devoured" the pamphlet and informed Kane that Ralph Waldo Emerson had expressed interest "in you & your subject."[60] Other reformers such as Horace Greeley, Frederick Douglass, and John Greenleaf Whittier publicly joined in Kane's campaign.[61] Kane's efforts on behalf of the Mormons both solidified his own growing reputation as a reformer and momentarily transformed the Mormon image (although the image of the suffering Saints quickly evaporated after the Mormons officially announced their practice of plural marriage in 1852).[62]

Kane's reform career also illuminates his most famous action—his intervention in the Utah War.[63] His involvement in Democratic, anti-Evangelical reform uniquely positioned him to mediate the Utah War crisis. In 1857, when President James Buchanan, a Pennsylvania Democrat with extensive ties to the Kane family, received reports of an allegedly rebellious Utah, the president dispatched the U.S. Army to establish federal supremacy and to replace Governor Brigham Young with a new appointee, Alfred Cumming. As tensions rose on both sides and as events threatened to spiral out of control, Kane convinced Buchanan to allow him to travel to Utah during winter 1857–58 in an unofficial capacity to negotiate peace between the Mormons and the federal civilian officials accompanying the army. Kane perceived the Utah War as a "Holy War" waged on the Mormons by an Evangelical nation, a belief that shaped his sense of mission in protecting the Latter-day Saints' religious liberty from the intrusions of federal officials and the U.S. Army.[64] A romantic sense of defending a downtrodden people also propelled Kane. He wrote in his travel diary, "Others may respect me less for being alone in the defence of a despised and injured people—but I respect myself more."[65] Kane's mediation in the Utah War ensured that the resolution of the Mormon Question would occur in the courts, the halls of Congress, and the realm of public opinion rather than on the battlefield.[66]

Transition of Kane's Reform Philosophy

While Kane began his career in Democratic, anti-Evangelical reform, he was a moving target. He remained neither Democratic nor as intensely anti-Evangelical as he had once been. But his companions in Democratic, anti-Evangelical reform were not stationary either. Indeed, Kane's political journey represented the larger political movement of the reform wing of the antebellum Democratic Party. As with Kane, many of his companions in Democratic reform passed through the Free

Soil movement in the late 1840s, returned to the Democratic Party, and then became Republicans (either in the 1850s, or in Kane's case, in 1861). Following the Civil War, Kane temporarily abandoned the mainstream Republican Party in 1872 for the dissident Liberal Republican movement before finally returning to the Republican Party. In supporting the Liberal Republicans, Kane not only expressed a preference for his old friend Horace Greeley (the Liberal Republican presidential nominee in 1872) but also manifested his Democratic ideals, as former Democrats were at the foundation of the Liberal Republican revolt.[67]

In his last twenty years, Kane's reform ethos changed as well, foreshadowing the spirit of the Progressive Era, with its confidence in social science, experts, and government solutions. In 1869, Pennsylvania Governor John W. Geary appointed Kane as the first president of the Pennsylvania Board of State Charities, a government entity mandated to regulate charitable organizations; this board became the foundation of modern state welfare agencies. Following his religious conversion experiences, Kane also moved closer to Evangelical reformers in some ways. For example, as he developed a community (which he named Kane) in the Allegheny Mountains of northwestern Pennsylvania from the mid-1850s until his death, he embraced temperance and battled to restrict the use of alcohol. Nevertheless, his continued involvement in Mormon issues ensured that Kane always remained deeply skeptical of Evangelical-inspired reform efforts.[68]

The Romantic Hero and the Honorable Gentleman

Besides his involvement in reform, Kane's life remains significant because he represents two nineteenth-century cultural types: the romantic hero and the honorable gentleman. An icon in both literature and in the nineteenth-century cultural imagination, the romantic hero exalted individuality, battled social injustices, and rejected religious, political, and social norms.[69] According to Ralph Waldo Emerson, who published a classic statement on the romantic hero in 1841, "Heroism works in contradiction to the voice of mankind." Furthermore, a hero was "negligent of expense, of health, of life, of danger, of hatred, of reproach, and knows that his will is higher and more excellent than all actual and all possible antagonists." In short, the romantic hero marched "to his own music."[70] Deeply influenced by transatlantic romanticism, Kane viewed himself within this context, and the ideal of the romantic hero shaped his actions. An iconoclast, he based his identity on standing against the crowd, on trusting his own conclusions rather than commonly held conventions, and on undertaking dangerous missions (such as during the Utah War and the Civil War) that defied his physical frailty.

The ideal of the romantic hero shaped Kane's concept of manliness. Reform often carried an unmistakably feminine aura, the result of the high profile of female reformers combined with reformers' support of women's rights.[71] Kane, who was described by contemporaries as "uncommonly small and feminine" and as "a little, weak, boyish, sickly looking fellow," combated the image of the effeminate reformer with flamboyantly masculine gestures.[72] At an 1850 New York abolitionist meeting, Kane publicly threatened to kill a Tammany Hall captain with a well-earned reputation for violence who attempted to disrupt the meeting.[73] An observer praised Kane's "instinctive manly honor" and described the scene (probably with some exaggeration): "Colonel Kane—a slight and fearless youth—made the notorious leader of the rioters quail."[74] In addition, the reformers' stance of protecting those who could not do so for themselves was seen by contemporaries as a manly act.[75] Kane wrote, "I have done a few manly deeds, and I have been abused for them." His accomplishments had "all been achieved not with but in despite of the majority of my fellow citizens."[76] Should Mormonism become popular, Kane would no longer be useful to the Saints, as his place would always be "in the ranks of the supporters of causes called desperate and at the head of unthanked and unrewarded pioneers of unpopular Reform."[77]

Kane's view of himself as a romantic hero closely relates to another cultural type: the man of honor, the chivalrous defender of the downtrodden. Honor-based cultures placed great emphasis on an individual's and on a family's public reputation; the opposite of honor was shame. In early America, upper-class men could defend their reputation from attacks through dueling. During the 1700s, the culture of honor deeply influenced both northerners and southerners, though the North moved away from this system during the first half of the nineteenth century, a result of both the integration of northerners into a market economy and the growing influence of Protestant Evangelicalism. While historians have generally associated the culture of honor with the South, Kane's actions demonstrate that the culture of honor retained its influence in the sectional borderlands and among elite northerners like Kane.[78] In addition, a man of honor—particularly one born to privilege, as was Kane—defended those lower on the social scale, and he thus related honor to his broader reform agenda. The seemingly odd combination of the sentimental defense of the oppressed, the iconoclasm and brash assertiveness of the romantic hero, and a high sense of honor formed Thomas's definition of masculinity.

Kane's immersion in the culture of honor particularly shaped his Civil War career. When he learned of the Southern attack on Fort Sumter in April 1861, Kane immediately recruited a regiment of soldiers from the mountains of northwestern Pennsylvania. Known as the Pennsylvania Bucktails, this regiment became one of the best-known units of the Union Army. During the next two years, before he retired because of injuries, he challenged a superior officer to a duel, rose to the rank of brigadier general, gained a reputation for personal courage, became seriously wounded in two battles, was taken prisoner of war, and played a key role at the battle of Gettysburg. Influenced by both the culture of honor and romanticism, Kane viewed himself as a chivalrous, medieval knight. His ethic of honor and attachment to romantic chivalry impelled not only his duel challenge but also shaped his perceptions of legitimate wartime tactics, his treatment of Confederates during the war, and his desire for rapid reconciliation with the South following the war. In addition, Kane saw the war as the culmination of his antislavery career. The rise of Copperhead sentiment in the North (northern Democrats who opposed the war) and the Republican embrace of emancipation prompted Kane, along with many of his companions in anti-Evangelical Democratic reform, to finally sever his relationship with the Democratic Party and become a Republican.[79]

Conclusion

Kane and his allies played key roles in the reform movements and debates at the center of American culture in the mid-nineteenth century. During the antebellum era, these reformers were Democrats who defined themselves against Evangelical reform and advocated a romantic humanitarianism that sought to relieve human suffering. Kane's own reform activities—most prominently, his opposition to slavery and his defense of the Mormons' religious liberty—sprang from this culture of anti-Evangelical, Democratic, romantic reform. Furthermore, Kane's life demonstrates the deep cultural influences of the romantic vision of the hero and the idea of honor. Understanding Kane's involvement in reform thus not only clarifies his relationship with the Latter-day Saints but also illuminates nineteenth-century social reform more broadly.

Matthew J. Grow (mjgrow@usi.edu) received his PhD from the University of Notre Dame. He is an assistant professor of history and director of the Center for Communal Studies at the University of Southern Indiana. This article is adapted from his book, *"Liberty to the Downtrodden": Thomas L. Kane, Romantic Reformer* (New Haven: Yale University Press, 2009). He is currently writing a biography of Parley P. Pratt with Terryl Givens for Oxford University Press.

1. John K. Kane to Elisha K. Kane, May 16, 1846, Elisha K. Kane Papers, American Philosophical Society, Philadelphia. This and many of the quotes in this article also appear in Matthew J. Grow, *"Liberty to the Downtrodden": Thomas L. Kane, Romantic Reformer* (New Haven: Yale University Press, 2009), 50–51.

2. Thomas L. Kane to John K. Kane and Jane Duval Leiper Kane, July 20–23, 1846, Thomas L. Kane Papers, American Philosophical Society.

3. Blessing, John Smith to Thomas L. Kane, September 8, 1846, Thomas L. and Elizabeth W. Kane Collection, L. Tom Perry Special Collections, Harold B. Lee Library, Brigham Young University, Provo, Utah (hereafter cited as Perry Special Collections).

4. Willard Richards to Thomas L. Kane, February 16–19, 1847, Perry Special Collections.

5. Orson Hyde to Thomas L. Kane, May 31, 1851, Perry Special Collections.

6. Scott G. Kenney, ed., *Wilford Woodruff's Journal, 1833–1898, Typescript* (Midvale, Utah: Signature Books, 1984), 5:171, entry for February 25, 1858.

7. Eleanor McComb [Pratt] to Thomas L. Kane, May 7, 1858, Perry Special Collections. Pratt had been murdered in Arkansas during the lead-up to the Utah War in May 1857.

8. For a longer discussion of this topic, see William MacKinnon's essay herein.

9. Descriptions of this visit, as well as E. Kent Kane's correspondence with Mormon leaders, are in the Kane Collection, Perry Special Collections. For more information on *Twelve Mormon Homes,* see Lowell C. Bennion and Thomas Carter's essay herein.

10. George Albert Smith to Israel Frank Evans, October 1, 1947, Israel Frank Evans Collection, Church History Library, The Church of Jesus Christ of Latter-day Saints, Salt Lake City.

11. See newspaper clippings and typescript of speech in Kane's Papers, Perry Special Collections.

12. Nicholas G. Morgan Papers, Special Collections, J. Willard Marriott Library, University of Utah; Albert L. Zobell Jr., *Sentinel in the East: A Biography of Thomas L. Kane* (Salt Lake City: Nicholas G. Morgan, 1965).

13. "Chance for an Outstanding Civic and Historical Attraction," *Kane Republican,* June 19, 1970, Church Information Service, Kane Memorial Chapel Files, 1970–1971, Church History Library.

14. Mormon History Association website, http://www.mhahome.org/awards/index.php.

15. For an expanded version of my arguments, see Grow, *"Liberty to the Downtrodden."*

16. Ralph Waldo Emerson, "Man the Reformer," in *The Works of Ralph Waldo Emerson: Nature, Addresses, and Lectures* (Boston: Houghton, Mifflin, and Company, 1855), 1:218.

17. The literature on antebellum reform is vast. For the historiography, see Glenn M. Harden, "'Men and Women of Their Own Kind': Historians and Antebellum Reform" (master's thesis, George Mason University, 2001). Classic older studies that linked Evangelicalism and reform include Gilbert H. Barnes, *The Anti-Slavery Impulse, 1830–1844* (New York: D. Appleton-Century, 1933); Whitney Cross, *The Burned-Over District* (Ithaca, N.Y.: Cornell University Press, 1950). For

studies of the "benevolent empire" and print culture, see Peter J. Wosh, *Spreading the Word: The Bible Business in Nineteenth-Century America* (Ithaca, N.Y.: Cornell University Press, 1994); Mark S. Schantz, "Religious Tracts, Evangelical Reform, and the Market Revolution in Antebellum America," *Journal of the Early Republic*, 17 (Autumn 1997): 425–66. For Evangelical reform in the South, see John W. Quist, *Restless Visionaries: The Social Roots of Antebellum Reform in Alabama and Michigan* (Baton Rouge: Louisiana State University Press, 1998). For Evangelical reform and politics, see Daniel Walker Howe, *The Political Culture of the American Whigs* (Chicago: University of Chicago Press, 1979); Richard Carwardine, *Evangelicals and Politics in Antebellum America* (New Haven: Yale University Press, 1993). While most monographs on antebellum reform have focused on Evangelical reform, broader surveys present a more complicated picture, though still slighting Democratic reformers. See Robert H. Abzug, *Cosmos Crumbling: American Reform and the Religious Imagination* (New York: Oxford University Press, 1994); Ronald G. Walters, *American Reformers, 1815–1860*, rev. ed. (New York: Hill and Wang, 1997); Steven Mintz, *Moralists and Modernizers: America's Pre-Civil War Reformers* (Baltimore: Johns Hopkins University Press, 1995).

18. On Democratic reform, see Jonathan Earle, *Jacksonian Antislavery and the Politics of Free Soil, 1824–1854* (Chapel Hill: University of North Carolina Press, 2004); Yonatan Eyal, *The Young America Movement and the Transformation of the Democratic Party, 1828–1861* (New York: Cambridge University Press, 2007); Daniel Feller, "A Brother in Arms: Benjamin Tappan and the Antislavery Democracy," *Journal of American History* 88 (June 2001): 48–74; Grow, "Liberty to the Downtrodden." Two recent influential histories of the early republic emphasize these competing reform traditions. Sean Wilentz focuses on Democratic reformers in *The Rise of American Democracy: Jefferson to Lincoln* (New York: Norton, 2005), while Daniel Walker Howe does the same for Evangelical Whig reformers in *What Hath God Wrought: The Transformation of America, 1815–1848* (New York: Oxford University Press, 2007).

19. On romanticism and reform, see John L. Thomas, "Romantic Reform in America, 1815–1865," *American Quarterly*, 17 (Winter 1965): 656–81; Stewart Winger, *Lincoln, Religion, and Romantic Cultural Politics* (Dekalb: Northern Illinois University Press, 2003).

20. "Death of General Thomas L. Kane," *Millennial Star* 46 (January 21, 1884): 42–44.

21. Thomas L. Kane to Brigham Young, September 24, 1850, Brigham Young Collection, Church History Library.

22. Thomas L. Kane to Brigham Young, Fall 1850, Perry Special Collections. Edward Geary's essay herein contains a Kane pedigree chart in the appendix.

23. Robert Patterson Kane to C. Dana, November 25, 1892 (?), Thomas L. Kane Collection, American Philosophical Society; Elizabeth W. Kane, biographical sketches of Thomas L. Kane, Perry Special Collections. For more on Comté's influence on Kane, see Edward Geary's essay herein.

24. Thomas L. Kane to John K. Kane, December 29, 1843, Perry Special Collections.

25. Thomas L. Kane to Jane D. Kane, January 23 and 31, February 1, 1844, Perry Special Collections.

26. Elizabeth continued, he "proclaimed himself a Communist; but was the unsparing critic of the Fourierite and other Socialist associated movements of the time; though he gave largely to many of them to assist them in working out their own salvation or damnation." Elizabeth W. Kane, draft biographical sketch of Thomas L. Kane, December 20, 1873, Perry Special Collections.

27. See John K. Kane, *Autobiography of the Honorable John K. Kane, 1795–1858* (Philadelphia: College Offset Press, 1949); Henry Simpson, *The Lives of Eminent Philadelphians* (Philadelphia: William Brotherhead, 1859), 614. The entry on John K. Kane in Simpson's *Lives* was almost certainly written by Thomas, who was thanked by Simpson in the acknowledgments for his assistance with the book.

28. John K. Kane to Elisha K. Kane, March 12, 1844, Perry Special Collections.

29. John K. Kane to Elisha K. Kane, May 14, 1844, Perry Special Collections.

30. Thomas L. Kane to Bessie [Elizabeth Kane Shields, his sister], n.d. [1844], Perry Special Collections.

31. Thomas L. Kane to Elisha K. Kane, June 8 and 11, 1845, Perry Special Collections.

32. Thomas L. Kane to John K. Kane, November 15, 1843, Perry Special Collections.

33. Thomas L. Kane to Jane D. Kane, December 24 and 31, 1843, Perry Special Collections. Some Protestant groups of this era, such as Presbyterians and Episcopalians, rented pews to their congregants as a source of church revenue.

34. Thomas L. Kane to Elizabeth D. Wood, May 8, 1852, Perry Special Collections.

35. Thomas L. Kane to Bessie Kane [his sister], [undated, about 1846?], Kane Family Papers, William L. Clement Library, University of Michigan, Ann Arbor.

36. Albert Post, "Early Efforts to Abolish Capital Punishment in Pennsylvania," *Pennsylvania Magazine of History and Biography* 68 (January 1944): 48–50. See also David Brion Davis, "The Movement to Abolish Capital Punishment in America, 1787–1861," *American Historical Review* 63 (1957): 23–46; Stuart Banner, *The Death Penalty: An American History* (Cambridge, Mass.: Harvard University Press, 2002).

37. See Grow, *"Liberty to the Downtrodden,"* 39.

38. Thomas L. Kane to John K. Kane and Jane Duval Leiper Kane, July 20 and 23, 1846, Thomas L. Kane Papers, American Philosophical Society.

39. John K. Kane to Elisha K. Kane, December 25, 1846, Elisha K. Kane Papers, American Philosophical Society; see Grow, *"Liberty to the Downtrodden,"* 41.

40. Kane, draft biographical sketch.

41. Thomas L. Kane to Brigham Young, December 2, 1846, Brigham Young Collection, Church History Library.

42. See Jonathan H. Earle, *Jacksonian Antislavery and the Politics of Free Soil, 1824–1854* (Chapel Hill, University of North Carolina Press, 2004). In a revisionist vein, Earle provides evidence for the contention that the impulse for much of antebellum reform—particularly the restriction of slavery—came not from evangelicals and Whigs, but rather from the world of Jacksonian Democracy, which Kane inhabited.

43. See Grow, *"Liberty to the Downtrodden,"* ch. 6.

44. On Kane's racial thought, see his unpublished manuscript, "The Africanization of America," Perry Special Collections.

45. On the Fugitive Slave Law, see Stanley W. Campbell, *The Slave Catchers: Enforcement of the Fugitive Slave Law, 1850–1860* (Chapel Hill: University of North Carolina Press, 1968).

46. Thomas L. Kane to Bessie [Elizabeth Kane Shields], November 27, [1850], Perry Special Collections; underlining in original.

47. "Manly," *Pennsylvania Freeman,* October 3, 1850, pasted in Elizabeth W. Kane, Journal, March 12, 1855, Perry Special Collections.

48. Often repeated in Kane family lore, this fact is supported by contemporary evidence. See William Wood to Thomas L. Kane, January 23, 1851, Perry Special Collections; Kane, draft biographical sketch. It is unclear whether Thomas actually served time in prison.

49. John Kane presided over two of the most controversial trials involving the Fugitive Slave Act, the 1851 trials resulting from the Christiana riot and the 1855 trial of Philadelphia abolitionist Passmore Williamson. See Thomas P. Slaughter, *Bloody Dawn: The Christiana Riot and Racial Violence in the Antebellum North* (New York: Oxford University Press, 1991); Nat Brandt with Yanna Kroyt Brandt, *In the Shadow of the Civil War: Passmore Williamson and the Rescue of Jane Johnson* (Columbia: University of South Carolina Press, 2007); Ralph Lowell Eckert, "Antislavery Martyrdom: The Ordeal of Passmore Williamson," *Pennsylvania Magazine of History and Biography* 100 (October 1976): 521–38.

50. For Kane's participation in the Underground Railroad, see William Still, *The Underground Rail Road* (Philadelphia: Porter and Coates, 1872; reprint, New York: Arno Press, 1968), 366.

51. "Thanksgiving among the 'Traitors,'" *Pennsylvania Freeman,* December 4, 1851.

52. Elizabeth W. Kane, draft biographical material of Thomas L. Kane, undated, 8, Perry Special Collections. For more information on Thomas and Elizabeth courtship and marriage, see Edward Geary's essay herein.

53. For the Kanes' involvement with women's rights, see Grow, *"Liberty to the Downtrodden,"* ch. 8; Darcee D. Barnes, "A Biographical Study of Elizabeth D. Kane" (master's thesis, Brigham Young University, 2002). Elizabeth's most influential writing, her 1874 *Twelve Mormon Homes,* defended polygamous women even though both of the Kanes deeply opposed plural marriage.

54. See Grow, *"Liberty to the Downtrodden,"* ch. 8.

55. For the largely Evangelical-led nineteenth-century campaigns against Mormonism, see Sarah Barringer Gordon, *The Mormon Question: Polygamy and Constitutional Conflict in Nineteenth-Century America* (Chapel Hill: University of North Carolina Press, 2002); Terryl L. Givens, *The Viper on the Hearth: Mormons, Myths, and the Construction of Heresy* (New York: Oxford University Press, 1997); and Gaines M. Foster, *Moral Reconstruction: Christian Lobbyists and the Federal Legislation of Morality, 1865–1920* (Chapel Hill: University of North Carolina Press, 2002).

56. Kane, draft biographical sketch, undated. On nineteenth-century communalism, see Donald E. Pitzer, ed., *America's Communal Utopias* (Chapel Hill: University of North Carolina Press, 1997).

57. Grow, *"Liberty to the Downtrodden,"* 277.

58. Elizabeth B. Clark, "'The Sacred Rights of the Weak': Pain, Sympathy, and the Culture of Individual Rights in Antebellum America," *Journal of American*

History 82 (September 1995): 463–93; Karen Halttunen, "Humanitarianism and the Pornography of Pain in Anglo-American Culture," *American Historical Review* 100 (April 1995): 303–34; Margaret Abruzzo, "Polemical Pain: Slavery, Suffering and Sympathy in Eighteenth- and Nineteenth-Century Moral Debate" (PhD diss., University of Notre Dame, 2005). Abolitionist literature graphically depicting cruelty to slaves created the "suffering slave" as an important cultural symbol. Kane had undoubtedly read much reform literature, and its influence was readily seen in his construction of Mormon image.

59. Charles Sumner to Thomas L. Kane, December 27, 1850, Perry Special Collections.

60. Wendell Phillips to Thomas L. Kane, November 19, 1851, Perry Special Collections.

61. Frederick Douglass, review of "The Mormons," *North Star*, October 3, 1850; John Greenleaf Whittier, "The Mormons and Their City of Refuge," *National Era*, August 15, 1850. For Greeley, see "The Mormons in the Wilderness," *New York Daily Tribune*, February 17, 1848, and Horace Greeley, to Kane, June 19, 1849, Perry Special Collections.

62. Grow, *"Liberty to the Downtrodden,"* chapter 5.

63. For more on Kane's involvement in the Utah War, see William MacKinnon's essay herein.

64. Thomas L. Kane to Brigham Young, July 18, 1858, Brigham Young Collection, Church History Library. For more on the Utah War, see William MacKinnon essay herein.

65. Thomas L. Kane, 1858 Diary, undated entry, Perry Special Collections, underlining in original.

66. On Kane and the Utah War, see Grow, *"Liberty to the Downtrodden,"* chs. 9 and 10; William P. MacKinnon, *At Sword's Point: A Documentary History of the Utah War to 1858* (Arthur H. Clark Company, 2008).

67. For Kane's political journey, see Grow, *"Liberty to the Downtrodden,"* especially chs. 6 and 12.

68. See Grow, *"Liberty to the Downtrodden,"* ch. 12.

69. On the romantic hero, see Peter L. Thorslev Jr., *The Byronic Hero: Types and Prototypes* (Minneapolis: University of Minnesota Press, 1962); Walter L. Reed, *Meditations on the Hero: A Study of the Romantic Hero in Nineteenth-Century Fiction* (New Haven: Yale University Press, 1974); Gerald N. Izenberg, *Impossible Individuality: Romanticism, Revolution, and the Origins of Modern Selfhood, 1787–1802* (Princeton: Princeton University Press, 1992); Thomas Carlyle, *On Heroes, Hero-Worship, & the Heroic in History*, ed. Michael K. Goldberg (Berkeley: University of California Press, 1993), xxxiii–xxxiv.

70. Ralph Waldo Emerson, "Heroism," in *The Works of Ralph Waldo Emerson: Essays, First Series* (Boston: Houghton, Mifflin, and Company, 1865), 2:236–37.

71. On the feminine perception of reform in Kane's Philadelphia, see Bruce Dorsey, *Reforming Men and Women: Gender in the Antebellum City* (Ithaca, N.Y.: Cornell University Press, 2002).

72. Juanita Brooks, ed., *On the Mormon Frontier: The Diary of Hosea Stout, 1844–1861*, 2 vols. (Salt Lake City: University of Utah Press, 1964), 1:177 (July 11, 1846); Nicholas B. Wainwright, ed., *A Philadelphia Perspective: The Diary of*

Sidney George Fisher, Covering the Years 1834–1871 (Philadelphia: Historical Society of Pennsylvania, 1967), 390 (May 17, 1861).

73. Wendell Phillips Garrison, *William Lloyd Garrison* (New York: Century Company, 1885–89), 3:292; Thomas L. Kane to Robert Patterson Kane, undated, Robert Patterson Kane Papers, American Philosophical Society.

74. [George William Curtis], "The Late Colonel Kane," *Harper's Weekly*, January 12, 1884, 19.

75. "Manly," *Pennsylvania Freeman*, October 3, 1850. For other discussions of reform and masculinity, see Dorsey, *Reforming Men and Women*; and James Robert Britton, "Reforming America and Its Men: Radical Social Reform and the Ethics of Antebellum Manhood" (PhD diss., University of Miami, 2003).

76. Thomas L. Kane to T. B. H. Stenhouse, draft, [1872], Perry Special Collections.

77. Thomas L. Kane to "My dear friends," [Brigham Young and other Mormon leaders], September 1850, draft, Perry Special Collections.

78. On the culture of honor, see Bertram Wyatt-Brown, *Southern Honor: Ethics and Behavior in the Old South* (New York: Oxford University Press, 1982); Bertram Wyatt-Brown, *The Shaping of Southern Culture: Honor, Grace, and War, 1760s–1890s* (Chapel Hill: University of North Carolina Press, 2001); Kenneth Greenberg, *Honor & Slavery: Lies, Duels, Noses, Masks, Dressing as a Woman, Gifts, Strangers, Humanitarianism, Death, Slave Rebellions, the Proslavery Argument, Baseball, Hunting, and Gambling in the Old South* (Princeton: Princeton University Press, 1996).

79. For more imformation on Kane's Civil War career, see Grow, *"Liberty to the Downtrodden,"* ch. 11.

FIG. 1. C. C. A. Christensen, *Winter Quarters,* tempera on muslin, 76¾ x 113¾ inches, c. 1865. This settlement of Saints contained nearly eight hundred dwellings and had a population of approximately thirty-five hundred people as of December 1846. The artist illustrates the first company to depart on their westward trek to the Great Salt Lake Valley. Gift of the Christensen grandchildren, Museum of Art, Brigham Young University.

"He Is Our Friend"
Thomas L. Kane and the Mormons in Exodus, 1846–1850

Richard E. Bennett

The study of Mormon history is anything but a static field of research. New sources of historical knowledge are continually coming to the fore, collection upon collection, document upon document, here a very little and perhaps there a great deal. New and revealing primary sources, like the Thomas L. and Elizabeth W. Kane Collection at Brigham Young University (BYU), are providing fresh historical insights. Thanks to the vision, foresight, and professional acumen of devoted archivists and librarians, such as David Whittaker at the Harold B. Lee Library, in acquiring, processing, and preserving such notable reflections as the Kane papers, the future of our history is indeed bright.

The purpose of this paper is to show how the Kane papers add to our present understanding of the early Mormon exodus era, particularly from 1846 to 1850. Specifically, this essay addresses what new information and insights they provide and especially how they enhance, correct, or confirm our knowledge of the following: first, the attitudes of President James K. Polk and his cabinet and others close to him toward the fleeing Latter-day Saints; second, the federal government's request for a five-hundred-man Mormon Battalion; third, the Mormon settlement at Winter Quarters at the Missouri River in winter 1846–47 (figs. 1 and 2); and fourth, Kane's lecture titled "The Mormons," given and published in Philadelphia in 1850. Last of all, this article considers what Kane's papers might suggest about the influence the Mormons had upon his life and thought.

Crossing Iowa

The martyrdom of Joseph Smith Jr. and his older brother Hyrum on June 27, 1844, in Carthage, Illinois, left The Church of Jesus Christ of Latter-day Saints suddenly leaderless and created a crisis of succession that sorely tested the allegiance of thousands. Meanwhile, persecution against the Mormons intensified rather than diminished. This caused Brigham Young (fig. 3), the interim leader by right of his ecclesiastical position as president of the Quorum of the Twelve Apostles, to set out on a course of exodus to the Rocky Mountains. Young believed the journey to be necessary for the salvation of his people and of the Church itself. Beginning in early February 1846, the majority of approximately fifteen thousand Latter-day Saints, some well prepared but many not so, left their homes in and around Nauvoo, Illinois, most without consideration or sale, to seek refuge in the West.[1]

The longer they traveled without a firm destination in mind, the greater the risk of discouragement, despair, and even death. The Saints'

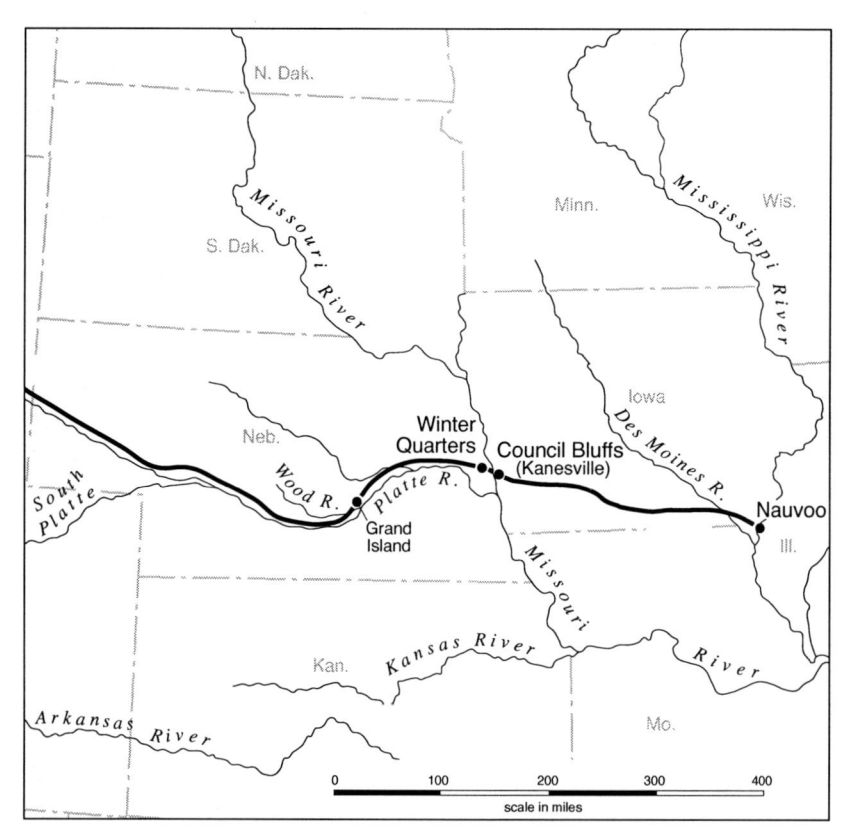

FIG. 2. Mormon Camps, 1846. Adapted from a map created by the Geography Department, Brigham Young University.

plan was to cross Iowa and reach Council Bluffs as quickly as possible. They would then ferry over the Missouri River and establish way stations at Grand Island and points farther west in present-day Nebraska. From these way stations, they would dispatch an express company of skilled farmers, builders, surveyors, and other pioneer laborers to some chosen valley in the Rocky Mountains in time to plant crops and build stockades and fortifications for the many thousands to follow. Funding to defray the enormous costs of so great an exodus composed primarily of faithful, but often destitute, people would have to come from the depleted tithing funds of the Church, the sale of the Nauvoo and Kirtland temples and other Church properties, contributions from the growing number of British converts, and from any work contracts that Church leaders could secure from the United States or British governments. All this had to happen in 1846 before the Saints could be interrupted by Missourians, Indians, or an interfering U.S. Army of the West, which was skeptical of Mormon intents and allegiances. This explains, in large measure, their very early wintry departure from Nauvoo in February 1846.[2]

FIG. 3. Brigham Young, steel engraving, c. 1853. Church History Library.

These expedition plans soon collided with reality, however. Instead of crossing Iowa in six weeks, as expected, the Saints took over three months. Incessantly wet, inclement weather created mud fields so deep that their heavily laden wagons sank to the axles.[3] Way stations had to be hastily established much sooner than planned, first in Garden Grove and then farther west at Mt. Pisgah, and crops had to be put in not only for the eighteen hundred in these advance companies but also for the many thousands soon to follow.[4] Money, supplies, and patience were fast running out, and "Brother Brigham's" 1846 enterprise was bogging down in a morass of mud, deteriorating health, poverty, and not a little ill will, as evidenced by increasing backbiting from detractors and defectors like James Strang, George Miller, and James Emmett, who viewed the Saints' mounting troubles as vindication of their own counterpoint claims and ambitions. By the time Brigham Young and his advance company of Saints reached what is now Council Bluffs, Iowa, on June 14, everyone knew that moving the entire Church farther west that season was entirely out of the question.[5]

Consequently, the immediate pressing issue Brigham Young faced was where in the wilderness the "Camp of Israel" (as they called themselves) could settle safely until spring 1847. The postponement of their original plans demanded a reformulation of their objectives and a serious reconsideration of how to survive the coming year with few or no provisions. Questions came to the forefront about how and where to raise money for supplies, purchase provisions, fix broken-down wagons, and attend to a thousand other physical needs, as well as how to live among wounded and warring Indian tribes, several of which were then being transplanted westward by government decree.

Beginning almost immediately, the Saints and their large herds of cattle began ferrying across the Missouri River, an arduous task that took months to complete. Those who could cross over that season could leave sooner for the Rocky Mountains in spring 1847. Abandoning all plans to reach Grand Island, Brigham Young decided to establish Winter Quarters on Indian lands—with or without government permission—on the west bank of the Missouri River near present-day Omaha. The several thousand Saints following behind, who had left Nauvoo during summer and early fall 1846, including the so-called "Poor Camps" of those forced out of their Nauvoo homes, would settle in various hollows and assorted encampments on the east side of the river. These small and scattered communities eventually coalesced into the city of Kanesville, predecessor to today's Council Bluffs, Iowa. Uprooted, distended, and scattered over hundreds of miles in unfamiliar, if not hostile, surroundings, the wounded Mormons—victims of persecution, distrust, and blatant religious prejudice, and in a country unsure of their loyalties and political allegiances—faced a very uncertain future.

To this difficult equation was now added yet another destabilizing factor. Not unlike the "trail of tears" then decimating so many displaced Indian tribes, the Mormons' forced migration exposed them to excessive toils and rigors of their journey; travel injuries; a lack of green vegetables and other nutritional foods; inclement weather; mosquito-infested, malaria-inducing sidebars and swamps of the Missouri River; and, not least of all, inadequate housing in the form of caves, hovels, hastily built cabins, mere wagon coverings, and tents. They were a people destined to suffer and die from overexposure, malnutrition, and poverty. And suffer and die they did in epidemic proportions in fall and winter 1846–47. The Mormon encampment at the Missouri must still be regarded as one of the most trying, dark, and difficult times in all of Mormon history.[6]

Meanwhile, the Latter-day Saints worried about the country they were leaving behind. Mormon haters like Senator Thomas Benton of Missouri were poisoning opinion against them in Washington,[7] an American war against Mexico was declared in May 1846 over control of California, a still unresolved debate existed with England over the Oregon Territories, and the U.S. Army of the West, commanded by General Stephen Watts Kearney, was waiting at Fort Leavenworth to receive orders from Washington. The Mormons had to wonder if they would be impeded by the American government they had come to distrust, if not disdain. Would they be caught in the middle of a political conflict that had little to do with them? Would they be forced to take sides in internecine Indian wars? Would Missouri yet again extend its hated shadow over Mormon intentions to build Zion? Could the Saints trust America any more than America could trust them? Both time and space had engulfed these weatherworn wanderers who desperately needed to find a winter quarters on possibly hostile Indian lands, secure provisions to last at least a year, and establish political goodwill with Washington.

"Possessed as You are of My Confidences"—
An Understanding Attitude

The U.S. Army of the West knew all about the Mormons and their wilderness wanderings, but instead of interfering, they came inviting. Thanks to intensive private negotiations in Washington led by Mormon agent Jesse Little, the fortuitous involvement of Thomas L. Kane, and the uniquely advantageous geographical location of the Mormon encampment at the Missouri, the Polk administration wished to signal a conciliatory attitude, a tone of compromise and understanding, born of political rather than humanitarian impulse. If the Mormons, restless and wandering but near the seat of action, could be persuaded to participate in the war against Mexico with a battalion of five hundred or more of their best and healthiest young men, then perhaps a deal could be made that would prove mutually beneficial. The Mormons needed money and provisions; the government desperately wanted more men close at hand to help wrest California for the Stars and Stripes.[8]

Onto this complicated stage of delicate negotiations entered Thomas Leiper Kane, an idealistic, twenty-four-year-old lawyer looking for a cause. He was born to socially elite parents in Philadelphia: John Kintzing Kane, a jurist and judge, and Jane Duval Leiper. His father, a leading Pennsylvania Democrat, had served as attorney general of the state before his recent appointment by President James K. Polk (fig. 4) to the U.S.

District Court for the Eastern District of Pennsylvania. Small in stature and ever delicate in health, Thomas had a philanthropic and compassionate nature. During his life he would become a crusader for antislavery, prison reform, women's rights, the abolition of capital punishment, and many other humanitarian causes. His mother once noted: "I do rejoice that the Almighty has given you such talents, with a heart to use them to benefit your fellow man; and if He only grants you health and strength, I feel assured your future course will be a source of pride to all of us."[9] A Protestant by birth and upbringing, Kane was more liberal in his Christian views and shied away from Evangelicals and everything he perceived as religious fanaticism.[10]

FIG. 4. James K. Polk, c. 1846. As eleventh president of the United States, Polk utilized Thomas L. Kane as an emissary to the Mormons after they left Nauvoo, Illinois. Library of Congress.

In 1846, Thomas's more famous brother, Elisha Kent Kane, who had just returned from a diplomatic mission to China, enrolled as a surgeon in the U.S. Navy. Elisha would later be remembered for his explorations in the high Arctic in search of the lost British explorer Sir John Franklin and for his scientific expeditions that opened the way for "the American route to the pole."[11] Both brothers were devoted patriots who were more committed to serving their country in trying and unpredictable circumstances than they were to enjoying the comforts of home.

Although the Kane papers do not reveal what specifically triggered Thomas Kane's interests in the Mormons, apparently his concerns on the subject had "weighed upon" his mind for many months.[12] By mid-1846, he had determined to find his own adventure and to help his country secure both Oregon and California for the Republic, and as a humanitarian, he planned to help a beleaguered body of religionists who were angry enough to consider aligning themselves with British, rather than American, interests.[13] Furthermore, at a church service in Philadelphia on May 13, Kane had met Jesse Little (fig. 5), a Mormon agent charged with seeking government contracts and whom Judge Kane described as "an honest man."[14] Little's instructions from Church leaders were that "if our government shall offer any facilities for emigrating to the western coast, embrace those facilities, if possible."[15] Thomas Kane provided Little access to administration officials, including President Polk. In the process, Kane became a friend and confidante of the Mormon emissary. As a result, young Kane was soon drawn into the midst of a very delicate round of negotiations involving an American administration seeking immediate military support for its war on Mexico and a Mormon leadership hoping for understanding and financial opportunity. Little indicated to President Polk that if the Mormons, who were in desperate, destitute circumstances, were unsuccessful in gaining support from Washington, they might seek for it elsewhere.

> [We] . . . are true hearted Americans . . . and we have a desire to go under the outstretched wings of the American Eagle. We would disdain to receive assistance from a foreign power, although it should be proffered, unless our government shall turn us off in this great crisis and will not help us, but compel us to be foreigners. Means for the gathering of poor we must obtain . . . and if I cannot get it in the land of my fathers, I will cross the trackless ocean where I trust I shall find some friends to help.[16]

Thus, Kane quickly became a trusted arbiter. When Little mentioned he was about to return to the Mormon "Camp of Israel" somewhere in western Iowa Territory, Kane determined to go with him as affidavit of his American loyalties on the one hand and his sympathies with the Mormons on the other. The two men departed Washington within days of one another on a journey of some two thousand miles. Kane planned to join up with Brigham Young, if not at Council Bluffs then wherever the Mormon companies might be on their westward trails, and accompany them all the way to Upper California.[17]

The Kane papers clarify the fact that President Polk wanted "definite information of the character of the leading Mormons," for the information he had received was "so various and conflicting," so "partial" or "prejudiced" as to make it "out of the question for the government to decide what course it would be proper, or even safe, to pursue in regard to them."[18] Moreover, Polk, while not wanting to distance himself from

FIG. 5. Jesse Carter Little. Little met Thomas L. Kane in 1846 and wrote him a letter of introduction to Brigham Young. Church History Library.

those in his administration and party who were critical of the Mormons, hoped to signal a working sympathy for the Latter-day Saints. Among those most wary of Mormon intentions were Senator Thomas Benton; John C. Edwards, governor of Missouri; perhaps Amos Kendall, former postmaster general; and William Medill, commissioner of the Office of Indian Affairs. Medill worried less about the possible collusion of the Mormons with western tribes and more about their contributing unknowingly to intertribal warfare, especially among the Sioux and Pawnee.[19] Yet new documents now make it clearer than ever before that many were sympathetic with the Mormons. "This much . . . seems to be conceded," Kane's father wrote to his traveling son,

> that they have been wronged by the State which they had chosen for their home, and that the honour of the nation requires that the wrong be not renewed where the power of the Union can be directly exerted for their protection. If then you are satisfied that your fellow travelers have not left their Americanism behind them, I think you will be safe in saying to them that they will carry with them the sympathies of their countrymen, and the guarantee of National Faith for their future repose.[20]

Judge Kane elaborated further on his feelings in another letter.

> Circumstances have made me much more familiar than I ever expected to be, with the character of the Emigrating Mormons and their habit and tone of life. My son . . . on a confidential errand from the President . . . has acquainted me from time to time with his observations regarding them. The result is, that I am thoroughly convinced of the general integrity and right mindedness of this persecuted sect—that they form a class of simple, industrious, kind spirited, and enterprising people . . . and in spite of their fanaticism, altogether deserving a different fortune. . . . They will carry to California abundant American feeling, and a determination to plant a permanent American colony in the Sacramento Valley.[21]

Taken at face value, such previously unknown statements reveal much about the government's sentiments and of the trust the president had in Thomas Kane. Wrote Polk in a confidential letter to Kane in June 1846: "Possessed as you are of my confidences you may have it in your power to import to those entrusted with the interests of the United States in that distant region, information of importance."[22] That same month, Judge Kane informed his son that "there is no man in whom the President has more absolute confidence." Judge Kane, who had once discouraged his son from becoming involved in the Mormon issue, was now convinced that his son might be "the means of doing a great good, not only to the people with whom you march, but the country under whose flag they are to live—for it is a good to the country, as well as the Mormons, to bind them together by a sense of mutual benefits."[23]

Thomas Kane later admitted he was granted authority to negotiate secretly on Polk's behalf and to do whatever necessary to ensure the loyalty of the Mormons to the government of the United States. "Invested with amusingly plenipotential powers civil and military, I 'went among the Mormons,'" he later wrote. "This is a little State Secret. Mr. Polk knew it. General Kearney knew it. One Col. Allen detailed by Kearney to march off a Battalion knew it. But probably no one else."[24] In bearing the goodwill and invitation of the president of the United States, Kane had to keep his mission secret from those in Washington who were opposed to federal assistance for Brigham Young and his Mormon followers.

As previously recognized, Jesse Little trusted Kane and recommended him "unhesitatingly" in his letters of introduction (fig. 6). Writing from St. Louis on June 22, 1846, Little said Kane bears "by my request to the President Papers of Great Value to us and enough for me to say that I have proved him well—and do most cheerfully recommend him as a true friend."[25]

"I Can See No Reason Why . . . Not"—
Thomas L. Kane and the Call of the Mormon Battalion

Kane caught up to the Mormon encampment in early July, a few days ahead of Little. Kane had traveled upriver from St. Louis, where he first conferred with General Stephen Kearney and then followed after Captain James Allen, who met with Mormon leaders for the first time at Mt. Pisgah on June 26, 1846. A gracious military officer, Allen gained local leader William Huntington's permission to address the Saints; on behalf of the president of the United States, Captain Allen invited the Mormons to enlist in the army of the West. "Shocked by [this] audacity to ask them to assist a government they popularly distrusted," Huntington said that he "followed [Allen] with an address, as the old saying is 'by answering a fool according to his folly.'"[26] Nonetheless, Huntington then provided Allen with a letter of introduction addressed to the authorities at Council Bluffs. Parley P. Pratt then galloped west to tell Brigham Young of Allen's appearance. As indicated earlier, Allen's invitation for a Mormon Battalion of five hundred of their most able-bodied men was not well received by the Saints initially. It took the earnest pleadings of their file leaders, the calm presentations of Captain Allen, and the assurances of newly arrived Thomas L. Kane, who was bearing the written promises of the president of the United States, to persuade the Saints to give up their men at a most difficult, trying time.[27]

In yet another revealing letter, Kane informed President Polk about the call of the battalion. "I have the honour to inform you that the happiest

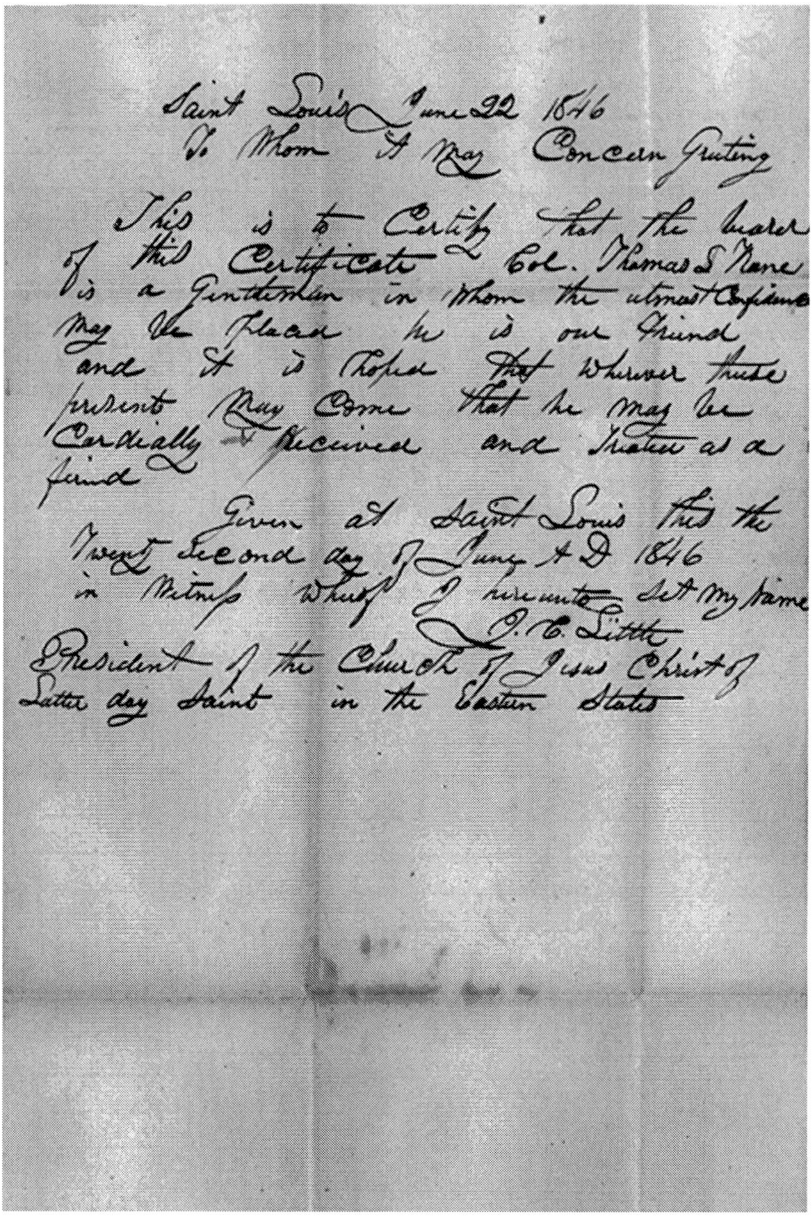

Saint Louis June 22 1846
To Whom It May Concern Greeting

This is to Certify that the bearer of this Certificate Col. Thomas L Kane is a Gentleman in whom the utmost Confidence may be Placed he is our Friend and it is hoped that wherever these presents may Come that he may be Cordially ~~&~~ Received and Treated as a friend

Given at Saint Louis this the Twenty Second day of June A D 1846 in Witness whereof I hereunto Sett my Name
J. C. Little
President of the Church of Jesus Christ of Latter day Saints in the Eastern States

FIG. 6. Letter of introduction from Jesse C. Little, June 22, 1846. In nineteenth-century American society, etiquette required that persons unknown to one another be introduced by a third party. In the case of Thomas L. Kane and the Mormons, Jesse C. Little acted as this third party, providing Kane with letters of introduction to Brigham Young and other Church leaders before Kane headed west to the Mormon settlements in Iowa Territory. L. Tom Perry Special Collections, Harold B. Lee Library, Brigham Young University.

results are to be anticipated from the wise policy observed by you with regard to the Mormon people," he wrote in cipher the night before the battalion marched away. He continued:

> The volunteers whom you have caused to be raised will be on the road to Santa Fe and the Pacific tomorrow or the day after . . . as true hearted Americans bearing the American flag.
>
> I arrived here just in time to be of service to Capt. Allen who was ordered by Col. Kearney to the duty of enrolling [the Mormons].
>
> ... The favour granted by you was at first imperfectly understood by some of the people and they therefore needed the strongest assurances to encourage in them promptitude of action.[28]

In return, Brigham Young negotiated a hard bargain. In addition to receiving cash in advance for the battalion enlistment, Young wanted permission from the federal government to stay on Indian lands, "any" Indian lands, either Pottawattamie on the Iowa side or Omaha on the west side of the Missouri River for at least two years (fig. 7).[29] It was critical that the Mormons winter on the west of the Missouri so as not to have to cross the river again the following spring when it would be swollen with the mountain spring runoffs. Young was concerned about having an early spring departure for the Rocky Mountains.

The Kane papers also confirm that Kane assisted in getting Captain Allen's permission ratified by the necessary Indian agents and departments as quickly as possible. "I have no hesitation in saying that while I can see no reason why the Mormon people should not winter in the valleys of this neighborhood," Kane wrote to President Polk, "I consider it exceedingly important to them to be allowed the privilege of so doing."[30] Judge Kane, in forwarding this letter to President Polk, added his own recommendations: "Circumstances which I have detailed to you in conversation makes it important that this arrangement . . . should be formally sanctioned by the Executive at the earliest day."[31]

Kane did more than write about the enlistment of the Mormon Battalion; we now know that he made several sketches of this important event. One of four he drew is entitled "Enlisting Camp of the Mormons, July 14, 1846" (figs. 8 and 9). It may well be the only contemporary drawing that captures the Mormon Battalion as it headed west to the encampment grounds on the east banks of the Missouri River in what is present-day Council Bluffs, Iowa. This drawing is also significant for evidencing Captain Allen's presence, the immense herds of Mormon cattle, and the various and scattered Mormon encampments at the "Bluffs."[32]

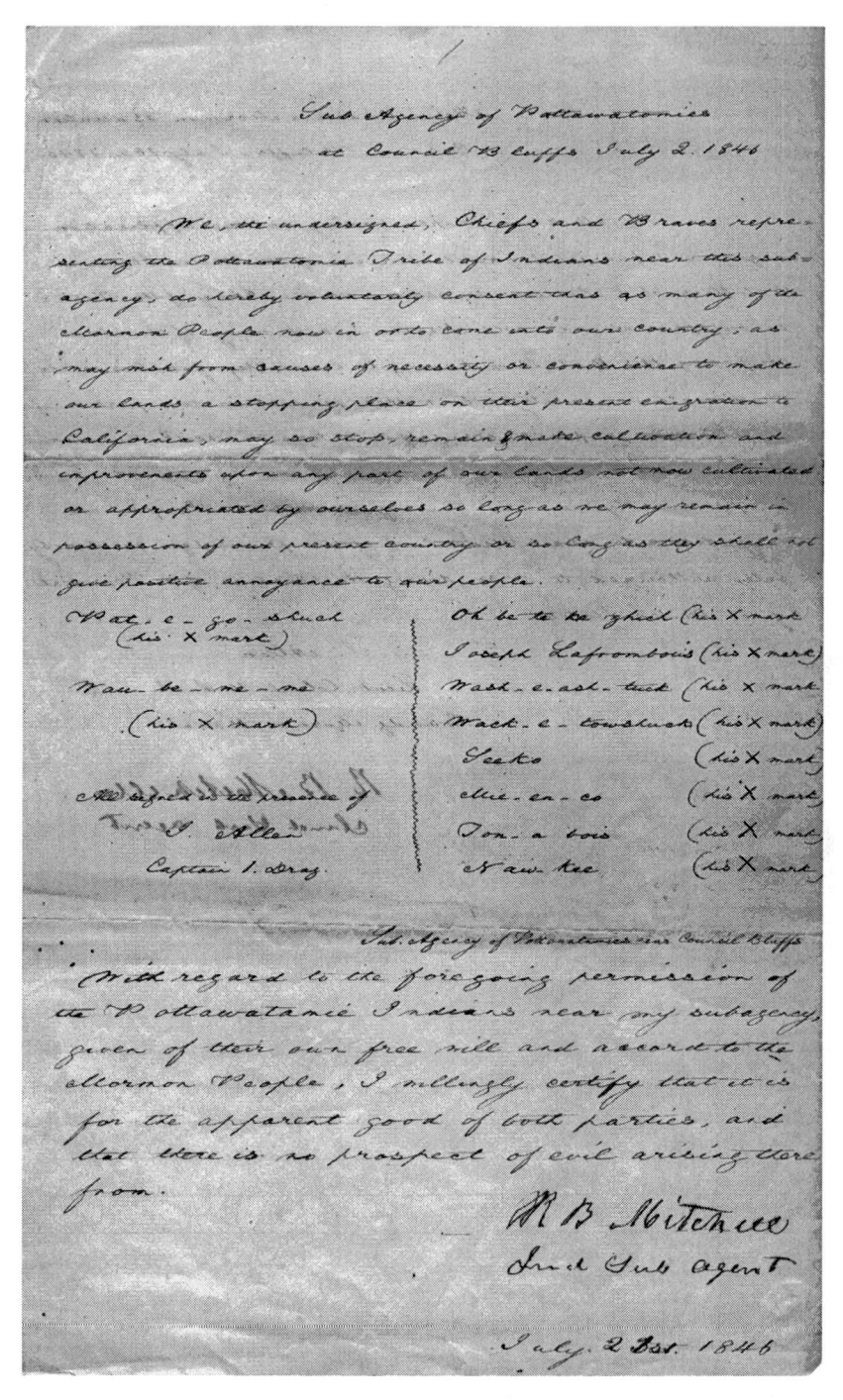

FIG. 7. Letter from Indian Subagent R. B. Mitchell, Council Bluffs, July 21, 1846. This letter was obtained for the Mormons by Thomas L. Kane, and it granted them permission to "stop, remain & make cultivation and improvements upon any part" of the land not already in use by the Native Americans themselves. L. Tom Perry Special Collections, Harold B. Lee Library, Brigham Young University.

FIG. 8. "Enlisting Camp of the Mormons, July 14, 1846." Kane included this sketch in a letter to his father dated July 25, 1846. It depicts the Mormon Battalion moving west to their Missouri River enlistment grounds near Council Bluffs. L. Tom Perry Special Collections, Harold B. Lee Library, Brigham Young University.

FIG. 9. Another sketch from Thomas Kane's papers. The text at the bottom reads, "My waggon—the first camp of the distant prairie of the Platte July 29th 1846 (Horseback Sunrise)." L. Tom Perry Special Collections, Harold B. Lee Library, Brigham Young University.

Winter Quarters—The Mormon Settlement

The Kane papers contain important corroborating information about Winter Quarters, the Mormon pioneer settlements in 1846–47 on lands now part of Florence, Nebraska, and Council Bluffs, Iowa. While Kane may have exaggerated in counting fifteen thousand Mormons at the Missouri River, there were indeed about seven hundred log and mud houses on the west bank. Correspondence between Kane and Brigham Young confirm the fact that the Mormons also wintered their large cattle herds "some 15 or 30 miles north."[33] Furthermore, the papers provide the names of 250 heads of households who petitioned for a post office in what later came to be called Kanesville, in honor of Thomas L. Kane.[34] The collection also documents that a Mr. Beach and a Mr. Eddy of St. Louis definitely operated "a very good store at Winter Quarters,"[35] which affirms the work of Bishop Newel K. Whitney while in St. Louis, Missouri, to establish trade and commerce with Missouri mercantile outlets. While it is true that Missouri expelled the Mormons from the state in winter 1838–39 due to the extermination order of Governor Lilburn W. Boggs, the irony is that many more Latter-day Saints would have died at Winter Quarters without provisions from Missouri in winter 1846–47.[36]

The Kane papers further reveal the names of leading Philadelphia residents, inspired and influenced by Thomas Kane, who donated a sum of $399.20 to the cause of the suffering Mormons at Winter Quarters. These included Kane's own father, Judge John K. Kane (who donated $50, a sum comparable to approximately $2,500 in today's currency), Joseph D. Browne ($50), and Thomas P. Cope ($25).[37] Thomas Kane was more than a mere publicist of Mormon difficulties; he was an active fundraiser in their behalf.

"Your Vindication Became My Own Defense"—Kane's 1850 Lecture

This evaluation of the unique contributions of the Kane papers would not be complete without looking at the circumstances surrounding Kane's famous lecture titled "The Mormons," which he delivered in Philadelphia in 1850 and eventually published for a very large reading audience.[38] A highly sympathetic, if not somewhat embellished, account of the Mormon plight, Kane's address focused on the terrible sufferings of the Mormon "Poor Camps" when they were driven from Nauvoo in fall 1846 and left no doubt as to the terrible injustices heaped upon them. Giving this lecture was a courageous act since Kane had a reputation to uphold and was addressing audiences not always friendly toward the Saints or those speaking in their behalf. But he did so even when he was extremely sick.

The germ of Kane's address had been planted in a letter he wrote to Josiah Quincy (fig. 10), former mayor of Boston and former president of Harvard University,[39] dated February 14, 1848. Kane's account in this letter captures a cruel moment in Mormon exodus history, one not addressed adequately even by those Mormons who lived through this ordeal. His descriptions are incomparable in evoking a genuinely sympathetic attitude toward the tattered remnants of a wounded and persecuted people who were being been driven from their Nauvoo homes at gunpoint into an unforgiving wilderness.

FIG. 10. Josiah Quincy. Quincy served as a member of the U.S. House of Representatives, mayor of Boston, and president of Harvard University. He was a friend of Thomas L. Kane. Library of Congress.

They [Mormon poor camps] compose, originally, the refuse, lame, aged, sick, and pauper members of the church, who were found unable to attempt the great California pilgrimage [the Mormon exodus west to the so-called "Upper California," which then included present-day Utah] of 1846. On this account, their friends who started at that date, concluded, it seems, an especial treaty or armistice for their benefit, with the anti-Mormon mob, and left them behind in Illinois under its protection. This treaty covenanted, . . . that they were in no wise to be molested until another asylum could be prepared for their reception beyond the Rocky Mountains. Just so soon, however, as the Mormon host has made a progress of some months upon its travels, and could safely be considered out of the way, the instrument:—oaths, seals, and ribbons—was broken by the anti-Mormons without ceremony or excuse, and the cripples who relied upon it, were ordered to take up their beds and walk. Upon this, the helpless beings, driven to desperation, made a remarkably resolute defence of their Holy City. . . . It was bombarded, however, by an overwhelming force.

. . . Few had enough to satisfy their hunger. Exposure and fatigue had combined to visit many of the nominally robust of them with the ague, and the bilious remittent fever. . . . I have not the satisfaction of a doubt that among those I looked upon thus shivering in the sharp night air of autumn, many whom the screening of a roof might have saved, died looking across the stream upon their comfortable homes, in which the orthodox bullies of the mob were celebrating their triumph in obscene and drunken riot.[40]

Kane's descriptions of these Mormon sufferings forestalled the growing tide of public anti-Mormon sentiments and earned a much-needed measure of American sympathy, at least until the public announcement in 1852 of the practice of polygamy.

The writing of his final essay is a story in and of itself. Suffice it to say that Kane almost died writing it. "I gave myself four weeks," he confided in a later letter to Brigham Young. "I was full of my subject, but suffered so much from pain and weakness as to be unable the major portion of the time to hold a pen in my hand. However, at it I went in spite of the entreaties of my friends and family." After giving the lecture, he fainted before reaching home and lay in bed for many days.[41] Only gradually did his health improve.

Conclusion

Why did Kane come to respect and admire the Mormon people so deeply? What began as a patriotic duty, a humanitarian goodwill gesture, developed into a genuine and profound friendship with and affinity toward this suffering people. His papers confirm at least five reasons.

First, Kane and the Mormons were partners in sickness. The Latter-day Saints fell ill and died at Winter Quarters at distressing rates. While there, Kane, ever prone to the ague and tuberculosis, also faced death and was kindly nursed back to health by his fellow sufferers. In September 1850, Kane wrote to his Mormon friends, "It is now four years since I left the camp where your kind nursing saved my life."[42]

Second, Kane was so extensively criticized for defending the Mormons that he almost unconsciously became one with them. "The personal assaults upon myself made your cause become so identified with my own, that your vindication became my own defence;" we became "'partners in iniquity'" so to speak, and "we were compelled either to stand or fall together. This probation it is that has made me feel our brotherhood and know how dear to me you have grown."[43]

Third, Kane and the Mormons shared much in common. "I have tried you and proved you and learned to love you," he remarked, "for all God has given you of his goodness. I have known too that my feelings were reciprocated & that you have all along felt toward me as I have felt toward you."[44] A genuine affection developed between Kane, Brigham Young, and the Mormon people.

Fourth, Kane's visit to the Mormon camps genuinely changed his outlook on life, thoroughly deepened his humanitarian impulse, and strengthened his religious convictions. "I think I have become morally a changed man," he wrote of his association with this people in peril.

Though I do not agree with our Religionists; with a less artificial formula of expression it is substantially true, I believe, that there is a crisis in the life of every man when he is called upon to decide seriously and permanently if he will die unto sin and live unto righteousness, and that till he has gone through this, he cannot fit himself for the inheritance of his higher humanity, and become truly pure and truly strong "to do the work of God persevering unto the end." Without endorsing the cant of preachers either, I believe that Providence brings about these crises for all of us by events in our own lives which are the evangelists to us of admonition and preparation. Such an event I believe was my visit to you.

I had many disregarded hints and warnings before, but it was the spectacle of your noble suffering for conscience sake made first a truly serious and abiding impression upon my mind, commanding me to note that there was something nobler and higher than the pursuit of interests of Earthly life, and taught me worthier the aspirations of a Spirit made after the image of Duty. I trust to seek the better part.[45]

Finally, Kane admitted his association with the Mormons had soured him from pursuing politics and encouraged him to pursue other humanitarian causes. "I have lost almost entirely the natural love for intrigue and curious management which I fear was once a noticeable defect of my character.... No, should I have lived, my place would have been in the ranks of the supporters of causes called desperate and at the head of unthanked and unrewarded pioneers of unpopular reforms."[46]

Thomas L. Kane lived longer than he ever anticipated, dying in 1883 at age sixty-one. During his lifetime, he maintained a steady correspondence with his friends in the Rocky Mountains. In 1857, he helped broker the essential compromise between the Mormons and Johnston's army during the march on Utah Territory by another U.S. Army. Kane went on to serve nobly in the Union Army during the Civil War. He wrote Brigham Young often and even advised him on such matters as the writing of his will and the establishment of Brigham Young Academy. Kane's influence and legacy continue into the twenty-first century at Brigham Young University. Although a friend to the Saints, Kane never aligned himself with them. Yet these last words express his feelings toward them: "I request you to receive my heart for deposit in your Salt Lake City Temple that after death it may repose where in metaphor at least it was when living."[47]

Richard E. Bennett (who can be reached by email via byustudies@byu.edu) earned his PhD from Wayne State University in Detroit, Michigan. He currently is Professor of Church History and Doctrine at Brigham Young University, director of research for the Department of Church History and Doctrine, and chair of the

Church History Board for BYU Studies. Prior to coming to BYU in 1997, he served as the department chair of the archives and special collections at the University of Manitoba in Winnipeg, Canada.

1. Richard E. Bennett, *Mormons at the Missouri, 1846–1852: "And Should We Die . . ."* (Norman: University of Oklahoma Press, 1987), 13–25.

2. See Bennett, *Mormons at the Missouri,* 24–25. See also Glen M. Leonard, *Nauvoo: A Place of Peace, A People of Promise* (Salt Lake City: Deseret Book; Provo, Utah: Brigham Young University Press, 2002), 551–86.

3. Richard E. Bennett, *Mormons at the Missouri,* 37.

4. Richard E. Bennett, *We'll Find the Place: The Mormon Exodus, 1846–1848* (Salt Lake City: Deseret Book, 1997), 31–40.

5. Bennett, *Mormons at the Missouri,* 45.

6. See Bennett, *Mormons at the Missouri,* 131–47. See also Evan L. Ivie and Douglas C. Heiner, "Deaths in Early Nauvoo, 1939–46, and Winter Quarters, 1846–48," *The Religious Educator,* 10, no. 3 (2009): 163–73.

7. Matthew J. Grow, *"Liberty to the Downtrodden": Thomas L. Kane, Romantic Reformer* (New Haven, Conn.: Yale University Press, 2009), 53–54.

8. Bennett, *Mormons at the Missouri,* 52–67.

9. Jane Kane to Thomas L. Kane, July 1846, Thomas L. and Elizabeth W. Kane Collection, L. Tom Perry Special Collections, Harold B. Lee Library, Brigham Young University, Provo, Utah.

10. Grow, *"Liberty to the Downtrodden,"* 47. For more on Kane's religious views, see Matthew Grow's essay herein.

11. As cited in "Register to the Thomas L. Kane and Elizabeth W. Kane Collection," prepared by David J. Whittaker, et al., L. Tom Perry Special Collections (2001), 2 vols., vol 1:14.

12. Thomas L. Kane to Elisha Kent [?] Kane, May 29, 1846, Kane Collection, Perry Special Collections. For more on Kane's motives for becoming invoved with the Mormon's, see Matthew Grow's and Edward Geary's essays herein.

13. Thomas L. Kane to Elisha Kent [?] Kane, May 29, 1846, Kane Collection, Perry Special Collections. See also Richard E. Bennett, "The Lion and the Emperor: The Mormons, the Hudson's Bay Company, and Vancouver Island, 1846–1858." *BC Studies* no. 128 (Winter 2000/2001), 47–52.

14. John K. Kane to William [Mathoit?], October 1, 1846, Kane Collection, Perry Special Collections.

15. Jesse C. Little to Brigham Young and the Council of the Twelve Apostles, July 6, 1846, quoted in Frank Alfred Golder, *The March of the Mormon Battalion from Council Bluffs to California: Taken from the Journal of Henry Standage* (New York: The Century Company, 1928), 74, 103.

16. Jesse C. Little to Brigham Young and the Council of the Twelve Apostles, July 6, 1846, quoted in Golder, *March of the Mormon Battalion,* 83.

17. Grow, *"Liberty to the Downtrodden,"* 48–50.

18. John K. Kane to Thomas L. Kane, June 18, 1846, Kane Collection, Perry Special Collections.

19. Bennett, *Mormons at the Missouri,* 52, 53, 55, 102–3, 258–59; Golder, *March of the Mormon Battalion,* 98–99.

20. John K. Kane to Thomas L. Kane, June 15, 1846, Kane Collection, Perry Special Collections.

21. John K. Kane to William Macleod [?], October 1, 1846, Kane Collection, Perry Special Collections.
22. James K. Polk to Thomas L. Kane, June 11, 1846, Kane Collection, Perry Special Collections.
23. James K. Polk to Thomas L. Kane, June 11, 1846, Kane Collection, Perry Special Collections.
24. Thomas L. Kane to Elizabeth D. Wood, May 19, 1852, Kane Collection, Perry Special Collections.
25. Jesse C. Little to "Dear Brethren," June 22, 1846, Kane Collection, Perry Special Collections. Little wrote a similar letter to Sam Brannan on the same day. Jesse C. Little to Sam Brannan, June 22, 1846, Kane Collection, Perry Special Collections.
26. William Huntington, "A History," June 26, 1846, as cited in Bennett, *Mormons at the Missouri: Winter Quarters*, 51.
27. Grow, *"Liberty to the Downtrodden,"* 58–59.
28. Thomas L. Kane to President James K. Polk, July 21, 1846, Kane Collection, Perry Special Collections. Forwarded to the president by John K. Kane, with his letter of support, August 18, 1846, Kane Collection, Perry Special Collections. "This sanction is desirable, not only to tranquilize the honest apprehensions of the mass[es], but to disprove the intimations and affected doubts of the few whose sympathies are adverse to the United States." Many times Kane wrote to his father in code lest anyone, Mormon or otherwise, discovered the full extent of his mission.
The Kane papers clearly show that Judge Kane was more instrumental in supporting his son's efforts in behalf of the Mormons than previously appreciated. Not only did he decode his son's writings, but he also often pled his cause and spoke ever favorably of the Mormons with the president himself.
29. Grow, *"Liberty to the Downtrodden,"* 63.
30. Thomas L. Kane to President James K. Polk, July 21, 1846, Kane Collection, Perry Special Collections.
31. John K. Kane to James K. Polk, August 29, 1846, Kane Collection, Perry Special Collections.
32. Thomas L. Kane to John K. Kane, letter of introduction for Orson Hyde, July 25, 1846, Kane Collection, Perry Special Collections. On the reverse side of the sketch is the following entry: "The eye is on a high hill. Capt. Allan's tent. [A] Immediately on the right at its foot begins the road that comes from [Mt.] Pisgah to the Missouri (B) and continues all along the Prairie Bottom, marked here & there by waggons drawn by ox teams . . . The distant line of timber. [C.] marks the course of the Missouri. Some trees small mark the course of a creek in the meadow at the right & front. The other marks mean waggons[,] tents or cattle the more speckly[,] generally cattle which crowd every hill-side and meadow, and the low speckles on the distant prairie bottoms are camps. The nos. 1.2.3.4.5.6. denote relative distance."
33. Brigham Young to Thomas L. Kane, August 2, 1846, Kane Collection, Perry Special Collections.
34. "To the Honorable Postmaster General of the United States," in an undated letter of Thomas L. Kane, Kane Collection, Perry Special Collections.
35. William S. Appleby to Col. T. L. Kane, June 20, 1848, Kane Collection, Perry Special Collections.

36. For more on this topic, see Richard E. Bennett, "'We Had Everything to Procure from Missouri:' The Missouri Lifeline to the Mormon Exodus, 1846–1850," *Mormon Historical Studies*, 8 nos. 1 and 2 (Spring/Fall 2007): 91–108.

37. William S. Appleby to Col. T. L. Kane, June 20, 1848, Kane Collection, Perry Special Collections. For a full treatment of the fundraising efforts of the Mormons in east coast American cities, in large part inspired by Kane, see Bennett, *We'll Find the Place*, 302–11.

38. Thomas L. Kane, *The Mormons: A Discourse Delivered before the Historical Society of Pennsylvania, March 26, 1850* (Philadelphia: King and Baird, 1850).

39. Quincy was mayor from 1823 to 1829 and president from 1829 to 1845.

40. Thomas L. Kane to Mr. Quincy, February 14, 1848, Kane Collection, Perry Special Collections.

41. Thomas L. Kane to Brigham Young, Fall 1850, Kane Collection, Perry Special Collections.

42. Thomas L. Kane to "My dear friends," September 1850, Kane Collection, Perry Special Collections.

43. Thomas L. Kane to "My dear friends," September 1850, Kane Collection, Perry Special Collections.

44. Thomas L. Kane to "My dear friends," September 1850, Kane Collection, Perry Special Collections.

45. Thomas L. Kane to "My dear friends," September 1850, Kane Collection, Perry Special Collections.

46. Thomas L. Kane to "My dear friends," September 1850, Kane Collection, Perry Special Collections.

47. Thomas L. Kane to "My dear friends," September 1850, Kane Collection, Perry Special Collections. For more on the Utah War, see William MacKinnon's essay herein. For more on Kane's Civil War service, see Matthew Grow's and Edward Geary's essays herein. For more on Kane's correspondence with Brigham Young see David Whittaker's essay herein.

Thomas L. Kane and the Mormon Problem in National Politics

Thomas G. Alexander

After the Mormons began to leave their temporary settlements on the Missouri in 1847 to settle in Utah, three key events marked Thomas L. Kane's experience with the problems of the Mormons in national politics: (1) the Mormons' quest for statehood or territorial organization in 1849 and 1850; (2) the dispute over federally appointed officials in 1851 and 1852; and (3) the conflicts created by the judicial administration of James B. McKean in the early 1870s. This essay will explore these instances in which Kane assisted the Mormons and the people of Utah in their dealings with the federal government.

The National Scene

To understand how Thomas L. Kane helped the Mormons navigate the rough terrain of national politics, it is necessary to consider the context of American politics and society during the second half of the nineteenth century. Whether slavery should expand into the areas of the Louisiana Purchase and the Mexican Cession was an issue that divided Americans during the 1840s and 1850s. This division can be seen in the political parties of the era. The Democratic Party split into free soil and proslavery Democrats, and the Whigs split into conscience Whigs and proslavery Whigs. In 1848 a significant number of Democrats, including Kane, left the Democratic Party to support the Free Soil Party, which opposed the expansion of slavery into the territories.[1]

By 1856 the Whig Party had died, and in its wake the Republican Party had arisen. The Republicans strongly opposed slavery in the territories and considered slavery and polygamy to be the "twin relics of barbarism." They hoped to eventually eradicate both, although at times they hedged on slavery in the states. Beginning with Abraham Lincoln's election in 1860, the Republican Party, with its decidedly anti-Mormon agenda, controlled the presidency and a closely divided Congress during most of the remainder of the nineteenth century.[2] Under this political system, Thomas L. Kane worked to influence the administration and Congress to treat his friends in Utah justly.

Although Mormons would have preferred to remain aloof from the controversies surrounding slavery and polygamy, after 1856 they could not do so. Under the United States system of dual sovereignty, the states have jurisdiction over such matters as qualifications for marriage, voters, and candidates for offices. Territories, as creatures of the federal government, however, do not enjoy the benefits of dual sovereignty. The federal government considers them colonies preparing for statehood. The president selects the territories' principal executive and judicial officers with Senate approval, and Congress may legislate for the territories as long as it protects individual rights guaranteed by the Constitution as interpreted by the Supreme Court. Territories do elect members of their legislature, city and county officers, and a delegate to Congress. The delegate can introduce legislation, speak on the floor of the House, and vote in committee. However, this person may not vote on the floor of the House. Working within the realities of American politics, Kane took up the Mormon cause, he tried to convince the administration and Congress to treat his friends in Utah fairly.

Quest for Statehood

Between July 1847, when the first Mormon settlers arrived in the region that would later become Utah, and September 1850, when Congress organized Utah Territory, the Latter-day Saints ruled the region with a provisional government as the State of Deseret.[3]

The Mormon quest for statehood officially began in 1849, though Kane had offered advice on the matter as early as April 1847.[4] In March 1849, the leadership in Utah drafted a constitution for what they called the State of Deseret.[5] After the public approved the constitution, the leaders sent two men to Washington to lobby for authorization of either a territorial or a state government. Dr. John M. Bernhisel (fig. 1), a physician of conservative disposition, left for the east on May 3.[6] Almon Whiting Babbitt (fig. 2), a local attorney who often did not seem to understand whom he represented, went east as the designated representative of the State of Deseret on July 27.[7]

Although Bernhisel carried a letter of introduction from the First Presidency of the Church to Senator Stephen A. Douglas of Illinois, who had previously aided the Mormons, Bernhisel and Mormon leader Elder Wilford Woodruff (fig. 3) met instead with Kane in Philadelphia on November 26, 1849. The purpose of the meeting was to plan for the campaign to legalize either a state or a territory. Kane told them that at Brigham Young's request, he had already applied to President James K. Polk for territorial government, but he had withdrawn the territorial petition on his "own discretion" after Polk told him that he did not favor the Mormons and that he would appoint outsiders to the territorial offices.[8]

However, Polk was now no longer in office, having turned the administration over to Zachary Taylor (fig. 4) and Millard Fillmore (fig. 5) on March 4, 1849. Kane offered Bernhisel and Woodruff tactical advice in dealing with the various politicians in their attempt to secure state or territorial government, urging the Mormons to take a neutral stand on the divisive slavery question. Kane also urged them not to align themselves with either party and promised that he would work with the Free Soil Party and that he would have his father, John K. Kane, and his friend George M. Dallas (fig. 6), the former vice president, work with the Democratic Party. Kane pointed out that

FIG. 1. John M. Bernhisel. Bernhisel was the first delegate from Utah Territory and served in the U.S. House of Representatives. Church History Library.

FIG. 2. Almon Whiting Babbitt. Babbitt served as lobbyist for the State of Deseret. He later served as the fourth secretary of Utah Territory (1853–56). Used by permission, Utah State Historical Society, all rights reserved.

Fig. 3. Wilford Woodruff, steel engraving, c. 1853. Woodruff met Thomas L. Kane in 1846. Church History Library.

Fig. 4. Zachary Taylor. As twelfth president of the United States, Taylor urged delay in the organization of Utah Territory. Library of Congress.

Fig. 5. Millard Fillmore, c. 1877. As thirteenth president of the United States, Fillmore approved the Utah Territorial Organic Act that made Utah a territory, and he also appointed the first group of Utah territorial officials, some of whom became the controversial "runaway officials." Library of Congress.

Fig. 6. George M. Dallas, c. 1844, by Currier and Ives. Dallas served as vice president to James K. Polk and was an influential friend of Kane's father, Judge John K. Kane. Library of Congress.

Mormons could count as "enemies" to Senators David R. Atchison and Thomas Hart Benton of Missouri, and intimated that the Mormons could expect little help from Illinois Senator Stephen A. Douglas (fig. 7), then serving as chair of the Senate Committee on Territories.[9]

Woodruff met again with Kane on December 4. Kane told Woodruff that Utahns would be better off "without any Government from the hands of Congress than [with] a Territorial Government. . . . You do not want," he said,

> Corrupt Political men from Washington strutting around you with military . . . dress. . . . You do not want two Governments with you. You have a Government now which is firm & Powerful and You are under no obligations to the United States. . . . Brigham Young should be your Govornor. . . . He has power to see through men & things. . . . [Under his leadership all associates will] work for the general good in all things and not act from selfish motives or to get some Petty office or a little salary.[10]

On the other hand, Kane suggested, if the people of Utah "did make up [their] minds to ask for a Territory [they] should use every exhertion in [their] power to get the assureance of the President that [their] Choice should be granted [them] in a Govornor & other officers." If they could not secure such a promise, he recommended that they not ask for territorial organization, but await "the result."[11]

Citing his frequent bouts of ill health, Kane told Woodruff he might not be able to continue to work as much as previously for the Mormons. Woodruff told him he would "Pray for his success in our behalf" and "also for his health strength & prosperity." Impressed with Kane's "wisdom," Woodruff wrote that he believed that the Pennsylvanian held "right views of things in General." After Woodruff returned to Utah in fall 1850, he read the entries from his journal of conversations with Kane to the Church's First Presidency and

FIG. 7. Stephen A. Douglas, c. 1855–1865. Douglas was a well-known orator and politician who represented Illinois as a congressman and as a senator. He championed such controversial bills as the Compromise of 1850 and the 1854 Kansas-Nebraska Act. Library of Congress.

FIG. 8. Truman Smith, daguerrotype, c. 1844–60. As a senator from Connecticut, Smith assisted unofficial Utah territorial delegate John M. Bernhisel in lobbying for Utah statehood. Library of Congress.

Quorum of the Twelve, as Kane had requested.[12]

Kane and Bernhisel continued to lobby Congress and the administration. By mid-January 1850, a perceptive Bernhisel understood that Congress would most likely not admit Deseret-Utah as a state, though Whig Senator Truman Smith (fig. 8) of Connecticut encouraged Bernhisel to believe, at first, that Congress might authorize Utahns to elect their own territorial officers. By this time, President Taylor had begun floating the idea of organizing California as a monster state (covering present-day California, Nevada, and Utah) that might be divided later. After assessing the situation, Bernhisel understood that Congress would not act until mid- to-late summer, at the earliest, on the application for statehood.[13]

Meanwhile, Almon W. Babbitt was managing to make a nuisance of himself, and neither Bernhisel nor Kane had much confidence in Babbitt's judgment or character. Kane said Babbitt lacked "wisdom, prudence and discretion."[14] Bernhisel witnessed such failings in Babbitt in an incident that took place early in 1850. By January a rumor had circulated that President Taylor would veto any bill "for the benefit of the Mormons." Imprudent as usual, Babbitt told Bernhisel that Fitz Henry Warren, the First Assistant Postmaster General, had made an appointment to introduce Babbitt to the president on January 11. Before the visit, Babbitt told Bernhisel he would ask the president if the rumor was true. If Taylor said yes, Babbitt would reply, "We might as well abandon our application for a government." Bernhisel urged Babbitt not to say anything to the president on the subject of state or territorial government.[15]

On the day after Babbitt's visit with Taylor, Bernhisel met with Babbitt again. Having ignored Bernhisel's advice, Babbitt and Warren had spoken with the president on the matter. Taylor had responded by commenting on "the absurdity of the Mormons asking for a State or Territorial government." Upset with Babbitt's lack of judgment, Bernhisel urged him again to remain quiet on the subject, telling him he would "entirely blast our prospects here" if he did not. Babbitt promised to drop the subject, and he asked Warren to do the same.[16] Nevertheless, in his message to Congress on January 21, 1850, President Taylor urged delay in the organization of Utah territory.[17]

By early March, Bernhisel had concluded they could not "get such a form of government, as will authorize us to choose our own officers." Under the circumstances, Bernhisel agreed with Kane that they "had better continue [their] provisional government." Under such a government, they could "enjoy peace and quiet, until [their] population" had grown large enough "to entitle [them] to admission . . . as a State."[18] Acting on Kane's advice, Bernhisel tried to induce Stephen Douglas to withdraw the application for territorial status. Unmoved by his attempt, Douglas told Bernhisel that Congress had a "duty to organize the territories" and that Congress and the nation could not settle the slavery question "until the territories were organized."[19] These comments undoubtedly reflected Douglas's views that adopting popular sovereignty in the territories would solve the slavery issue.

By late March 1850, Bernhisel had been left on his own to try to influence Congress to meet the Utahns' needs. Babbitt was visiting Nauvoo and Council Bluffs, and Kane had grown so ill that after he had delivered a lecture on the Mormons to the Historical Society of Pennsylvania on March 26, 1850, his physician ordered him to go to the West Indies for his health.[20] Kane's lecture and its publication in pamphlet form appeared at a crucial time during congressional consideration of Utah's application for state or territorial government. The address provided such a positive treatment of the Mormons and their persecution that, although it did not soften Taylor's resolve, it did help to shape public opinion in the Mormons' favor.[21]

Bernhisel secured the help of Senator Truman Smith, who tried to bypass Douglas's Territorial Committee by inserting an amendment in an appropriation bill to legalize the State of Deseret. That failed, and Douglas introduced bills to organize Deseret Territory, which the senators renamed Utah, and New Mexico Territory. Douglas's bill, amended in both the Senate and the House, languished until after President Taylor's death on July 9, 1850. Thereafter it moved with deliberate speed through the two houses. The newly installed president, Millard Fillmore, who proved as well-disposed toward Utahns as they could realistically expect, signed the Utah Territorial Organic Act on September 9, 1850, as part of the multifaceted Compromise of 1850.[22]

Fig. 9. Willard Richards, steel engraving, c. 1853. Member of the Twelve, Church Historian, and a counselor to Brigham Young, Richards became territorial secretary, pro tem, in 1851. Church History Library.

Fig. 10. Zerubbabel Snow. Snow served as supreme court associate justice for Utah Territory, 1850–54. He later became the attorney general in 1869. Used by permission, Utah State Historical Society, all rights reserved.

Fig. 11. Seth M. Blair. The first U.S. district attorney for Utah, Blair was nominated by President Millard Fillmore in 1850 and served until he was called on a Church mission in 1854. *Pioneers and Prominent Men of Utah*, 245.

Fig. 12. Joseph L. Heywood. Heywood was appointed U.S. marshal for Utah by President Millard Fillmore in 1850. He later helped settle southern Utah. *Pioneers and Prominent Men of Utah*, 121.

The Federal Appointees

Unfortunately, Kane's prediction of the intense grief that Utahns would suffer with officials appointed from outside the territory proved all too accurate, as the relationship with the first set of officials demonstrated. On September 16, 1850, Bernhisel sent President Fillmore a list of men Utahns recommended as their territorial officials. These included Brigham Young as governor, Willard Richards (fig. 9) as territorial secretary, Zerubbabel Snow (fig. 10) as supreme court chief justice, Heber C. Kimball and Newel K. Whitney as associate justices, Seth M. Blair (fig. 11) as U.S. attorney for Utah, and Joseph L. Heywood (fig. 12) as U.S. marshal for Utah. In his letter submitting the recommendations, Bernhisel argued that Utahns had a "right, as American citizens, to be governed by men of their own choice, entitled to their confidence, and united with them in opinion and feeling."[23]

FIG. 13. Daniel Webster. An esteemed statesman, Webster served as U.S. representative from New Hampshire, as U.S. representative and senator from Massachusetts, and twice as U.S. secretary of state. Library of Congress.

Babbitt successfully undercut Bernhisel's argument and recommendations by sending his own recommendations to Secretary of State Daniel Webster (fig. 13) dated September 21, 1850, seven days before Fillmore sent his nominations to the Senate. Styling himself "Delegate from the Territory of Utah," Babbitt provided a different list of candidates, which he may have discussed earlier with Webster and perhaps even with Fillmore. This discussion seems probable because, with one exception, the list coincided with the nominations Fillmore actually made. The exception was Henry R. Day of Missouri, whom Babbitt recommended as territorial secretary. Fillmore appointed Day as an Indian subagent rather than as secretary.[24]

Following Babbitt's and Bernhisel's recommendations, Fillmore nominated Young as governor, Blair as attorney, and Heywood as marshal. Kimball (fig. 14) and Whitney (fig. 15) were rejected as justices, though this is understandable as neither was an attorney. From Babbitt's list, Fillmore nominated Joseph Buffington of Pennsylvania as chief justice.

FIG. 14. Heber C. Kimball, steel engraving, c. 1853. Utah Territory representative John Bernhisel recommended to President Fillmore that Kimball serve as an associate justice in the territory. Church History Library.

FIG. 15. Newel K. Whitney. Bernhisel also recommended that Whitney serve as another associate justice in the territory. Church History Library.

When Buffington refused to serve, Fillmore nominated Lemuel G. Brandebury, whom Babbitt also had recommended. For the other associate justices, Fillmore followed Babbitt's list and nominated Zerubbabel Snow of Ohio and Perry E. Brocchus (fig. 16) of Alabama. Instead of Richards or Day, Fillmore nominated Broughton D. Harris of Vermont as territorial secretary.

Utah's first territorial chief justice, Lemuel G. Brandebury of Carlisle, Pennsylvania, arrived in Utah on June 7, 1851, earlier than any of the other appointees from outside the territory. Before accepting the judgeship in Utah, Brandebury had lobbied unsuccessfully for appointment as recorder of the General Land Office in Washington, D.C., and for a position in the Treasury Department solicitor's office.[25] In 1851, Pennsylvania friends campaigned for his appointment as chief justice of Utah Territory. Letters and petitions poured in from members of the Pennsylvania congressional delegation.[26] Although Brandebury sent two letters to Fillmore withdrawing his application, the president nominated him on March 12, 1851. Congress confirmed the appointment, and despite his reluctance, Brandebury agreed to serve.[27]

On August 17, Associate Justice Perry E. Brocchus, a Democrat from Alabama, arrived in Utah, the last of the outside appointees to reach Salt Lake City. He had practiced law in Alabama and served as a law clerk in

FIG. 16. Perry E. Brocchus. President Millard Fillmore appointed Brocchus as a supreme court justice for Utah Territory in 1850. He left Utah in 1851, soon after arriving. Special Collections Deptartment, J. Willard Marriott Library, University of Utah.

the solicitor's office in Washington, D.C. Beginning in 1847, the ambitious Brocchus had lobbied the Polk administration for appointment as a supreme court justice in both Minnesota and Oregon territories. He failed in his efforts to secure either appointment, and he did not apply for the Utah judgeship. Nevertheless, Fillmore appointed Brocchus on September 28, 1850, with the first judicial list.[28]

Among the three justices appointed on the first list, only one, Zerubbabel Snow, was a Latter-day Saint. (Zerubbabel's brother Erastus was a member of the Quorum of the Twelve.) Snow, a Democrat like Brocchus and Babbitt, had joined the Church in 1832. He lived in Ohio at the time of his appointment as an associate justice. Significantly, Snow's file contains fewer letters of support than Brandebury's and Brocchus's.[29] Interior Secretary Alexander H. H. Stuart wrote to Fillmore on the same day the president nominated Snow. Stuart repeated allegations from two clerks who said Snow was "a man of bad character, of no talent, and has always been a *loco foco*," a pre–Civil War designation for a radical Democrat.[30] Fillmore acted in spite of Stuart's letter and did not rescind the nomination. Snow arrived in Salt Lake City on July 19, accompanied by Bernhisel and Babbitt. With them also came territorial secretary Broughton D. Harris and Indian agents Henry R. Day and Stephen B. Rose.[31]

Brigham Young's nomination as governor caused more of a stir. Young was recommended by Babbitt and Bernhisel and also had the endorsement of Kane, who spoke directly with Fillmore, defending Young from a number of unflattering newspaper attacks. Kane had recommended Kimball and Richards, and he had provided Fillmore with information "upon which to base his defence against . . . assailants" of the three. Kane also had written a confidential letter in support of Young that someone leaked in a garbled and uncomplimentary form to a newspaper.[32] After a series of attacks and counterattacks appeared in party newspapers, Kane succeeded in blunting the effects of the assaults, convincing Fillmore to maintain the nomination.[33] In his defense of Young and others, Kane also found it necessary to mount a rearguard action in the press against Babbitt's "improper conduct and [to disavow] his improper associations," presumably for fear he would undermine the nomination.[34]

Flight of the Runaways

After the flurry of disputes over the appointment of Young, the arrival of the territorial officials in Salt Lake City seemed a tame affair. Kane wrote a letter of introduction to Young praising Brocchus and Brandebury.[35] The Mormons greeted the officials with social events and dinners.[36] Then on September 8, 1851, Brocchus spoke in a session of the semiannual conference of The Church of Jesus Christ of Latter-day Saints, and relationships deteriorated rapidly. Although no transcript of his message has survived, summaries exist, and historians have commented widely on its content. Fortunately, we have a lengthy summary by Wilford Woodruff, who may have prepared it for his diary from shorthand notes.

According to Woodruff, Brocchus maintained a good rapport with the congregation until he came to the discussion of the violent attacks against Mormons in Missouri and Illinois. He deplored the persecution, but justified the failure of the federal government to come to the Mormons' aid, arguing that the government "had No power"—we probably would use the term "authority"—to do so. He told the people if they "wanted redress" for their wrongs, they should "Apply to Missouri & Illinois," where they had received these wrongs. "This part of the speech," Woodruff wrote, "stir[r]ed the Blood of the whole congregation." Then, Woodruff wrote, "Much was said By the speaker which was Calculated to Stir the Blood of the people And offend them."[37]

Brocchus did not seem to understand that Mormons had sought redress in both states, but had received neither judicial, legislative, nor executive assistance in Missouri and only token executive assistance in Illinois. Rather, local militias had forced Mormons to flee both states with the loss of hundreds of thousands of dollars in property and hundreds of lives, principally from disease, starvation, malnutrition, and freezing weather. Young arose after the speech and commented that "Judge Broc[c]hus was either profoundly Ignorant or wilfully wicked" in denying the culpability of the federal government in failing to redress the grievances of the Latter-day Saints in the two states.[38]

Brocchus's speech and Young's reply engendered a vigorous response. Fearing for their lives in a hostile community, Brocchus, Brandebury, Harris, and Day left the territory for the United States on September 28,

1851.[39] The flight of the secretary and judges had serious consequences for Utahns. Harris took with him the money Congress had appropriated for the territorial government. Young and the territorial legislature tried to force him to leave the money, but the judges ruled against them. The absence of the two judges left only Snow to preside over all district court business for a territory whose settlements stretched, in 1851, from Brigham City on the north more than three hundred miles to Cedar City on the south and from Fort Bridger (now in Wyoming) on the east nearly seven hundred miles to Carson Valley (currently in western Nevada) near the California border on the west.

In an attempt to apprise Fillmore of the seriousness of the runaways' actions, shortly after the judges left, Young wrote to the president outlining the steps he had taken, after waiting more than a year following the passage of the territorial organic act, to inaugurate the government of Utah Territory. Young admitted he had moved with dispatch and without approval of the territorial secretary, who had not yet arrived, to order a census and the apportion of the territory into districts for the election of the legislature and a delegate. Young had begged Harris, Brandebury, and Brocchus not to leave the territory. Harris's intentions particularly distressed him because the secretary planned to take the funds with him that Congress had appropriated for the payment of legislative expenses, a course Young "considered . . . illegal." In an attempt to thwart Harris's action, Young, with the secretary's approval, called the legislature into an extraordinary session. Harris, however, refused to prepare a roll for the legislature or to perform other duties prescribed in connection with the session, and he secured a ruling from the territorial supreme court sustaining his decision to carry the money from the territory.

In his letter to Fillmore, Young faulted the government for failing to execute "those laws in times past, for our protection." He accused some unnamed officials of "abuse of power . . . even betraying us in the hour of our greatest peril and extremity, by withholding the due execution of laws designed for the protection of all the citizens of the United States." As a proximate case in point, the governor cited the actions of the runaway officials who deprived the territory "of a Supreme Court," of the official seal, of publication of laws, and of other statutory benefits. In addition, Young faulted the judges for their failure to take up their judicial duties after they arrived in the territory. He recommended that the president appoint people who had some knowledge of conditions in Utah, and he also suggested the government forward territorial funds through Charles Livingston, a non-Mormon merchant doing business in Salt Lake City, who could see to the payment of legislative and other expenses. The legislature approved a memorial supporting Young's allegations.[40]

Three weeks after the judges left, Young wrote to Fillmore again. The governor explained the administrative and legal problems caused by the flight of the judges and secretary and the lack of instructions from Washington on Indian affairs. In the exigency of the situation, he appointed Willard Richards as territorial secretary pro tem.[41]

With the flight of the judges, the people of Utah faced the difficulty of finding courts to try offenders or judges to preside in the territory. As a stopgap measure, Governor Young vested responsibility for all of the territorial district courts in Judge Snow. Then, to help relieve the pressure on Snow, in 1852 the territorial legislature extended the jurisdiction of the county probate courts to include civil and criminal cases.[42] In addition, justices of the peace adjudicated cases within their jurisdictions. Most of the federal judges considered Utah's probate court jurisdiction illegal.[43] In 1874 the U.S. Supreme Court agreed, and in the same year Congress abolished the jurisdiction in a provision of the Poland Act.[44]

While Young and others argued their case from far-distant Utah, Bernhisel returned to Washington to defend his Mormon constituents. On December 12, he met with Fillmore. Bernhisel asked the president whether anyone had preferred charges against Young. Fillmore said the runaway officials had done so verbally, and he had told them to "reduce their charges to writing and send them to the State Department." He told Bernhisel that when the runaways had lodged their charges, "he would give [Bernhisel] an opportunity to answer."[45]

Eager to secure support from someone friendly to the Mormons with political connections, Bernhisel wrote to Kane first on December 11, 1851, to apprise him that Brandebury and Harris had arrived in Washington.[46] On December 17, Bernhisel wrote Kane again. This second letter was the first the Pennsylvanian had read that outlined details of the charges against the Utahns. He resolved to assist the Mormons and considered it his duty to ask for the closest scrutiny of the charges by a congressional committee. Kane drafted a letter to Fillmore and a resolution for the House of Representatives on the matter. The resolution asked the president to refer the charges to a special congressional committee with authority to subpoena persons and papers to investigate the matter. Kane sent copies to Bernhisel, cautioning that they must conduct the defense "wisely and temperately."[47]

As Fillmore requested, Brandebury, Brocchus, and Harris published their grievances in letters to President Fillmore and Secretary of State Webster in the *Congressional Globe*. The runaway officials also wrote to others elaborating on these and some additional charges. The letters are significant as much for what they reveal about the runaway officials as about conditions in Utah. Clearly anti-Mormon in his views and unfeeling in his attitude toward the people he had sworn to serve, Brocchus gave his version of his speech. He obviously had failed to understand the deep feelings of the people about the violence they had suffered in Missouri and Illinois and about the failure of President Taylor to honor their applications for state or territorial government. Moreover, Brocchus had cast aspersions on Utahns' patriotism by telling them "if they could not offer a block of marble [for the Washington Monument] in a feeling of full fellowship with the people of the United States, . . . they had better not offer it at all."[48]

The runaways' charges attacked both the Mormon leadership and the Mormon people. As was usual in such charges, the runaways alleged that Young successfully commanded "unlimited sway over the ignorant and credulous," by which the runaways meant all the Latter-day Saints. The runaways criticized the deep resentment of the Mormon people for the abuse they suffered in Missouri and Illinois and the feelings against the government for appointing judges from outside the territory. The officials criticized the way in which Young conducted elections and superintended the census to apportion representatives.[49]

Some of the comments were self-contradictory. The runaway officials asserted that the governor had not appointed local judicial and executive officers as required by the territorial organic act, then commented on decisions made by the allegedly nonexistent judges with whom they disagreed. The runaways alleged first that no elections were held; then they said the people had elected officials obedient to Young. The runaways complained that the legislature was not scheduled to meet until January 1852, but then pointed out it had met September 22, 1851. They alleged from rumors—and without evidence—that various murders had been committed with the approval of Church leaders. Brocchus's speech, they insisted, was designed to "arrest that flow of seditious sentiment which was so freely pouring forth from their bosoms toward the country to which they owed their highest patriotism and their best affections."

The letter told also of the disputes between the legislature and Governor Young on the one side and Secretary Harris and Babbitt on the other. The legislature and the governor sought reimbursement for the expenses incurred in legislative meetings and territorial business, but Harris and Babbitt refused to part with the money Congress had appropriated for these purposes. Eventually, a local court ordered Babbitt's property seized and sold to settle the debt, but Harris left Utah with the money entrusted to him, which he deposited with the assistant U.S. Treasurer in St. Louis.[50]

Taking the opportunity Fillmore promised him, after receiving a copy of the charges from the State Department, Bernhisel penned a response on December 27. This letter added very little to a letter to Fillmore that Bernhisel had sent on December 1, in which he denied the charges of seditious statements and accused Brocchus of insulting the people of the territory in his speech by questioning their patriotism.[51]

Moreover, Bernhisel informed Fillmore and Kane of the falsity of specific charges against Young. Since the charges included allegations that Young had conducted a fraudulent census, Bernhisel secured a statement from the superintendent of the census that said the "returns are all in good and regular form," including all information required by census takers.[52] Bernhisel then supplied information on the conduct of elections. He pointed out that Young had ordered the elections in conformity with the provision of the Utah territorial organic act that authorized him to conduct the first election "'in such manner,'" time, and place "'as the Governor shall appoint and direct.'"[53]

"A Plain Statement of Facts"

Energized by the need to act, Kane collaborated with Bernhisel and also with Jedediah M. Grant (fig. 17), the current mayor of Salt Lake City and a member of the Church's First Council of the Seventy, whom the Utah leaders sent to Washington to help deal with this problem. Grant arrived in Washington on December 8, 1851. After consulting with Bernhisel, Grant went to Philadelphia, where he met with Kane later that month.[54]

Early in their discussions, Kane learned from Grant something that disturbed him. Grant explained for the first time of the practice of polygamy among the Mormons, which, according to Kane, made it impossible "truthfully to refute the accusation of their enemies that they tolerate polygamy or a plurality of wives among them." He felt deeply pained and humiliated "by this communication for which [he] was indeed ill prepared." Nevertheless, he wrote, he retained "personal respect and friendship" toward Bernhisel and the Mormons.[55] More important, however, this information did not dim Kane's resolve to assist the Mormons.

In February 1852, at Kane's suggestion, Kane and Grant decided to draft what the Pennsylvanian called "'a plain statement of facts' over Mr. Grant's signature," which met with Bernhisel's "entire approbation."[56] Grant published the first letter in the *New York Herald*, and it was published as a pamphlet, together with two other letters signed by Grant that defended the Mormons against the runaways.[57] The letters, written in a folksy style, emphasized the friendly treatment bestowed on the officials that had been reciprocated with verbal attacks and officiousness. (For example, the locals had sponsored elaborate balls and banquets for Brandebury, Harris, and Snow that Governor Young and local dignitaries had attended.) Grant and Kane used sarcasm and ridicule in the first letter with a description of Brandebury's shirt, which "came about as near to being *the* great unwashed . . . [and] the most Disrespectful Shirt, ever was seen at a celebration."[58]

From there, Kane and Grant moved to refute the runaways' charges against Mormons by attacking Brocchus's September 8 speech. The two letter writers characterized the speech as self-serving and offensive, claiming Brocchus had insulted Mormon women and questioned Mormons' patriotism. Kane and Grant then professed astonishment that "neither Brandebury nor Harris" disavowed Brocchus's actions. Rather, both officials announced their intensions to return with Brocchus. Moreover, in spite of the actions of the U.S. Marshal and the territorial legislature in their attempts to induce Harris to distribute the money due the legislature for "mileage, stationery, &c." from the $24,000 he carried for the purpose, the secretary refused. Instead, he wrote the legislators "an insulting letter," alleging "they were illegally elected and constituted."[59]

FIG. 17. Jedediah M. Grant. Grant served as a member of the Church's First Presidency and as mayor of Salt Lake City. He worked with Kane to defend the Mormons in print. Church History Library.

In the second letter, Kane and Grant turned specifically to the charges made in the reports of Brandebury, Brocchus, and Harris. Listing the charges seriatim, Kane and Grant labeled them either as true or false. On some charges they explained their answer, and on most they asked for a trial to examine the allegations on the evidence. They agreed that "almost the entire population" of Utah consisted of Mormons but denied that the Church controlled "the opinions, the actions, the property, and even the lives of its members" and denied that it had usurped and exercised "the functions of legislation and the judicial business of the Territory."[60]

Kane and Grant denied that the Church had disposed of the "public lands upon its own terms." Rather, the Mormons claimed the land only as squatters, by which they owned only "a certain right of preëmption in for our Improvements." Because of "the delay of Congress in legislating . . . [they] remain without Titles to [their] Homes."[61]

The letter writers claimed the Mormons had made a mistake in coining money. From lack of expertise in purifying the gold, they said, the coins were worth less than the stamped amount. Rather than circulating at their stamped value, as the runaways had insisted, the coins circulated at their actual value in gold.[62] Kane and Grant then acknowledged that the Church did ask members to pay tithing, but did not require it of nonmembers. Tithing, they asserted, "is a Free Will Offering purely, [calculated] by the giver, and is not accepted from those who are not in full communion."[63]

To the charge that the Mormon community levied "enormous taxes" on nonmembers, Kane and Grant replied with an explanation. They agreed in rather convoluted language that Mormons did levy high taxes on liquor and that this fell inordinately on those who consumed large amounts. The tax burdened non-Mormons more than Mormons because the latter did not drink as much alcohol as the former.[64] Kane and Grant also denied that they made the rules and teachings of the Church the basis of "all the obligations of morality, society, of allegiance, and of law."[65]

The second letter ended in a peroration designed to blunt the substance of the charges. The thesis of the section lay in the opening, which charged "the enemies of Religious Liberty" with using "the old Trick" of "persuading the ignorant to confound the two notions of *Spiritual* or strictly Religious influence, and *Material* or Political influence." Although they "often go hand in hand, . . . they are two things entirely distinct and independent of each other." The substance of the argument was that Mormons followed Brigham Young not because he or others forced them to do so, but because they believed his leadership had helped preserve and promote their community and that the missionaries sent out under his direction would spread American civilization throughout the world.[66]

The third letter included a defense against a number of charges. It argued for Mormons' true patriotism by citing their backgrounds and family connections to the colonial founders and American revolutionaries.[67] It defended Young's leadership as salutary and approved by the majority. It also denied that his influence derived from violent abuse.[68] Kane and Grant attacked the attempt of the runaways to blame the entire Mormon community for the violence of some in the community. They explained the murders of John M. Vaughn and James Monroe, by the cuckolded husbands Madison Hamilton and Howard Egan, as the result of the two defiling the marriage bed through "adultery."[69] Both Hamilton and Egan stood trial for the murders, and in both cases the juries found them not guilty. In Egan's trial, his attorney, George A. Smith, argued that in similar cases of the murder of adulterers in New Jersey and Louisiana, juries had returned similar verdicts.[70] Kane and Grant also offered an oblique defense of plural marriage.[71]

After the letters were published in pamphlet form, Grant sent a copy to Fillmore with a cover letter. The letter argued for religious and political liberty and insisted that "we contradict every single statement of the Delinquent officers, and by wage of law or battel [sic] will equally rejoice to be brought to prove their falsehood.—We call for the Examination under oath."[72]

Kane and Grant's first letter along with Bernhisel's lobbying led Fillmore to side with the Utahns against the runaway officials. On March 17, 1852, Bernhisel met with Fillmore at the president's request. The discussion led Bernhisel to conclude that Fillmore appeared eager "to do justice to the people" of Utah and that he would not remove Young as governor.[73]

Fillmore did, however, ask Bernhisel about the murder of John M. Vaughn. Amos E. Kimberly, a friend of Vaughn's, had written to Fillmore, blaming the entire Mormon community for the murder.[74] Unlike Grant, who excused the murder because Vaughn had committed adultery with Hamilton's wife, Bernhisel deplored the murder. He pointed out that the courts had tried the murderer and the jury had returned a verdict of not guilty. He explained that after a previous incident of adultery between Vaughn and another married woman, Young had actually intervened to protect Vaughn after he had professed repentance, promised to reform, and submitted to rebaptism.[75]

By early May it had become clear that Fillmore, Webster, and Congress had all accepted the Mormon view of the dispute. Kane, Grant, and Bernhisel had played crucial roles in shaping public opinion on the question, and Fillmore seems also to have accepted Young's explanation of his actions. Fillmore decided to retain the Mormon appointees Young, Blair, Heywood, and Snow. After some failed or withdrawn nominations, the Senate confirmed Lazarus H. Reed as chief justice to replace Brandebury, Leonidas Shaver to replace Brocchus, and Benjamin G. Ferris to replace Harris.[76] Reed and Shaver proved exceptionally popular in Utah, while Ferris remained only six months before leaving the territory and writing an anti-Mormon exposé.[77]

In the short run, Utahns won this skirmish, though the charges of sedition and the flight of the officials came back to haunt them in Ferris's exposé and again in 1857, when President James Buchanan sent an army to Utah with a new set of federal officials. In the case of the original runaways, however, on June 15, 1852, Congress passed a law prescribing forfeiture of pay for territorial officials who left their posts without permission, and Secretary of State Webster recommended that Brocchus return to Utah or resign. Public opinion as expressed in the press remained predominantly anti-Mormon, although a few articles supported the Saints.[78]

"Federal Authority versus Polygamic Theocracy"

The case of the runaways did not end Kane's assistance to the Mormons. Kane again became their mediator with the U.S. government during the Utah War in 1857 and 1858. He accomplished this task admirably as William MacKinnon has shown in a number of publications, including his essay herein.[79] Between 1858 and 1871, Kane involved himself in a number of business and military affairs. From 1861 to 1863, he served as a commander of Pennsylvania units in the Civil War, reaching the rank of Brigadier General (and Brevet Major General) of Volunteers.[80] Calls for help from the Mormons tailed off, as did correspondence with them until 1869, when he began to lobby Congress and various presidents to try to defeat anti-Mormon legislation.

Kane became even more intensely involved in Mormon relations with the federal government following President Ulysses S. Grant's 1870 appointment of James B. McKean (fig. 18) as chief justice of the Utah Territorial Supreme Court.[81] McKean became extremely unpopular with the Mormons and in 1872 admitted he had gone to Utah on a mission from God to suppress Mormonism.[82] Grant undoubtedly shared McKean's views on the need to suppress Mormon polygamy and to control theocratic government. Grant's appointment of anti-Mormon judges to Utah Territory, such as Cyrus M. Hawley, Obed F. Strickland, and Jacob S. Boreman, seems to parallel those feelings. U.S. Attorney William Carey and his assistant Robert N. Baskin (fig. 19)

FIG. 18. James B. McKean. Appointed chief justice of the Utah Territorial Supreme Court in 1870 by President Ulysses S. Grant, McKean was antagonistic toward the Mormons and the practice of polygamy. Several of his actions and court decisions illegally disadvantaged the Mormons. Library of Congress.

had intense dislike for Mormons. On the other hand, some of Grant's appointees such as Samuel A. Mann, Philip H. Emerson, George C. Bates, and Sumner Howard got along well with Mormons.[83]

Some of the actions McKean took to suppress the Mormon influence he so strongly opposed were clearly illegal. For instance, ruling that territorial district courts were United States district courts, he authorized the U.S. Marshal to empanel grand juries on an open venire rather than under the Utah Territorial court statute of 1852. Under McKean's ruling, rather than having the judge of the county probate court select potential jurors from a list of men from the tax rolls as territorial law required, the marshal simply walked along the street and picked men to serve on the grand jury. This practice led to juries packed with anti-Mormons who returned indictments against Mormons.[84]

One of the earliest of these indictments challenged the legality of actions taken under a warrant issued by a previous federal judge, Chief Justice John F. Kinney (fig. 20). Acting on Kinney's warrant, in 1862 a posse led by deputy marshal Robert T. Burton had tried to free William Jones and two other men held as prisoners at Kingston Fort in South Weber by an apocalyptic religious group headed by Joseph Morris. In the attempt to free the prisoners, Burton's posse killed

FIG. 19. Robert N. Baskin. Baskin served as an assistant U.S. Attorney. He later served as mayor of Salt Lake City and as chief justice of the Utah State Supreme Court. Used by permission, Utah State Historical Society, all rights reserved.

FIG. 20. John Fitch Kinney. Kinney served as Chief Justice of the Supreme Court of Utah Territory from 1854 to 1857 and again from 1860 to 1863. Used by permission, Utah State Historical Society, all rights reserved.

several members of the group, including Isabella Bowman. One of McKean's packed grand juries indicted Burton for Bowman's murder, but later in the trial the petit jury found Burton not guilty.[85]

In April 1871, after the grand jury indictment, but before Brigham Young knew the petit jury would free Burton, Young turned to Kane for help. With Kane's connections in Washington, Young hoped the Pennsylvanian might be able to induce Grant to rid the territory of a judge who had "rendered himself so obnoxious to the people by his tyrannical and high handed measures." McKean had, Young said, become "the acknowledged standard bearer" of a "miserable clique of pet[t]ifogging carpetbaggers with their packed grand jury."[86]

In September 1871, a similarly packed grand jury indicted Mormon leaders Brigham Young, George Q. Cannon, and Daniel H. Wells, along with Godbeite leader Henry W. Lawrence under territorial law that prohibited "lewd and lascivious cohabitation and adultery."[87] After admitting Young to $5,000 bail, McKean denied the motion of Young's attorney, Thomas Fitch, to quash the indictment. In a long statement of his intent, McKean asserted that although "the case at bar is called, 'The People versus Brigham Young,' its other and real title is, 'Federal Authority versus Polygamic Theocracy.'"[88]

Fitch filed a bill of exceptions to what he considered McKean's outrageous statement. It seems clear that McKean had perverted the territorial laws because "Mormons [through the Utah legislature] had not intended the adultery and lewd and lascivious cohabitation laws to apply to their plural marriage system." In addition, McKean refused to recognize the marriage exception to the testimony of plural wives against their husbands.[89]

U.S. Attorney George C. Bates, who would have had to prosecute the accused, questioned the indictments because the grand jury did not indict Mormon leaders under the Morrill Act of 1862, which prohibited polygamy. Instead, the indictments were given under local laws that the territorial legislature had passed to punish adultery and prostitution instead of plural marriage.[90]

In October 1871, McKean began excluding all potential Mormon jurors from petit as well as grand juries by asking them whether they believed in the revelation authorizing plural marriage. Young recognized that McKean's action placed him and other Church leaders in additional jeopardy, and Young turned again to Kane. Apparently loath to trust the U.S. mail, Young sent his son John W. Young with a letter to Kane pleading for help. McKean's rulings, the Mormon leader wrote, "have deprived the old settlers here of the right to sit on all juries, and in other ways deny to us the rights belonging to the common people." He believed that by excluding Mormons from juries, McKean and his associates "have at last succeeded in what they trust will be a death blow to Mormonism." Owing to the actions of the grand jury, Young expected "to be a prisoner in the Military Post, Camp Douglass, long before" the letter reached Kane.[91]

McKean and his associates, especially Robert N. Baskin, who served for a time as assistant U.S. attorney, had long hoped to indict Young for something more serious than polygamy. They got their opportunity by working with William Adams Hickman, a confessed murderer. In September 1868, Hickman's Taylorsville bishop excommunicated him from the Church *in absentia* for his felonious activities. In September 1870, Hickman murdered a man who threatened his family in Tooele County. Indicted for the murder, Hickman agreed with McKean and Baskin to turn states' evidence against Young and others in return for his freedom. On the basis of Hickman's stories to Baskin, McKean secured indictments against Brigham Young, Daniel H. Wells, and Hosea Stout for the murders of Richard Yates and several others during the Utah War. McKean asserted he had evidence other than Hickman's testimony, but the prosecuting attorney provided none.[92]

The letter John W. Young carried to Thomas L. Kane apprised him of the danger created by McKean's action. In a letter replying to Young, Kane said he was considering coming to Utah to meet with Young, which he eventually did during winter 1872–73. In the meantime, in view of the indictment, Kane advised Young to retain the best legal counsel available. Kane suggested hiring William M. Evarts, who had served as chief counsel for Andrew Johnson in his impeachment hearings and as U.S. attorney general during the early years of the Grant administration.[93]

Later in the fall, Kane contacted William H. Hooper, who served as Utah's territorial delegate from 1859 to 1861 and again from 1865 to 1873. On Kane's suggestion, Hooper agreed to introduce a bill "providing for appeals in criminal causes from the Territorial courts to the Supreme Court of the United States." Kane also met with "influential parties" to lobby in support of Hooper's bill and other pro-Mormon matters.[94]

Fearing for Young's life under McKean's rulings, Kane urged Young to hide out and to restrict information on his location to close friends. "In the present crisis," Kane wrote, "I can think of nothing as essential to the safety of your people as your personal security." In addition, he suggested George A. Smith, John Taylor, Orson Pratt, and others with names familiar to the public go into hiding. "We do not want," he wrote, "your persecutors to get hold of any man with name enough to help them to a sensation trial." Kane expected that "political friends of ours may originate more than one measure in Congress for the relief of Utah." He also encouraged Young not to engage in "duplicity" but rather to remain open about the Church's beliefs and practices and to be certain that his followers did the same.[95]

Although Kane had urged Young to remain in hiding, the Church president did not do so. Instead, he turned himself in. McKean refused to admit him to bail, but because of Young's ill health, the judge sentenced him to house arrest rather than incarcerating him at Fort Douglas with several of the others who had been indicted.[96]

After learning of Young's arrest, Kane began preparing notes for an argument for removing McKean, and Kane lobbied with Congress and Grant either to provide legislative relief or to remove McKean and other supporters. Kane pointed out that friends in California had agreed to serve as sureties for bail equal to a hundred times the bail accepted for Jefferson Davis, the former president of the Confederacy. Yet McKean still refused to grant bail. McKean should not require Young, Kane argued, to submit to imprisonment for an indefinite period designed to break down his health before he could obtain an acquittal on the charges. Kane met with Pennsylvania Senator Simon Cameron, and Cameron met with Grant to argue Kane's case. Kane also met with Secretary of State Hamilton Fish and with Grant. Instead of securing help, Kane found that Grant seemed bent on prosecuting Young.[97]

After Young had spent several months in house arrest, which the other indicted leaders spent at Fort Douglas, the United States Supreme Court ruled against McKean's theory of jury empanelling. In the federal case of *Clinton v. Englebrecht*,[98] the Supreme Court ruled that the territorial federal courts had to follow local law in empanelling juries. Contrary to McKean's ruling, the Supreme Court said, the territorial courts were merely legislative courts of the territory created by federal statute and thus subject to territorial law. This decision provided the legal basis for throwing out 130 indictments found by McKean's grand juries, and it vacated judgments in his petit juries as well.[99] Significantly, the *Englebrecht* decision invalidated the indictments for lewd and lascivious association and adultery against Young, Cannon, Wells, and Lawrence, and the indictments for murder against Young, Wells, and Stout.

Thwarted in his efforts to try the Mormons for polygamy and for murder, in 1873 McKean mounted a rearguard action against Brigham Young. To do so, McKean accepted the divorce suit of Ann Eliza Webb Dee Young (fig. 21), Brigham's twenty-fifth wife.[100] Failing to recognize that under federal statutes Brigham's marriage to Ann Eliza was illegal, McKean ordered the prophet to pay alimony of five hundred dollars per month pending the outcome of the litigation. Brigham refused to do so on the grounds that she was not his legal wife, but that she had been sealed to him in a religious rather than a civil ceremony. Refusing to accept his plea, McKean fined Brigham twenty-five dollars and sent him to the territorial penitentiary in Sugar House for a night. Recognizing that accepting the marriage as legitimate would undermine federal statutes that prohibited polygamy, the U.S. attorney general later ordered the case dismissed.[101]

Conclusion

After the failure of McKean's judicial crusade, Kane continued to work for the Mormons on a number of other matters. These included the attempt to secure statehood in 1872 and several bills designed to undermine local control. He helped, for instance, to mitigate the impact of the Poland Act of 1874, since the act as finally passed authorized the judges of the county probate courts to remain involved in the selection of jury panels instead of turning over the entire empaneling to the U.S. marshal. Kane also tried, unsuccessfully, to derail the Edmunds Act.

In retrospect it seems clear that, although he failed in a number of his efforts, Kane played a crucial role in helping the Mormons in their dealings with Washington from 1849 until his death in 1883. As citizens of a territory, Mormons in the Great Basin could not vote in national elections, they had to accept whatever appointees the president and Senate chose to send to them, and their delegate to Congress had only limited power. Kane used his personal prestige and political connections to overcome these obstacles. His efforts to secure the appointments of Young, Snow, Blair, and Heywood to territorial offices had undoubtedly helped. Kane's assistance in thwarting the efforts of the runaway officials to undermine local government and interests proved invaluable. Most particularly, his advice to Bernhisel and especially his work with Jedediah Grant in drafting the

FIG. 21. Ann Eliza Young, lithograph, c. 1869–75. Ann Eliza filed for divorce from Brigham Young in 1873. A highly publicized trial followed, and the U.S. Attorney General ordered the case dismissed two years later. Library of Congress.

three letters to the *New York Herald* helped immeasurably. Although Kane also provided advice in the campaign to thwart McKean and Baskin in their effort to undermine local democratic government in Utah and to lodge spurious charges against Young and other Church leaders, his extensive efforts in Washington proved of little help, largely because the Grant administration supported McKean's efforts. It is unclear just whether Kane's public efforts in support of the Mormons in this case had any influence on the Supreme Court in the *Englebrecht* decision. Significantly, however, he did assist in helping to remove the most obnoxious features of the Poland Act of 1874.

Kane's efforts proved to be as successful as one might expect in a representative democracy. This was particularly true since the people of Utah had little political clout. On balance, Kane's personal prestige and political connections helped the Mormons a great deal.

Thomas G. Alexander (who can be reached via email at byustudies@byu.edu) earned his PhD at the University of California at Berkeley and is the Lemuel Hardison Redd Jr. professor of Western American history emeritus at Brigham Young University. He served as assistant director, associate director, and director of the Charles Redd Center for Western Studies (1972–1992). As an author, coauthor, editor, or coeditor of twenty-two books and monographs and more than a hundred and thirty articles, he specializes in Utah history, Western history, environmental history, and Mormon history. The author wishes to thank David Whittaker and the staff of the L. Tom Perry Special Collections for their help in supplying documents and giving assistance in the preparation of this paper and the lecture that accompanied it. Thanks also to William MacKinnon, Matthew Grow, and Bruce Africa for comments on an earlier version of this paper.

1. For a general discussion of these matters, see Michael F. Holt, *The Rise and Fall of the American Whig Party: Jacksonian Politics and the Onset of the Civil War* (New York: Oxford University Press, 1999); Joseph G. Rayback, *Free Soil, the Election of 1848* (Lexington: University of Kentucky Press, 1970); Daniel Walker Howe, *The Political Culture of the American Whigs* (Chicago: University of Chicago Press, 1979). On Kane's support for the Free Soil Party, see Matthew J. Grow, *"Liberty to the Downtrodden": Thomas L. Kane, Romantic Reformer* (New Haven: Yale University Press, 2009), 93–112.

2. On these matters, see Eric Foner, *Free Soil, Free Labor, Free Men: The Ideology of the Republican Party before the Civil War* (New York: Oxford University Press, 1995); Michael F. Holt, *The Political Crisis of the 1850s* (New York: Wiley, 1978); and Michael F. Holt, *The Fate of Their Country: Politicians, Slavery Extension, and the Coming of the Civil War* (New York: Hill and Wang, 2004). On the presidents after the Civil War, see Brooks D. Simpson, *The Reconstruction Presidents* (Lawrence: University Press of Kansas, 1998).

3. Dale L. Morgan, *The State of Deseret* (Logan: Utah State University Press with the Utah State Historical Society, 1987), 13–66.

4. Grow, "Liberty to the Downtrodden," 81.

5. Peter Crawley, "The Constitution of the State of Deseret," *BYU Studies* 29, no. 4 (Fall 1989): 10. The enormous state they proposed encompassed the land from the Sierra Nevada to the crest of the Rockies, covered all the Great Basin, included present-day Arizona south to the Gila River, and extended over a swatch of southern California to a seaport at San Diego. Morgan, *State of Deseret*, 31, 35–36, 128.

6. Morgan, *State of Deseret*, 67.

7. Morgan, *State of Deseret*, 39.

8. Wilford Woodruff, *Wilford Woodruff's Journal, 1833–1898 Typescript*, ed. Scott G. Kenney (Midvale, Utah: Signature Books, 1983), 3:513–14. This entry and those cited in the next four footnotes are summaries that Woodruff wrote of his discussions with Kane and that he placed at the end of the year rather than at their respective dates.

9. Woodruff, *Journal*, 3:513–14.

10. Woodruff, *Journal*, 3:515–16. Woodruff's spelling has been retained.

11. Woodruff, *Journal*, 3:516. Woodruff's spelling has been retained.

12. Woodruff, *Journal*, 3:516 (entry at end of year); 3:579 (October 27, 1850).

13. John M. Bernhisel to Thomas L. Kane, January 17, 1850, Thomas L. and Elizabeth W. Kane Collection, L. Tom Perry Special Collections, Harold B. Lee Library, Brigham Young University, Provo, Utah.

14. Bernhisel to Kane, January 17, 1850, Perry Special Collections.

15. Bernhisel to Kane, January 17, 1850, Perry Special Collections.

16. Bernhisel to Kane, January 17, 1850, Perry Special Collections; Almon W. Babbitt to Brigham Young, July 7, 1850, as quoted in Morgan, *State of Deseret*, 82.

17. Morgan, *State of Deseret*, 73.

18. John M. Bernhisel to First Presidency, March 5, 1850, as quoted in Morgan, *State of Deseret*, 74.

19. John M. Bernhisel to Brigham Young, March 27, 1850, as quoted in Morgan, *State of Deseret*, 75.

20. Morgan, *State of Deseret*, 76.

21. Thomas L. Kane, *The Mormons: A Discourse Delivered before the Historical Society of Pennsylvania, March 26, 1850* (Philadelphia: King and Baird, 1850). A second printing in 1850 added more positive information on the Mormons by answering questions Kane had encountered by those who showed interest in the religious group.

22. Morgan, *State of Deseret*, 78–81. On the compromise, see Holt, *Fate of Their Country*.

23. John M. Bernhisel to Millard Fillmore, September 16, 1850, as quoted in Morgan, *State of Deseret*, 86.

24. Almon W. Babbitt to Daniel Webster, September 21, 1850, in "Letters of Application and Recommendation during the Administrations of James Polk, Zachary Taylor, and Millard Fillmore, 1845–1853," General Records of the Department of State, RG 59, microfilm 873, reel 4, National Archives, Washington, D.C. (hereafter cited as "Letters of Application").

25. Pennsylvania Congressmen [illegible, perhaps Jehu Glancy Jones], Thaddeus Stevens, and Joseph Casey to Treasury Secretary William M. Meredith, March 8, 1850, in "Letters of Application," reel 9.

26. Twelve Congressional Representatives from Pennsylvania to Millard Fillmore, n.d. [1851], in "Letters of Application," reel 9; Representative Moses Hampton to Millard Fillmore, February 25, 1851, in "Letters of Application," reel 9; Representative Joseph Casey to Solicitor of the Treasury John C. Clark, February 6, 1851, in "Letters of Application," reel 9; John C. Clark to Millard Fillmore, February 7, 1851, in "Letters of Application," reel 9.

27. Lemuel G. Brandebury to Millard Fillmore, February 17 and February 25, 1851, in "Letters of Application," reel 9; List entitled "Chief Justices,—Utah Territory," in "Records Relating to the Appointment of Federal Judges, Attorneys, and Marshals for the Territory and State of Utah, 1853–1901," RG 60, microfilm 680, reel 1, National Archives, Washington, D.C. (hereafter cited as "Records Relating to the Appointment").

28. "Associate Justices,—Utah Territory," in "Records Relating to the Appointment," reel 1.

29. Z. Snow to David K. Carter [sic], September 17, 1850, in "Letters of Application," reel 82. C. W. Belden et al. to Millard Fillmore, September 23, 1850, in "Letters of Application," reel 82.

30. Alexander H. H. Stuart to Millard Fillmore, September 28, 1850, in "Letters of Application," reel 82.

31. Jenson, Church Chronology, 43.

32. Thomas L. Kane to Brigham Young, Heber C. Kimball, and Willard Richards, July 29, 1851, Perry Special Collections. I have been unable to determine which newspaper published the letter. Kane simply called the newspaper the "Republic." It was possibly the *Baltimore Republican and Argus*.

33. Millard Fillmore to Thomas L. Kane, July 4, 1851; and Thomas L. Kane to Millard Fillmore, July 11, 1851, in *Frontier Guardian*, September 5, 1851, both cited in Matthew Grow to author, December 8, 2008.

34. Kane to Young, Kimball, and Richards, July 29, 1851, Perry Special Collections.

35. Thomas L. Kane to Brigham Young, April 7, 1851, cited in Matthew Grow to author, December 8, 2008.

36. Gene A. Sessions, *Mormon Thunder: A Documentary History of Jedediah Morgan Grant* (Urbana: University of Illinois Press, 1982), 323–25.

37. Woodruff, *Journal*, 4:61–62. For comments by other historians on Brocchus's talk, see B. H. Roberts, *Comprehensive History of The Church of Jesus Christ of Latter-day Saints, Century 1* (Salt Lake City: Deseret News Press, 1930), 3:522–23; Clifford L. Ashton, *The Federal Judiciary in Utah* (n.p.: Utah Bar Foundation, 1988), 1–2; Norman F. Furniss, *The Mormon Conflict, 1850–1859* (New Haven: Yale University Press, 1960), 24–26.

38. Woodruff, *Journal*, 4:62–63; Roberts, *Comprehensive History*, 3:522–23.

39. For the date of their flight I have relied on Roberts, *Comprehensive History*, 3:534.

40. Brigham Young to Millard Fillmore, September 29, 1851, in *Appendix to the Congressional Globe*, 32nd Cong., 1st Sess. (January 9, 1852), 91–92; "Memorial Signed by the Members of the Legislative Assembly of Utah, to the President of the United States," September 29, 1851, in *Appendix to the Congressional Globe*, 32nd Cong., 1st Sess. (January 9, 1852), 92–93.

41. Brigham Young to Millard Fillmore, October 20, 1851, in *Appendix to the Congressional Globe,* 32nd Cong., 1st Sess. (January 9, 1852), 86.
42. On this matter, see James B. Allen, "The Unusual Jurisdiction of County Probate Courts in the Territory of Utah," *Utah Historical Quarterly* 36, no. 2 (Spring 1968): 132–42.
43. A number of other territories with scattered populations including Nevada, Washington, Nebraska, Colorado, Idaho, and, to a limited extent, Montana later made similar provisions for expanded probate court jurisdictions. Only the probate court jurisdiction in Utah, however, seems to have elicited much opposition. Earl S. Pomeroy, *The Territories and the United States, 1861–1890: Studies in Colonial Administration* (Philadelphia: University of Pennsylvania Press, 1947), 59–60.
44. *Ferris v. Higley* 87 U.S. 375 (1874); Poland Act, 18 U.S., *Statutes at Large,* 253 (1874).
45. John M. Bernhisel to Thomas L. Kane, December 17, 1851, Perry Special Collections. On the date of the arrival of Brandebury and Harris, see Jedediah M. Grant to Brigham Young and Council, December 30, 1851, in Sessions, *Mormon Thunder,* 91.
46. John M. Bernhisel to Thomas L. Kane, December 11, 1851, Perry Special Collections.
47. Thomas L. Kane to John M. Bernhisel, December 29, 1851, Perry Special Collections.
48. "Extract of a letter from a judicial officer [Perry E. Brocchus] of the Government at Great Salt Lake City," September 20, 1851, in *Appendix to the Congressional Globe,* 32nd Cong., 1st Sess. (January 9, 1852), 85–86.
49. "Extract of a letter from a judicial officer [Perry E. Brocchus] of the Government at Great Salt Lake City," September 20, 1851, in *Appendix to the Congressional Globe,* 32nd Cong., 1st Sess. (January 9, 1852), 85–86.
50. Lemuel G. Brandebury, Perry E. Brocchus, and Broughton D. Harris to Millard Fillmore, December 19, 1851; Broughton D. Harris to Daniel Webster, January 2, 1852; Broughton D. Harris to Millard Fillmore, January 2, 1852, in *Appendix to the Congressional Globe,* 32nd Cong., 1st Sess. (January 9, 1852), 86–90.
51. Bernhizel [sic] to Millard Fillmore, December 1, 1851, in *Appendix to the Congressional Globe,* 32nd Cong., 1st Sess. (January 9, 1852), 85; John M. Bernhisel to Millard Fillmore, December 31, 1851, in *Appendix to the Congressional Globe,* 32nd Cong., 1st Sess. (January 9, 1852), 91. Judge Snow also wrote to Fillmore in anticipation of the judges' flight, referring the president to Bernhisel, who was then in Washington, for further information. Zerubbabel Snow to Millard Fillmore, September 22, 1851, in *Appendix to the Congressional Globe,* 32d Cong., 1st Sess. (January 9, 1852), 86.
52. Joseph C. G. Kennedy, Superintendent of the 7th Census to John M. Bernhisel, January 27, 1852, included in John M. Bernhisel to Thomas L. Kane, February 4, 1852, Perry Special Collections.
53. John M. Bernhisel to Thomas L. Kane, February 7, 1852, Perry Special Collections.
54. Kane to Bernhisel, December 29, 1851, Perry Special Collections.
55. Kane to Bernhisel, December 29, 1851, Perry Special Collections; Grant to Young and Council, December 30, 1851, in Sessions, *Mormon Thunder,* 92–93.

56. Bernhisel to Kane, February 4, 1852, Perry Special Collections.

57. The *Herald* published only the first one, which is probably why the men issued a pamphlet with the other letters.

58. Sessions, *Mormon Thunder,* 325. All three letters are reproduced in an appendix in Sessions, *Mormon Thunder,* 319–68. Perry Special Collections has a copy of the original pamphlet.

59. Sessions, *Mormon Thunder,* 333. The first Kane-Grant letter "afforded a great deal of amusement" in Washington. Bernhisel learned Secretary of the Treasury Thomas Corwin was "delighted with it, saying that it is the best thing he ever read . . . and that he does not believe a 'whit' of the charges preferred by the late officers." The public became gleeful over Grant and Kane's characterization of Brandebury's filthy shirt, and rumors circulated that "Brandebury [had become] . . . very wroth about 'that shirt.'" John M. Bernhisel to Thomas L. Kane, March 18, and March 29, 1852, Perry Special Collections.

60. Sessions, *Mormon Thunder,* 338, 339.

61. Sessions, *Mormon Thunder,* 338, 339. There was no federal office in Utah Territory until 1868.

62. Sessions, *Mormon Thunder,* 338, 339–40.

63. Sessions, *Mormon Thunder,* 340.

64. Sessions, *Mormon Thunder,* 338, 340–41.

65. Sessions, *Mormon Thunder,* 338–39, 341–42.

66. Sessions, *Mormon Thunder,* 342–50.

67. Sessions, *Mormon Thunder,* 359–60.

68. Sessions, *Mormon Thunder,* 355–57.

69. Sessions, *Mormon Thunder,* 360–62.

70. The cases were *New Jersey v. Mercer* and *Louisiana v. Horton.* Robert Wynn, "Howard Egan: Outlaw or Guide?" http://www.robertwynn.com/EganH.htm. On the Egan case, see Kenneth L. Cannon II, "'Mountain Common Law': The Extralegal Punishment of Seducers in Early Utah," *Utah Historical Quarterly* 51, no. 4 (Fall 1983): 308–27.

71. Sessions, *Mormon Thunder,* 362–63.

72. Jedediah M. Grant to Millard Fillmore, May 1, 1852, in Sessions, *Mormon Thunder,* 369.

73. John M. Bernhisel to Thomas L. Kane, March 18, 1852, Perry Special Collections.

74. On the general view of violence, see D. Michael Quinn, *The Mormon Hierarchy: Extensions of Power* (Salt Lake City: Signature Books, 1997), 241–61; Jon Krakauer, *Under the Banner of Heaven: A Story of Violent Faith* (New York: Doubleday, 2003).

75. John M. Bernhisel to Millard Fillmore, April 8, 1852, enclosed in John M. Bernhisel to Thomas L. Kane, April 9, 1852, Perry Special Collections.

76. John M. Bernhisel to Thomas L. Kane, May 11, 1852, May 19, 1852, May 29, 1852, August 16, 1852, Perry Special Collections.

77. On Ferris, see "Benjamin G. Ferris," Wikipedia, http://en.wikipedia.org/wiki/Benjamin_G._Ferris.

78. Furniss, *Mormon Conflict,* 32–33.

79. For more on this topic, see William MacKinnon's essay herein.

80. On these matters, see Grow, *"Liberty to the Downtrodden,"* 207-35. For more on Kane's Civil War service, see Matthew Grow's and Edward Geary's essays herein.

81. For an article on McKean and his career in Utah, see Thomas G. Alexander, "'Federal Authority versus Polygamic Theocracy': James B. McKean and the Mormons, 1870-1875," *Dialogue: A Journal of Mormon Thought* 1, no. 3 (Autumn 1966): 85-100. I should point out I do not now agree with many of the conclusions I arrived at in defense of McKean. Rather, I now believe that he was an anti-Mormon bigot and that many of his actions were clearly illegal and aimed at undermining Mormonism.

82. "In January, 1872, in the Ebbett House, in Washington, Judge McKean avowed his principles to Judge Louis Dent, brother-in-law of the President, in these precise words: 'Judge Dent, the mission which God has called upon me to perform in Utah, is as much above the duties of other courts and judges as the heavens are above the earth, and whenever or wherever I may find the Local or Federal laws obstructing or interfering therewith, by God's blessing I shall trample them under my feet.'" Edward W. Tullidge, *Life of Brigham Young; or, Utah and Her Founders* (New York: Tullidge and Crandall, 1876), 420-21.

83. On Grant and the people of Utah, see Thomas G. Alexander, "A Conflict of Perceptions: Ulysses S. Grant and the Mormons," *Newsletter of the Ulysses S. Grant Association* 8 (July 1971): 29-42. Elizabeth Kane's manuscript account of the 1868 visit of President Grant to the Kane home in Kane, Pennsylvania, is in the Kane collection, Perry Special Collections.

84. Alexander, "'Federal Authority,'" 86-87.

85. On the Morrisites and Burton's trial, see *Utah History Encyclopedia*, ed. Allan Kent Powell (Salt Lake City: University of Utah Press, 1994), s.v. "The Morrisites."

86. Brigham Young to Thomas L. Kane, April 16, 1871, Perry Special Collections.

87. Alexander, "'Federal Authority,'" 89.

88. Alexander, "'Federal Authority,'" 89-90; Orson F. Whitney, *History of Utah* (Salt Lake City: George Q. Cannon and Sons, 1892-1904), 2:592; "The U.S. District Court," *Salt Lake Tribune*, September 19, 1871, [3]; "New Phase of the Mormon Question," *Salt Lake Tribune*, October 9, 1871, [1].

89. Orma Linford, "The Mormons and the Law: The Polygamy Cases," *Utah Law Review* 9, no. 2 (Winter 1964): 331; 12 *Statutes at Large*, 501; "Third District Court," *Salt Lake Tribune*, October 8, 1874, [4]; *Friel v. Wood*, 1 Hagan (Utah), 160 (1874).

90. Whitney, *History of Utah*, 2:604-6, 620, 678.

91. Brigham Young to Thomas L. Kane, September 27, 1871, Perry Special Collections.

92. Robert N. Baskin, *Reminiscences of Early Utah* (Salt Lake City: Privately printed, 1914), 37; Whitney, *History of Utah*, 2:629-33, 663-64, 666-71. On Hickman's excommunication and turning states evidence, see *Utah History Encyclopedia*, s.v. "William Adams Hickman."

93. Thomas L. Kane to Brigham Young, October 12, 1871, Perry Special Collections. On Evarts see "William Maxwell Evarts," Civil War Landscapes Association, http://civilwarlandscapes.org/cwla/per/civil/wme/wmef.htm.

94. Thomas L. Kane to Brigham Young, November 30, 1871, Perry Special Collections. There are several drafts of this letter in the Kane Collection.

95. Kane to Young, November 30, 1871, Perry Special Collections.

96. Thomas L. Kane, "Notes of Communication to Prest. Young when he was urged to seek refuge," n.d. [probably 1872], Perry Special Collections.

97. Thomas L. Kane, "Notes of Communication," Perry Special Collections; Grow, *"Liberty to the Downtrodden,"* 260–62.

98. The case in question involved a judgment of $59,063.25 in McKean's court against Salt Lake alderman and justice of the peace Jeter Clinton. Saloonkeeper Paul Englebrecht had refused to pay a city liquor tax that he considered exorbitant, and Clinton had ordered the destruction of his liquor stock as a punishment. Englebrecht had appealed to McKean's court, and one of the packed juries had ruled against Clinton. The Utah Territorial Supreme Court made up of McKean and anti-Mormons Obed F. Strickland and Cyrus M. Hawley had sustained the award against Clinton. Clinton appealed successfully to the United States Supreme Court. *Clinton v. Englebrecht*, 80 U.S. 434, 1872.

99. *Clinton v. Englebrecht*. On the fallout from this decision, see Cyrus M. Hawley to George H. Williams, November 9, 1872, in "Department of Justice Selected Documents from the Appointment Clerk Files Relating to Utah Judges," vol. 1, RG 60, National Archives, Washington, D.C. (microcopy, Utah State Archives, Salt Lake City); McKean to Williams, November 12, 1873, in "Department of Justice Selected Documents"; "Decision in the Engelbrecht Case," *Salt Lake Tribune*, October 5, 1871, [2]; "The Jury Question," *Salt Lake Tribune*, April 3, 1873, [2]; "Important Proceedings in Court," *Salt Lake Tribune*, October 22, 1873, [4]; "Judge McKean Sustained by the Supreme Court," *Salt Lake Tribune*, December 10, 1873, [1]; "A Judicial Nondescript," *Salt Lake Tribune*, January 8, 1874, [4]; "The Jury Bill," *Salt Lake Tribune*, February 1, 1874, [2]; "Territorial Marshal," *Salt Lake Tribune*, May 8, 1874, [4]; "Grand and Petit Jurors," *Salt Lake Tribune*, July 23, 1874, [4]; "Third District Court," *Salt Lake Tribune*, December 19, 1874, [4].

100. Leonard J. Arrington, *Brigham Young: American Moses* (New York: Alfred Knopf, 1985), 420–21. Even though Orson F. Whitney's *History of Utah* identifies Ann Eliza as Brigham's nineteenth wife, I have counted his wives on Arrington's list and determined she was the twenty-fifth.

101. Whitney, *History of Utah*, 2:757–60; "The Impending Suit," *Salt Lake Tribune*, July 31, 1873, [2]; "The Divorce Suit," *Salt Lake Tribune*, August 1, 1873, [2]; "Important Divorce Case," *Salt Lake Tribune*, July 25, 1874, [4]; "Revelation!" *Salt Lake Tribune*, August 26, 1874, [4]; "Third District Court," *Salt Lake Tribune*, February 26.

"Full of Courage"
Thomas L. Kane, the Utah War, and BYU's Kane Collection as Lodestone

William P. MacKinnon

> This young man KANE . . . now gratuitously and voluntarily asks to be heard by the present Administration before his bosom friend, and mild, meek, and humble Christian companion BRIGHAM YOUNG is removed from the office of Governor of Utah. . . . As soon as he lectures the President on his duties on Mormonism, I may refer to him again, but trust the necessity will not exist.
>
> —"Verastus" to Editor, *New York Daily Times*, May 24, 1857[1]

> Col. Kane from his long association with that people, has much influence with the Mormons, and especially with their chief. He thinks he can do much to accomplish an amicable peace between them and the United States. . . . He is full of courage, and if his judgment is correct, he may be able to avert a war of extermination against a poor deluded race.
>
> —James C. Van Dyke to President James Buchanan, December 9, 1857[2]

I am here not only because of my interest in the Thomas L. Kane papers but also out of respect and affection for David J. Whittaker. As the Curator of Nineteenth-Century Western and Mormon Americana, Whittaker has not only acquired and organized one of the great concentrations of materials bearing on this subject, he has published a three-volume register of these Kane materials that is itself a remarkable scholarly work.[3] This study is a collector's item, and after a half-century of research and writing in this field, I think I know a master of his discipline when I see one.[4] Accordingly, I congratulate both BYU and its Harold B. Lee Library for supporting not only Whittaker but also his efforts to acquire outstanding source materials.

For a comprehensive understanding of the complicated—even daunting—subject of Thomas L. Kane's Utah War involvement, one needs to plunge into the work of Kane's first biographer, Albert L. Zobell Jr.; the Utah War analyses of my former collaborator, the late Richard D. Poll; my own book titled *At Sword's Point;* and, above all else, Matthew J. Grow's splendid new biography, *"Liberty to the Downtrodden."*[5]

This article, however, is *not* meant to be a complete explication of Kane's Utah War involvement but rather has a more limited focus. In addition to honoring David Whittaker and remembering Thomas L. Kane, I will explore the significance of Kane's role in helping to resolve peacefully the Utah War of 1857–58 by exploring five questions:

- What was the Utah War?
- When and how did Thomas L. Kane become involved in it?
- What were his motives?
- Was Kane a Latter-day Saint?
- What was the significance of his efforts?

In dealing with these five questions, I will discuss the Kane collection at Brigham Young University and show how it is an indispensable tool for pursuing this subject. I view this collection not only as the Eldorado of Kane primary sources, but also as a sort of basic compass essential to navigating Kane's very complex psyche as he, in turn, maneuvered through a murky and still poorly understood federal-territorial conflict.

The Utah War: What Was It?

In one sense, the Utah War was President James Buchanan's (fig. 1) 1857 effort to replace Brigham Young as governor of Utah Territory and to install his successor with an army escort of twenty-five hundred troops.[6] It was a change that Young resisted with guerrilla tactics until a controversial but peaceful settlement was reached a year later, largely through the unofficial mediating efforts of Thomas L. Kane, who shuttled between Salt Lake City and Fort Bridger for that purpose.

The war did not just well up soon after President Buchanan's inauguration because of a single critical incident. Instead, the confrontation was nearly ten years in the making, with Mormon-federal relations—already poor in Missouri and Illinois before the 1847 arrival of Mormons in the Salt Lake Valley—steadily deteriorating immediately thereafter. By Buchanan's inauguration on March 4, 1857, virtually every interface between the territorial and federal governments had become a battleground.

There were conflicts over the selection and performance of mail contractors; relations with Utah's Indian tribes; matters of land ownership and the accuracy of federal surveys; financial stewardship of congressional appropriations for the territory; the administration of Utah's federal courts and criminal justice system; and, perhaps most important, the background, competence, and behavior of appointees to federal office

FIG. 1. James Buchanan, c. 1857. Fifteenth president of the United States, Buchanan squared off against Brigham Young during the Utah War. Library of Congress.

in Utah. In addition to these administrative pinch points, there were highly public, event-driven upsets over the 1852 polygamy announcement; the uneven treatment of emigrants passing through Utah to the Pacific Coast; responsibility for a series of uninvestigated, unprosecuted murders; repeated congressional rejection of statehood for Deseret; and a related controversy over whether Young was seeking Mormon independence outside the Union.

At the heart of these clashes was the disconnect implicit in conflicting philosophies of governance: Young's vision of Utah as a millennially oriented theocracy operating under his autocratic leadership; and the U.S. government's view of Utah as a federal territory functioning under republican principles as a congressional ward through a federally sworn governor. What Governor Young perceived as a form of intolerable colonialism, the federal establishment viewed as the normal path to statehood established by the Northwest Ordinance of 1787.[7]

In a sense, the conflict was the armed confrontation over power and authority during 1857–58 between the civil-religious leadership of Utah Territory, led by Governor Young, and the federal leadership of President James Buchanan—a contest that pitted perhaps the nation's largest, most experienced territorial militia (Nauvoo Legion) against an expeditionary force that ultimately grew to involve almost one-third of the U.S. Army. It was the nation's most extensive and expensive military undertaking during the period between the Mexican and Civil wars. In my view, it was *not* a religious crusade against Mormonism to eradicate polygamy, an effort that came only after the Civil War.[8] Neither was it a campaign to suppress a Mormon "rebellion," a term that Buchanan used warily as do I, although at the point in fall 1857 when Governor Young declared martial law, forbade free travel within and across Utah (fig. 2), and issued orders to kill U.S. Army officers and their mountaineer guides, it becomes more difficult to avoid the "R" word.

When I entered this field of study in 1958, I used the term "Utah Expedition" for not only the United States Army brigade commanded by

PROCLAMATION
BY THE GOVERNOR.

CITIZENS OF UTAH—

We are invaded by a hostile force who are evidently assailing us to accomplish our overthrow and destruction.

For the last twenty five years we have trusted officials of the Government, from Constables and Justices to Judges, Governors, and Presidents, only to be scorned, held in derision, insulted and betrayed. Our houses have been plundered and then burned, our fields laid waste, our principal men butchered while under the pledged faith of the government for their safety, and our families driven from their homes to find that shelter in the barren wilderness and that protection among hostile savages which were denied them in the boasted abodes of Christianity and civilization.

The Constitution of our common country guarantees unto us all that we do now or have ever claimed.

If the Constitutional rights which pertain unto us as American citizens were extended to Utah, according to the spirit and meaning thereof, and fairly and impartially administered, it is all that we could ask, all that we have ever asked.

Our opponents have availed themselves of prejudice existing against us because of our religious faith, to send out a formidable host to accomplish our destruction. We have had no privilege, no opportunity of defending ourselves from the false, foul, and unjust aspersions against us before the nation. The Government has not condescended to cause an investigating committee or other person to be sent to inquire into and ascertain the truth, as is customary in such cases.

We know those aspersions to be false, but that avails us nothing. We are condemned unheard and forced to an issue with an armed, mercenary mob, which has been sent against us at the instigation of anonymous letter writers ashamed to father the base, slanderous falsehoods which they have given to the public; of corrupt officials who have brought false accusation against us to screen themselves in their own infamy; and of hireling priests and howling editors who prostitute the truth for filthy lucre's sake.

The issue which has been thus forced upon us compels us to resort to the great first law of self preservation and stand in our own defence, a right guaranteed unto us by the genius of the institutions of our country, and upon which the Government is based.

Our duty to ourselves, to our families, requires us not to tamely submit to be driven and slain, without an attempt to preserve ourselves. Our duty to our country, our holy religion, our God, to freedom and liberty, requires that we should not quietly stand still and see those fetters forging around, which are calculated to enslave and bring us in subjection to an unlawful military despotism such as can only emanate [in a country of Constitutional law] from usurpation, tyranny, and oppression.

Therefore I, Brigham Young, Governor and Superintendent of Indian Affairs for the Territory of Utah, in the name of the People of the United States in the Territory of Utah,

1st:—Forbid all armed forces, of every description, from coming into this Territory under any pretence whatever.

2d:—That all the forces in said Territory hold themselves in readiness to march, at a moment's notice, to repel any and all such invasion.

3d:—Martial law is hereby declared to exist in this Territory, from and after the publication of this Proclamation; and no person shall be allowed to pass or repass into, or through, or from this Territory, without a permit from the proper officer.

{ L.S. } Given under my hand and seal at Great Salt Lake City, Territory of Utah, this fifteenth day of September, A. D. Eighteen hundred and fifty seven and of the Independence of the United States of America the eighty second.

BRIGHAM YOUNG.

FIG. 2. Proclamation by the Governor, September 15, 1857. As the U.S. Army approached Utah's northeastern frontier, Governor Brigham Young proclaimed martial law, forbidding entrance to Utah without permission from him or other territorial officers. This extraordinary decree, aimed at the army's Utah Expedition, shocked the country and soon resulted in Young's indictment for treason by a federal grand jury at Fort Bridger (dropped without trial in 1859). L. Tom Perry Special Collections, Harold B. Lee Library, Brigham Young University.

Albert Sidney Johnston (fig. 3) but also for the broader conflict itself. Decades later professor Richard D. Poll led me to understand that the label Utah Expedition overlooks the fact that there was a large group of people engaged on the other side who had nothing to do with the army, specifically Utah Territory's Mormon population. Since then I have used the term "Utah War," and have reserved "Utah Expedition" solely for the uniformed federals and camp followers involved.

The flip side of this parochialism is the term "Johnston's Army," an ethnocentric label used in Utah and few other places. To me it is an understandable but unfortunate term that trivializes the war by personalizing it in much the same way that "Seward's Folly" was once used to ridicule the federal government's purchase of Alaska.[9] The term is especially inappropriate in my view since Johnston was not the expedition's initial commander and, once appointed, there were efforts on two occasions to supersede him.[10] I was surprised to learn through researcher Ardis Parshall that the war's participants did not even use the term Johnston's Army. The label took root in Mormon Utah only decades later for political and cultural reasons, and the term "Buchanan's Blunder" also came into vogue.[11] Elder Boyd K. Packer used the latter label at the semiannual general conference in October 2008, so old ways are sometimes enduring.[12]

FIG. 3. Albert Sidney Johnston, commander of the U.S. Army's Utah Expedition. Johnston was a key figure during Kane's involvement in this armed Mormon-federal confrontation. In the midst of the campaign, Johnston was promoted from colonel to brevet brigadier general. He died at the battle of Shiloh in April 1862 as the Confederacy's senior general in the field. Library of Congress.

While on the subject of terminology, I would note that within the institutional army there is an aversion to using the term "war" for this conflict. The military prefers to call it a campaign or an expedition. The army's logic is that there was neither a congressional declaration of war nor pitched battles between massed troops and wholesale bloodletting on the scale of Civil War battles. Quite true, but I continue to think that "war" is an appropriate, common-sense term—as with the way we discuss the "Indian Wars." Consider the following points: (1) for years Camp Floyd, Utah, near Salt Lake City, was the nation's largest army garrison; (2) the confrontation was so costly that it virtually bankrupted the U.S. Treasury and devastated Utah's economy; (3) the conflict's financing forced the resignation of the secretary of war, John B. Floyd (fig. 4); (4) the citizens' move south—an effort to flee the approaching army—put thirty thousand Mormon refugees on the road from northern Utah to Provo and perhaps beyond; (5) Brigham Young and scores of others were indicted by a federal grand jury for treason; and (6) the Mountain Meadows massacre alone, the conflict's greatest atrocity, was one of the worst incidents of organized mass murder against unarmed civilians in the nation's history. For me "Utah War" is an appropriate term.

Kane's Involvement: When and How?

My guess is that most people who are aware of Thomas L. Kane's famous Utah War involvement think of this as an activity that began midway through the conflict with his January 4, 1858, departure from Philadelphia for Salt Lake City via Panama and California. How, as well as when, all this came about is not well understood. The fact is that Kane entered the picture in March 1857 even *before* the conflict started. He did so in response to a letter written by Young on January 7, 1857, asking for his help in lobbying the incoming president whose name Young had just learned after a two-month postelection communications lag. Young wanted to ensure that he kept his gubernatorial appointment, the term of which had expired in 1854.[13]

After reading Richard E. Bennett's article, readers might not find this request by Young a strange one in view of Kane's earlier substantial service to the Church, especially through his 1846 trip to Iowa and 1850 lecture on Mormonism in Philadelphia. But, surprisingly, there are telltale signs that Messrs. Young and Kane had not communicated with one another for quite some time—perhaps as long as a year or more.[14] Young had been busy with, if not distracted by, a host of church, political, and medical problems. Kane, in turn, had been preoccupied with illness as well as daunting personal and family responsibilities—even tragedies.[15]

FIG. 4. Secretary of War John B. Floyd. Floyd resigned from Buchanan's cabinet in December 1860 for Utah War financial irregularities, an imbroglio that resulted in his indictment (later quashed) for malfeasance in office. He subsequently became an unsuccessful Confederate brigadier. Library of Congress.

What drove Young to reestablish contact with Kane by letter in early January 1857 were two factors: the realization that his hold on Utah's governorship was extremely precarious, given President Pierce's refusal to reappoint him; and the imminent inauguration of Pierce's successor—Buchanan—would undoubtedly churn the federal patronage, including the positions of territorial appointees. With the March 4 inauguration fast approaching and severe time lags in winter mail service between Salt Lake City and the Atlantic Coast, Young realized that he had a very narrow window of opportunity during which to influence the incoming president's appointment decisions. To Kane he wrote:

> Again do I venture to break the silence of intervening months, and draw upon your time and perhaps patience long enough to read a line or two from your old friend. Well, we in the mountains are still alive. . . . In regard to other matters, through the Providence of God and doubtless the influence and favor of *kind friends* I am still Governor of Utah. In this I shall ever appreciate the kindness of Col. Kane and shall hold myself in readiness to reciprocate whenever opportunity shall occur.[16]

Young closed this long letter with another, even more convoluted summation about his gubernatorial role, "We thus recommend ourselves to you honestly believing that we are as willing to serve our country (this part of it) as we are to have anybody else to serve it for us, and better acquainted with the merits and conditions of the people, better capable of doing it correctly."[17] On January 31, concerned that weather might delay this letter's eastbound passage, an anxious Young wrote a follow-up message to Kane. Young commented, "We are satisfied with the appointment of Buchanan as future president, we believe he will be a friend to the good, Pres. Fillmore was our friend, but Buchanan will not be a whit behind."[18]

When he received Young's first letter in late March, Kane swung into action, doing so at a time when the new president and his cabinet were exhausted and beleaguered—working feverishly night and day to fill thousands of federal appointments ranging from those for country postmasters to territorial governors. Kane's first overture came through a March 21 letter to Buchanan pleading that he retain Young as Utah's governor. Kane proposed that Buchanan do so not by reappointing him—an act that would have triggered a controversial confirmation process in the U.S. Senate—but rather by the technical gambit of taking no action to remove or replace him.[19] On April 1, one of Young's agents in New York reported to him,

> I had a long talk with Col. Kane yesterday; he informed me that he received a letter from you a short time since. He has written to the President and also to Judge Black Attorney General of the U.S. in relation to Utah, and the [negative] reports, urging your reappointment, how it will terminate [turn out] he says he cannot at present determine, but he

will do his best, and use his utmost endeavors and influence for you and the Welfare of Utah. His feelings are good.[20]

Two weeks later Elder John Taylor, also in New York, added the following news:

> Col. Kane has been using all his influence with the administration; he is a true friend. In an interview that I had with him lately, he informed me that he had received a letter from you & was desirous to carry out your request as far as possible, he did not think it prudent, however to recommend all [your nominees]; but seemed more desirous to first secure the governorship.[21]

Kane himself reported to Young that,

> there exists where there shd. not be a spirit of determined hostility to your interests. The best thing that can be done at present, as I am advised, is to obtain delay—at any price. I have accordingly procured an influential friend to represent to Mr. Buchanan how complicated as well as embarrassing the whole Utah question was to be considered.... This is about the drift of my own letter.... Mr. Buchanan is a timorous man, as well as just now an overworked one.[22]

Notwithstanding Kane's upbeat interactions with Mormon leaders on the Atlantic Coast, his lobbying efforts on Young's behalf took place during a period of great personal turbulence. Kane was beset by a continued grief over the recent death of his older brother Elisha, an internationally famous explorer; the financial and emotion collapse of his father-in-law; his own prolonged illness; and plans for an expedition to the Arctic inspired by Elisha that his family considered and rejected on March 27.[23] Although Thomas was neither the Democratic Party stalwart nor the Buchanan intimate that his father was, the younger Kane had good reason to assume the president would give his letter and offer to visit the White House careful thought as the cabinet focused on Utah affairs.

When his overtures to Washington were met with silence, Kane interpreted this as an embarrassing, offensive rebuff compounded by what he perceived as indiscreet handling of his correspondence by the administration. The latter resulted in humiliating public ridicule by the venomous, debauched Judge W. W. Drummond through pseudonymous letters about Kane written to various newspapers. After attempting to build a backfire against Drummond by collecting and forwarding to the administration material damaging to the judge's reputation collected by Elders John Taylor and George A. Smith, Kane notified Brigham Young of the failure to influence Buchanan.[24] Kane then withdrew from Mormon affairs, and retreated with his family from Philadelphia to Pennsylvania's mountains. What Kane and Young did not know was that on March 19 and 20

Buchanan and his cabinet had already received three new batches of materials from Utah that—true or not—destroyed any remaining vestiges of Young's political viability. These were inputs that one Buchanan cabinet secretary informed Utah Territorial Delegate John M. Bernhisel were interpreted as a Mormon "declaration of war." What followed in short order was the administration's decision to appoint a new governor and to provide him with some sort of substantial military escort.[25]

In May, a few weeks before General Winfield Scott (fig. 5) issued orders to the army launching the Utah Expedition, Kane received Young's second letter—the one written at the end of January. On May 21, in what almost sounds like a valedictory letter, he replied to Young in fatalistic fashion:

FIG. 5. Brevet Lieutenant General Winfield Scott, the army's general in chief at mid-century. In 1857 he unsuccessfully opposed a move on Utah until 1858 and was unaware of Kane's involvement until reports from Fort Bridger reached him in early summer 1858. From the 1862 class album, United States Military Academy Library, West Point.

> I am still without good news to communicate. We can place no reliance upon the President: he succumbs in more respects than one to outside pressure. You can see from the papers how clamorous it is for interference with Utah affairs. Now Mr. Buchanan has not heart enough to save his friends from being thrown over to stop the mouths of a pack of Yankee editors. . . . I thank you for writing to me. I am growing old enough to prize the friends whom Time has left me. . . . Yet this writing, my friend Young;—does it keep down the miles of waste which seem to be growing up between us every year? I wish I had your hand to grasp. I write myself, and it seems but form.[26]

Several years later, after Kane had criticized Bernhisel for also withdrawing from Washington during spring 1857—thereby creating a lamentable vacuum in Mormon lobbying capabilities at a crucial time[27]—Bernhisel countered with a polite criticism of his own communicated to one of Buchanan's closest political confidantes. That advisor, in turn, reported Bernhisel's comments to Kane:

[He] expressed great regret that you had not thought of going out [to Utah] at an earlier date; and he had no doubt that had you gone there during the latter part of the summer [of 1857] and given them assurances of the prosecution of offenders and of the pardon from the President of such persons as they might desire, his belief was that you could have exerted a powerful influence in persuading his people to return to their allegiance to the U.S.[28]

This, then, was how Kane first came to become involved with what soon unfolded as the Utah War. This is not the place to describe the equally complex story of how Kane spent summer 1857, how and why Young reached out to him again in August and September 1857, and how Kane ultimately returned to the fray of Mormon affairs with two trips to the White House on November 10 and December 26, 1857, the genesis of his 1858 mediating mission to Utah.[29] It is relevant, though, to plumb the depths of his motivations in undertaking such a task.

Kane's Motives: The "Why" Question

Why, at the end of December 1857, would Kane return from the White House to Philadelphia, quit his job as clerk of his father's U.S. district court, and—to the accompaniment of Judge Kane's disapproval and predictions of failure—convince his wife of his need to hurry off at age thirty-five in the dead of winter to Utah in pursuit of a dangerous humanitarian mission of uncertain character and indeterminate length among a people whose religion he did not share? All this was to be done while leaving Elizabeth and their two children as virtually destitute boarders in his parents' home. In his essay, Richard Bennett describes the motivations behind Thomas's somewhat similar 1846 visit to the migrating Mormons in western Iowa and the reasons for his attachment to the Mormons in terms of such drivers as empathy for and bonding with a sickly, beleaguered people. I do not challenge the accuracy of any of these early factors in the relationship Kane had with the Mormons but would add that in 1846 Kane was also strongly interested in the fanciful possibility that if he reached the Pacific Coast with Young's pioneer party, he might somehow become governor of California. Before reaching Iowa, Kane had written to a brother:

> At one time or other a government representative may be wanting [in California]. Who so fit for one as I?—above all if on the journey I shall have ingratiated myself with the disaffected Mormon army before it descends upon the plains—and according to the promptings of occasion, be or be not the first Governor of the new territory of California.[30]

If one accepts the assumption that most of these same motivations were still present in Kane's mind during late 1857, it is important to ask whether there were any other factors influencing his decision to intervene in Utah. In my view there were several new drivers to be considered in assessing Kane's Utah War role.

Chief among these factors was the devastating impact of Elisha Kent Kane's death in February 1857 during a fruitless attempt to recover his long-deteriorating health in Havana. Thomas was in Cuba with Elisha during his brother's final illness—the very time when Brigham Young was reaching out to him. He accompanied the body home to Philadelphia and immediately plunged into not only deep grief but also the complex role of Elisha's legal and literary executor as well as the keeper of his reputational flame. Because of Elisha's notoriety as a naval surgeon, Arctic explorer, would-be rescuer of Sir John Franklin's fatal British expedition to that region, and best-selling author, his funeral cortege through New Orleans, Louisville, Cincinnati, Pittsburg, and other cities produced an event unmatched in American mourning during the period between the funerals of Presidents Washington and Lincoln.[31] This example and the knowledge that during the Mexican War Elisha had undertaken a confidential, dangerous government mission to carry dispatches to General Winfield Scott in the field as he had done earlier in a diplomatic mission to China, provided a powerful motivator for Thomas to emulate, if not match, his brother's accomplishments. Hence Thomas's quixotic, unsuccessful attempt to mount an Arctic expedition of his own during late March 1857, shortly after Elisha's death and only a few weeks after his March 12 burial and Thomas's March 21 letter on behalf of Young to Buchanan. By the end of the year, the prospect of substantial bloodshed in Utah provided still another opportunity for a dramatic adventure—one made all the more compelling, if not appealing, by the daunting nature and the blunt skepticism of his prominent, overshadowing father.[32]

Having at least introduced the subject of Thomas L. Kane's famous older brother and widely respected father, I am not going to wade deeper into the murky diagnostic waters of psychohistory. What I can do, though, is discuss Kane's mediating mission to Utah in terms of the observations of those in close proximity to him as well as his own explanation.

In that connection, it is important to understand that on December 9, 1857, James C. Van Dyke, the president's shadowy political confidante, wrote to Buchanan to brief him on Kane's mood and thinking. This took place soon after news of the Nauvoo Legion's successful raid on the Utah Expedition's supply trains reached Washington and the day after the president sent his first annual message to Congress, but before Kane's fateful Christmas visit to the White House. Although at approximately the same time territorial delegate Bernhisel had described visiting Kane in a "sick room" in which he was beset by personal "anxieties and troubles," Van Dyke reported a different view to Buchanan:

> Col. Kane from his long association with that people, has much influence with the Mormons, and especially with their chief. He thinks he can do much to accomplish an amicable peace between them and the United States. He is willing to make an expedition to Salt Lake this winter, even at his own expense, if hostilities have not advanced to such a point as would render useless any efforts on his part. He has conversed with me much, on this subject, and my conclusion from all he has said has been, that it would not be an unprofitable thing if you would have a consultation with him, and hear his views. . . . He is full of courage, and if his judgment is correct, he may be able to avert a war of extermination against a poor deluded race.[33]

Buchanan, of course, did meet with Kane on December 26, and Kane later recorded that he had explained his motivations to the President by saying, "I will not be a disappointed man unless I fail to prove myself."[34] As Kane was confiding this driver to Buchanan, Kane's wife recorded in her diary the news that,

> God has mercifully brought out of them [our adversities] one great blessing already, in uniting Tom and me in the bonds of a common [Christian] faith. Tom thinks he may be of service to Him by bringing about a peace between Utah & the U.S. and went to Washington last night to see the President about it. May God give him wisdom to do right, and may His peace be with him. And oh, may He guide Papa.[35]

After he returned from Utah in June 1858, Kane told territorial delegate Bernhisel that "he would have the world know that he m[a]de his journey at his own expense, in the interest of the whole United States, and of humanity as well as the friends he loves in Utah."[36]

The longest, most interesting assessment of Thomas L. Kane's motives came from his younger brother, John, who was studying in Paris at the time of Thomas's decision to go to Utah. On January 21, 1858, with awareness that his older brother had indeed left for the West, John wrote to his siblings and parents:

> I am glad the family did not make him unhappy by useless remonstrances . . . [and unlike father] I am moreover not so sure of an unsuccessful termination to the affair. I have great confidence in Tom's long head and unbounded energy and however impossible a thing may seem I regard the fact of Tom's having undertaken it as more than half a success. Then too when I reflect that Tom is never so well as when exposed to what would kill most men of his build, and that hard life in open air (no matter how hard) always agrees with him better than the most tranquil of sedentary existence. . . . At home Tom's big soul was preying on his body. The loss of dear Elish. and the crushing blow which this finan-

cial crisis gave to his hopes of organizing a new [Arctic] expedition were killing him by inches. He is too great a man to occupy himself with trifles.... Now he has got an object large enough and noble enough to draw his thoughts away from the poor self on which they were fading and I cant help hoping that his physical man will improve in consequence. However be the result of what it may the object is grand and noble and does him and the family honor and I for one say God bless and speed him with all my heart.[37]

Such was the combination of drivers that propelled a sickly, overshadowed, ambitious, restless, and religiously struggling Thomas L. Kane from the comforts and boredom of Philadelphia to the wilderness perils of the American West. Here was an unconventional mission on behalf of a beleaguered Mormon people whom both President Buchanan and territorial delegate Bernhisel feared might kill Kane in southern Utah, scene of the Mountain Meadows massacre less than three months earlier.[38]

Was Kane a Latter-day Saint?

In spring 1858, when it became known on the Atlantic Coast that Thomas Kane was in Utah and somehow engaged in the war, there was a great deal of speculation as to whether this unclear involvement stemmed from membership in the Latter-day Saint church. Was Thomas a closet Saint? Many newspaper commentators as well as troops at Fort Bridger thought so, but the fact is that he was not. The clearest, most concise assessment of that question appears in an article by David J. Whittaker. He explains that, although Thomas had been baptized in 1846 for health while visiting the Mormons in Iowa, this was not a religious commitment or affiliation—just an act of mercy extended to what appeared to have been a visitor dying of malaria. As Whittaker also notes, Elizabeth Kane's diary at BYU makes clear that the relevant question for the Utah War period was not whether Thomas was a Mormon but rather whether he was even a Christian.[39]

In his essay, Richard Bennett comments that at the time of Thomas Kane's 1846 mission to Iowa "he embraced no one particular Christian faith." Twelve years later, just before Kane was to leave Utah to return home, Brigham Young made a highly tactful attempt to invite Kane to investigate Mormonism (fig. 6) by writing, "For your own eye":

> Though our acquaintance from its commencement, which now dates from many years past, has ever been marked by that frank interchange of views and feelings which should ever characterize the communications of those who have the welfare of mankind at heart, irrespective of sect or party, as I am well assured by a long and intimate

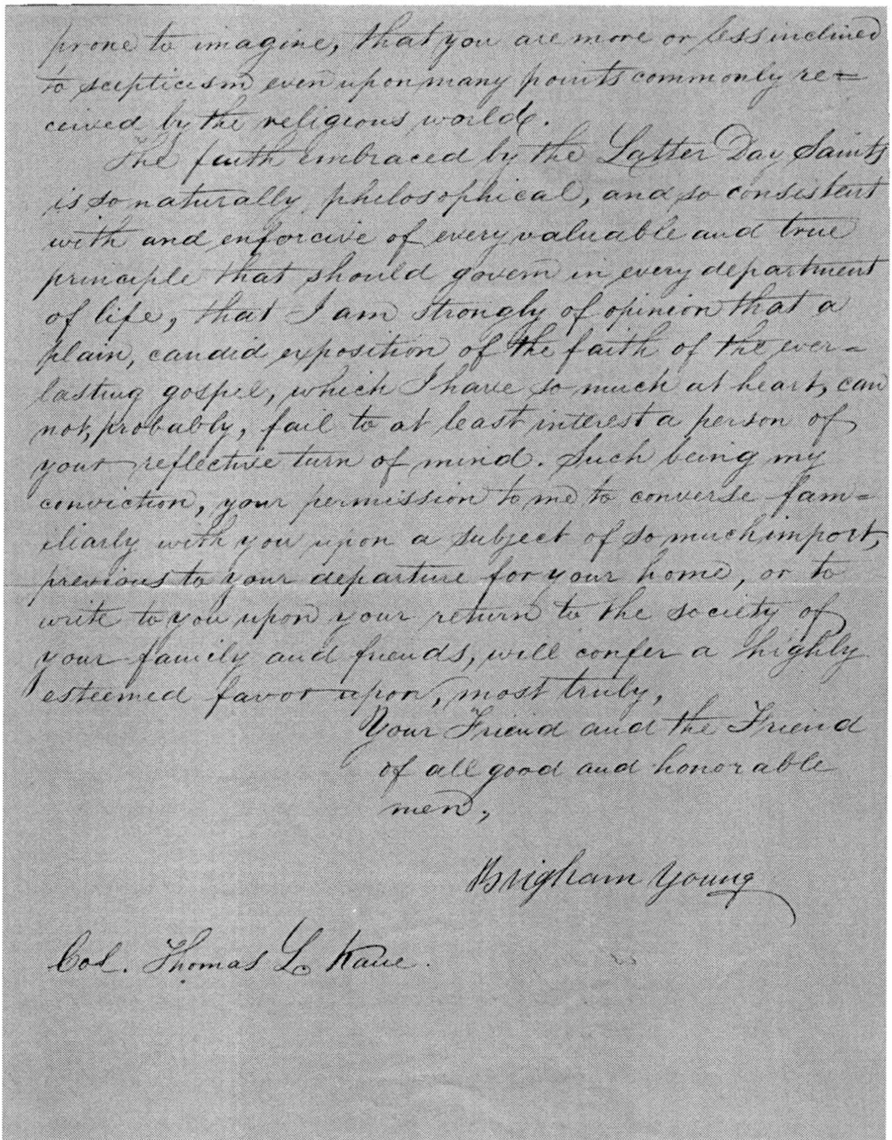

FIG. 6. Letter from Brigham Young to Thomas L. Kane, May 8, 1858. During Kane's involvement as a mediator between the Mormons and the federal government following the Utah War, there was much speculation about whether Kane had been secretly baptized as a Mormon. In this letter, Young invited Kane to learn more about the beliefs and doctrines of the people Kane had so ardently defended, something Young would not have done if Kane had already been baptized. L. Tom Perry Special Collections, Harold B. Lee Library, Brigham Young University.

acquaintance, is a feeling signally shared by yourself in common with your best friends; yet, so far as I can call to mind, I do not remember to have ever, either in correspondence, or in familiar conversation, except, perhaps, by a casual and unpursued remark, alluded to matters of religious belief, as entertained by myself and others who are commonly called "Mormons"; nor do I remember that you have ever overstepped the most guarded reserve on this subject in all your communications with me. So invariably and persistently has this peculiarity marked our friendly and free interchange of views upon policy and general topics, that I have at times imagined, and still am prone to imagine, that you are more or less inclined to scepticism even upon many points commonly received by the religious world.

The faith embraced by the Latter Day Saints is so naturally philosophical, and so consistent with and enforcive of every valuable and true principle that should govern in every department of life, that I am strongly of opinion that a plain, candid exposition of the faith of the everlasting gospel, which I have so much at heart, cannot, probably, fail to at least interest a person of your reflective turn of mind. Such being my conviction, your permission to me to converse familiarly with you upon a subject of so much import, previous to your departure for your home, or to write to you upon your return to the society of your family and friends, will confer a highly esteemed favor upon, [me].

Matthew J. Grow, Kane's latest biographer, argues that "Kane rejected Young's overtures; for him Mormonism would always remain in the realm of reform not personal belief."[40]

While Kane was in Utah, even President Buchanan waded into the fray of controversy over Thomas's religious affiliation, doing so, in his typical indirect fashion, through his party's political organ, the *Washington, D.C., Union*. On May 20 or 21, 1858, Kane's brother Pat visited the president to complain of the *Union*'s lack of support for Thomas's humanitarian mission to Utah. Elizabeth Kane recorded that at that session Buchanan "with his own hand wrote a notice to the *Union*, saying that Tom was no Mormon, but a worthy brother of Elisha's, a noble enterprise—etc. etc." An unsigned editorial in these words appeared in the *Union*'s May 21 issue.[41]

Kane arrived home on June 19, 1858, and, before departing for Washington two days later to see Buchanan, he devastated Elizabeth by announcing that he had lost the newfound religious commitment that had so enraptured her at the time of his departure six months earlier. In her journal she recorded:

Tom and I had a good deal of talk together. I said in my diary that "I was so happy and unhappy". What made me unhappy was this. Tom told me the first moment we were alone, like my dear honest darling, that the hope that had dawned on him of being a Christian was gone.—Now what distresses me is not the same trouble as I used to have, because I am sure it is only a cloud veiling the sun. I *know* that my prayers won't fall to the ground, I *know* that he will be a Christian, and if I exulted in the answer to my prayer too soon, I can wait patiently. Late or soon it shall be answered. Not all the men on earth, nor all the fiends in hell could persuade me against Christ's words "Ask and ye shall receive". I know that I ask a prayer that is a right one, and the answer I *will* have. True it is that for six years I have prayed daily for this one thing, but sometimes it has been more habit, not always the "strong crying and tears" with which I prayed last night. I need no special revelation, no messenger from heaven to tell me what I feel in the depth of my soul that my Savior hears, and is my advocate. I know my prayer will be granted. My grief is that the only comfort in his trouble is not his now. All my letters dwelt on that comfort. What can he do? And how hard it will be to shut up in my own breast again all the sympathies that went out to my brother Christian. He was so much nearer me! I don't know how to talk to him, for my thoughts have so moulded themselves around that hope that I – Oh dear poor Tom! I think I must not show you my diary. It would pain you now. I am glad I did not know he had lost his staff till now. I could not have borne his absence.[42]

In 1859, James C. Van Dyke, Buchanan's political advisor, related to Kane a conversation he had with Delegate Bernhisel during Kane's late December 1857 visit to the White House:

His [Bernhisel's] remarks upon your influence with the Mormons were so pointed an[d] decided that I felt some curiosity to know how it was that you had ingratiated yourself into the affections of this strange people. I remarked to him, "How is it that Col. Kane has such influence with your people?" I said jocosely, "He is no Mormon, and does not, I believe, approve of those peculiarities in their religion which appear to be the principal obstacle to a cordial affiliation between you and the rest of the U.S." He said, "Oh no! he is no Mormon, and of late years has treated us very coldly; we think on account of our religion which we all very much regret; but our friendship for and confidence in him is of a different nature."[43]

Kane's Mediating Mission: Significance and Impact

The last of my five questions investigates the significance and impact of Thomas L. Kane's Utah mission. Did it make a difference? Was it important? At one point, soon after Kane's late-February arrival in the Salt Lake Valley, Elder George A. Smith wrote to one of the prime movers in the Mountain Meadows massacre to describe sarcastically Kane's plea for Mormon leaders to negotiate with rather than fight the army:

It turns out that Col Tho. Kane's message is an unofficial one, he designs [intends] our good & is a warm friend, but he wants us to spare the lives of the poor soldiers camping about Bridger. Mr. Buchanan would like us to feed them, and not destroy them until he can get sufficient reinforcements to them to destroy us? This is as near I can learn the design of the President of the United States.

Smith summarized his assessment with the single word "Bah!"[44]

But when the smoke cleared, President Buchanan felt that Kane's effort had indeed been beneficial, although consistent with his convoluted style he could barely bring himself to say so publicly. At the end of 1857, Buchanan had crafted two letters of introduction for Thomas Kane to take west as an expression of goodwill and a means of introducing him to any federal officers whom he encountered. Given the criticism of his Utah policy then developing in Congress, what Buchanan had written for Thomas in his cautious, lawyerly, and secretive fashion was a model of what in today's presidential politics and intelligence work would be called plausible deniability. The letters were a means of distancing Buchanan from Thomas if his secret mission should become known, controversial, or a failure while providing signs that on at least a personal basis he had wished Kane well—thin gruel and cold comfort. From the distance of Philadelphia, George Plitt and John W. Forney—jaundiced former friends of the president—and Pat Kane immediately recognized the letters as such. Elizabeth Kane recorded their reactions and commented: "[They] think Mr. B. has behaved badly. His exceedingly noncommital letters are, they say, 'Buck all over, so that if Mr. K. succeeds, he may approve him, if he fails disavow him.'"[45] When a controversy indeed arose in summer 1858 over Kane's role and authority, Buchanan again turned to the *Washington Union* to make his case while protecting his anonymity:

> Dr. Kane, [was] a mere private citizen without power or authority of any sort.... He was a personal acquaintance of the President and possessed his esteem, and hence, we believe, took with him letters of introduction to officers of the army from Mr. Buchanan as from an [private] individual. But he went neither as agent of the President nor as officer of the government; neither as secret agent nor as public officer; but simply on an individual, self-imposed mission, as a private citizen, philanthropist, well-wisher of the Mormons, or what you will. He took no message from the President, other than the President had publicly announced [in his 1857 annual message], in regard to the Mormons.[46]

Old Buck's only recorded public utterance appreciation came in a single, muted sentence buried in his December 1858 second annual message to Congress: "I cannot, in this connection, refrain from mentioning the valuable services of Colonel Thomas L. Kane, who, from motives of pure benevolence, and without any official character or pecuniary compensation, visited Utah during the last inclement winter for the purpose of contributing to the pacification of the Territory."[47]

My view is that Kane's intervention made an indispensable difference in the outcome of this confrontation and that Buchanan, although fundamentally silent in public, was vastly relieved. Absent Kane's gratuitous intervention, the result could well have been substantial bloodshed beyond what had already taken place in Utah during fall 1857—a carnage roughly equivalent to what prompted for Utah's eastern neighbor the enduring label "Bleeding Kansas."[48]

Although Kane's March 21 letter to Buchanan and his November and December visits to Washington appeared to have had little or no overt influence on the President's thinking, Kane did have an impact on Brigham Young's decision making at a crucial juncture in the war. At first it appears that Kane's late-February/early-March discussions with Young and his counselors in Salt Lake City were fruitless. Elder Smith's "Bah!" reaction may not have been unique among the views of senior Mormon leaders. However, as discussed below, I believe that, beneath the surface, Kane's arguments for a peaceful resolution of the armed standoff prepared the way for the marked change in Young's then confrontational posture that took place immediately after Kane left for Camp Scott on March 8.[49]

As Kane was departing Salt Lake City, exhausted messengers arrived to inform Young of a surprise attack on the Church's Salmon River Mission in southern Oregon Territory (Fort Limhi) by two hundred Bannock and Northern Shoshone warriors. Mormon losses had been two killed and five wounded, together with hundreds of cattle and horses. Kane apparently took little note of the incident, preoccupied as he was with his departure on a daunting, lonely trek to Fort Bridger across 113 miles of mountainous terrain in bad weather. But Young understood immediately the implications of the bad news from Fort Limhi. It meant his inability to count on Lamanite allies in any coming fight with the Utah Expedition and the loss of safe access to a northern escape route to Montana's Bitterroot Valley or perhaps even to the Pacific Coast. With the north closed to him by this catastrophe, the army approaching from his east, California to the west inflamed over the Mountain Meadows massacre, and the army's Ives Expedition ascending the Colorado River from the south, Young realized he was trapped.[50]

He immediately did two highly unexpected things. First, he sent one of his sons galloping east to intercept Kane on the trail to deliver a note offering to donate or sell large quantities of flour to the army as a goodwill gesture.[51] Then he began to consider plans for a mass Mormon exodus from northern Utah that by March 21 would be refined into what became known as "the Move South." Without Kane's foundational arguments in Salt Lake City and his immediately subsequent presence on the trail to Fort Bridger, it is unlikely that Young would or could have undertaken to send the conciliatory flour signal to Albert Sidney Johnston as he did. I would argue that there is also a likelihood that Kane's determination in December to broach the notion of a Mormon exodus to Young when he reached him in February had a real but unclear influence on that leader's March decision to launch the Move South.[52]

Even more consequential to the outcome of the war was Kane's pivotal role during April in persuading Alfred Cumming (fig. 7), Young's gubernatorial successor, to change his hostile attitude toward the Mormons. As a result, Cumming agreed to Kane's proposal that he travel from Fort Bridger to Salt Lake City to take up his office unescorted by the army and accompanied only by Kane and two servants. It was a highly symbolic, unthreatening gesture that permitted Young to yield the governorship with some semblance of dignity while allowing Cumming, in turn, to declare to the Buchanan administration that federal authority had indeed returned peacefully to Salt Lake City.[53]

FIG. 7. Alfred Cumming, governor of Utah Territory, 1857–61. Coincidentally (and confusingly), Cumming's nephew of the same name was a captain in the Utah Expedition's 10th Infantry. Church History Library.

Finally, I would note that by traveling to the White House in June 1858 while deathly ill to brief Buchanan in person on conditions in Utah and to do so even before the president's own official peace commissioners had returned from the West, Kane provided Buchanan with the wherewithal to do something he had contemplated for some time—to declare victory in Utah, halt the massive military reinforcements already on the march to the territory from Kansas, and begin to wind down an enormously expensive and embarrassing armed confrontation. Buchanan declared "the Mormon problem" had been resolved to his satisfaction, a position that permitted him to turn attention from his then-controversial and expensive military intervention in Utah to other issues such as statehood for Kansas and Indian conflicts in both the Pacific Northwest and Southwest.[54]

No one else could have done all this, especially under such daunting circumstances. Kane's accomplishments were those of a person uniquely willing to champion the Mormon cause with an unmistakable idealism abetted by a hidden manipulativeness that matched James Buchanan's own such behavior. Although he did not know the half of what Kane had done, it was a performance that prompted one New York war correspondent to write a dispatch from Utah that, in turn, prompted his distant editor to argue that the nation owed a substantial debt of gratitude to a largely unknown Colonel Kane:

> We are not yet apprised of the precise nature and extent of Col. KANE's negotiations with the Mormon leaders, but they were certainly followed by an invitation to Governor Cumming to visit Salt Lake City—an invitation which the Governor immediately accepted . . . Without doubt they [Mormon leaders] have been greatly influenced by the counsels of Col. KANE.

Another newspaper dubbed Kane the "Peace Maker" and attributed to him "the close of the Mormon war" with enormous cost savings to the federal government (fig. 8).[55]

At the end of 1857, Buchanan lacked a plan for resolving the Utah War except for the application of more force. Small wonder that when Kane returned in June 1858 to meet for five days with Buchanan and his cabinet, the president was vastly relieved and grateful. As Kane later related the scene to Elizabeth, upon first seeing him the president immediately ushered out Pennsylvania's politically powerful Senator William Bigler, exclaimed "Colonel Kane!" and took his hand with "effusion." When Kane asked, "Well, Sir, Have I been as good as my word?" Buchanan gushed, "Better—More than as good as your word," following which Kane reported "more effusion and words of thanks."[56]

BYU's Kane Collection: Observations and Lessons Learned

In thinking about lessons to be learned from BYU's Kane collection—or at least those I have derived from using these materials—four principal observations come to mind:

Importance of the Collection. I want to re-emphasize the importance of these materials. Although there are ten or more concentrations of Thomas L. Kane's papers in various repositories across the United States, BYU's collection is enormously important and clearly the most vital to understanding his role in the Utah War. I have found BYU's holdings essential to grasping not only crucial aspects of what happened but also the reasons events took place.

I will mention just one example. Richard Bennett's article touched on Thomas's 1846 Iowa visit in terms of Kane's illnesses and certain distinctive behaviors such as his use of family members as intermediaries with the White House; attempted exercise of presidential authority and power; and extreme secretiveness, including the use of codes and ciphers. To be aware of this Kanesean style during the Mexican War brings meaning to its reappearance twelve years later in the Kane documents generated during the Utah War. In effect, all of this permits historians and biographers to discern a distinct pattern of operation.

Necessity of Looking beyond Kane's Papers. My second point is that to understand Thomas's role in the Utah War it is important to consult not only *his* papers at BYU but also those in Provo generated by his spouse and siblings. For example, Elizabeth's diary is an indispensable source by which to understand the depth of family sacrifices implicit in Kane's travel to Utah. It is also the sole means by which one can grasp Thomas's fragile religiosity and the family's deep ambivalence about President Buchanan's dealings with him.[57] Thomas L. Kane's papers alone are not enough; they are necessary, but not sufficient, to provide a rounded understanding of the man. (Would that President Buchanan or one of his cabinet members had kept a diary as Elizabeth Kane did!)

BYU's Holdings—Only Part of the Puzzle. In somewhat the same vein, my third point is that, as important as BYU's Kane collection is, researchers seeking a rounded picture of the man and his Utah involvement will need to venture beyond the Harold B. Lee Library. No single repository has holdings sufficiently broad to permit a full understanding of such an extremely complex man. Among the high-yield collections that can and should be consulted in addition to BYU's are those at:

• The American Philosophical Society (Philadelphia, Penn.)
• Church History Library, The Church of Jesus Christ of Latter-day Saints (Salt Lake City, Utah)
• Yale's Beinecke Rare Book and Manuscript Library (New Haven, Conn.)
• The University of Michigan's William L. Clements Library (Ann Arbor, Mich.)
• Stanford University Libraries (Stanford, Calif.)
• Pennsylvania State Archives (Harrisburg, Penn.)
• The Huntington Library (San Marino, Calif.)
• Private collections (various locations)

I will mention just one example of the extent to which materials to be found outside of Provo shed important light on Kane. Until quite recently, his crucial interactions with President Buchanan during December 1857 were almost wholly unknown. Until BYU acquired Elizabeth's diary, historians were not sure of how and when they took place and certainly were unaware of what Kane told his family upon returning home from

"To Col. Thomas L. Kane"

Much Honor'd Sir,
                    I'd fain address my pen
To you, a lover of your fellow men.
I dare presume; but beg you'll pardon, Sir:
I trust you will, if I, presuming, err.

    You plead the rights of man—you fain would see
All men enjoy the sweets of liberty.
Goodness is greatness—knowledge—pow'r; and thou
Perchance art greatest of your nation now.
And while that nation sinks beneath its blight;
You, like a constellation, cheer the night.

    If you can quell the raging ocean's wave,
You may, perhaps, your fallen country save.
If you can cleanse corruption's growing stream,
Hope on, your nation's honor, to redeem—
Give back our martyr'd Prophet's life again
And from th' escutcheon, wipe that dreadful stain.

    Your civil pow'rs—your Officers of State,
On freedom's shoulders, throw a deadly weight;
With suicidal acts, they've trampled down,
Our Charter'd Rights, and God Almighty's frown
Is resting on them; and the bitter cup
They've dealt, they'll drink; and drink it wholly up.

    Though for a while you may avert the blow,
The deed is done, which seals their overthrow—
The pois'nous canker-worm is gnawing where
No skill—no med'cine can the breach repair.

    What have they done? O blush, humanity!
What are they doing? <u>All the world can see.</u>

    Where is the Banner which your nation boasts?
Say, Is it waving o'er the gentile hosts?
Where are the Statesmen that have never swerv'd?
By whom the Constitution's Rights preserv'd?

    Here in the mountains, 'neath the western sky,
Columbia's Banner proudly waves on high.
And here are <u>men with souls</u>—men just and true—
Men worthy of our noble sires and you:
They have preserv'd our sacred Constitution
'Midst fearful odds and cruel persecution.

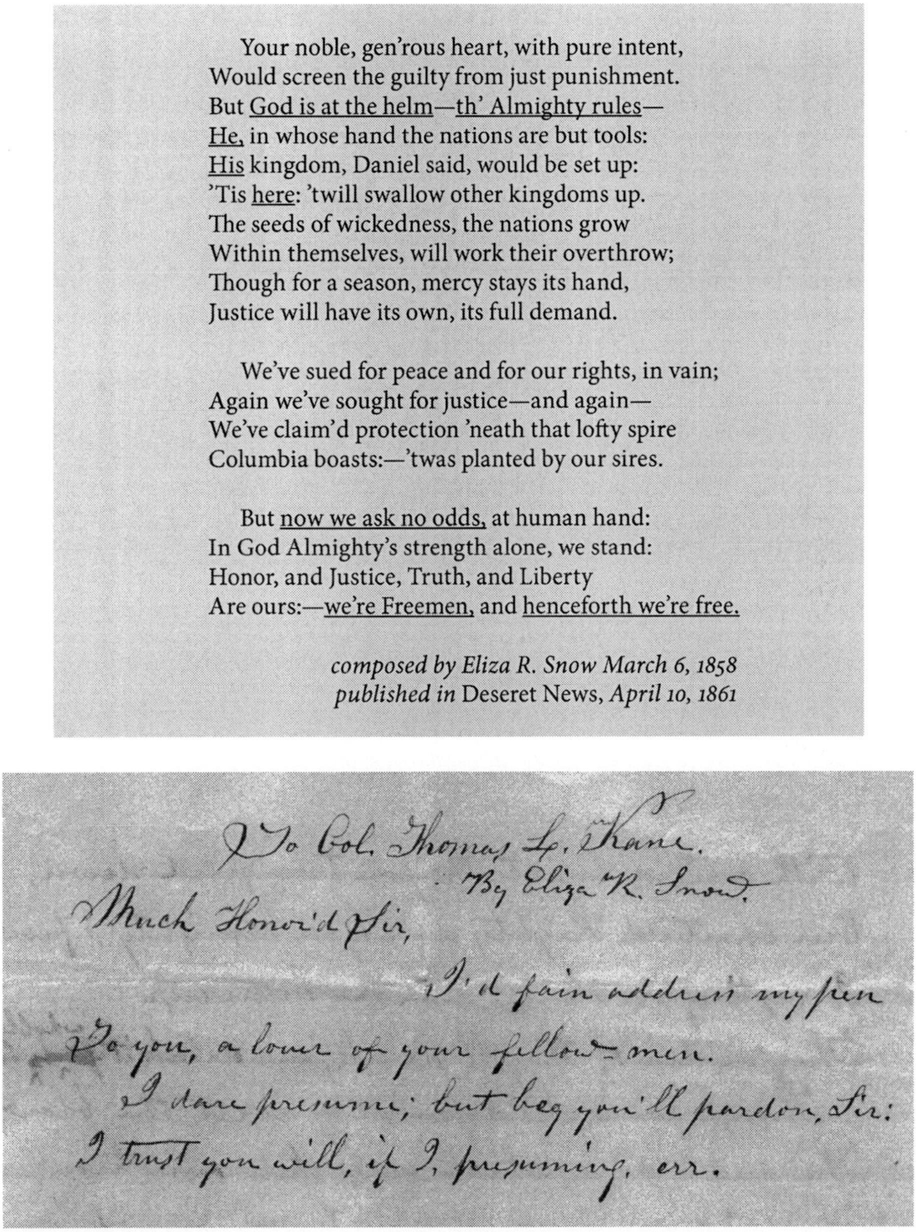

> Your noble, gen'rous heart, with pure intent,
> Would screen the guilty from just punishment.
> But <u>God is at the helm</u>—<u>th' Almighty rules</u>—
> <u>He,</u> in whose hand the nations are but tools:
> <u>His</u> kingdom, Daniel said, would be set up:
> 'Tis <u>here</u>: 'twill swallow other kingdoms up.
> The seeds of wickedness, the nations grow
> Within themselves, will work their overthrow;
> Though for a season, mercy stays its hand,
> Justice will have its own, its full demand.
>
> We've sued for peace and for our rights, in vain;
> Again we've sought for justice—and again—
> We've claim'd protection 'neath that lofty spire
> Columbia boasts:—'twas planted by our sires.
>
> But <u>now we ask no odds,</u> at human hand:
> In God Almighty's strength alone, we stand:
> Honor, and Justice, Truth, and Liberty
> Are ours:—<u>we're Freemen,</u> and <u>henceforth we're free.</u>
>
> *composed by Eliza R. Snow March 6, 1858*
> *published in* Deseret News, *April 10, 1861*

FIG. 8. Opening lines of "To Col. Thomas L. Kane," a poem by Eliza R. Snow, plural wife of Joseph Smith and later Brigham Young and poet laureate of Mormonism. Snow mixes multiple messages here: gratitude laced with skepticism for Kane's efforts; a litany of Mormon grievances; defiance; a veiled declaration of Mormon "independence"; and hints of the broader national civil conflict to come. A typescript of the complete poem precedes this detail of Snow's original handwritten version. L. Tom Perry Special Collections, Harold B. Lee Library, Brigham Young University. For another published text and analysis, see Jill Mulvay Derr and Karen Lynn Davidson, eds., *Eliza R. Snow: The Complete Poetry* (Provo and Salt Lake City: Brigham Young University Press and University of Utah Press, 2009), 571–74.

Washington. Supplementing this important behind-the-scenes glimpse provided by Elizabeth are astonishing pieces of the puzzle to be found in each of the repositories listed above. Perhaps the most arcane information about the December Buchanan-Kane meeting, though, comes from an indirect source, a letter written to the president by Judge Kane on December 31 to thank him for seeing his son and to comment on what Thomas told him of their White House conversation. This document is now in a private collection in California. Here Judge Kane commented matter-of-factly that, in the course of his presidential interview, Thomas indicated his intent to discuss with Brigham Young what could be interpreted as a Mormon mass exodus from Utah.[58] With this piece of the puzzle at hand, it is now possible to understand—or at least to speculate about—an enigmatic, cryptic sentence that later appeared in two letters that Young wrote to agents in Washington and Liverpool during Kane's visit to Salt Lake City. The sentence was, "We continue to keep our eyes on the Russian possessions [Alaska]."[59]

And the Lost Shall Be Found—More to Come. My fourth and final observation is there are far more Kane documents that will indeed be discovered in the years to come. My confidence that wonderful additional discoveries await us is the reason that my September 2008 Arrington Lecture at Utah State University on the future of Utah War studies was an optimistic talk.[60]

One of the missing documents that I expect to surface is the text of a lecture on Utah that Kane delivered at the New-York Historical Society in March 1859. In many respects, the very fact of Kane's New York lecture reflects the complexity of his character and personality while demonstrating the need to consult multiple sources to understand them. With this lecture, Kane rendered Governor Cumming an enormous service, and he did so by traveling to Manhattan in the dead of winter while struggling with another of his episodic life-threatening illnesses.[61] Kane did so because he believed that retention of Cumming as governor was essential to the well-being of the Latter-day Saints and to the tranquility of Utah. Yet Kane was hardly an admirer of Cumming, a four-hundred-pound alcoholic of limited talent who had successfully alienated not only Albert Sidney Johnston, his military protector, but former colleague Isaac I. Stevens, governor of Washington Territory.

Kane's personal disdain for Cumming and cynicism about his susceptibility to manipulation were such that in April 1858, when he first introduced the new governor to Brigham Young, George A. Smith recorded that "Col. Kane visited Gov. Young [and] told him that he had caught the fish, now you can cook it as [you have] he had a mind to." On May 1,

General D. H. Wells reported to Young on a recent discussion with Kane in which Cumming was described as "the poor old man" and "the Old Man," a descriptor that Wells used in such a way that it appears to have been Kane's as well as his own way of speaking about the new governor. Kane and Young frequently exchanged comments about Governor Cumming's drinking problem, yet Kane in March 1859 was willing to leave what territorial delegate Bernhisel had once called his "sick room" in Philadelphia and travel to Manhattan to lecture the world on Alfred Cumming's courage.[62]

It was a gambit that generated such extensive publicity that it made it virtually impossible for President Buchanan—a leader whom Kane had once described to Young as "a timorous man"—to remove Cumming. This was Kanesean wire-working on an even grander scale than Kane's May 1858 arrangement for dispatches to Albert Sidney Johnston to be delivered only by uncommunicative Mormon couriers, a system that Kane devised because he knew it would enrage the colonel and "tend to add fuel to the fire between Cumming and Johns[t]on."[63] Here one sees the combination of nobility and manipulation that had permitted a younger Kane to plan a mission of compassion to Iowa in 1846 while simultaneously dreaming of becoming governor of California with the armed might of his new, hopefully ingratiated Mormon friends behind him.[64]

And so I believe strongly that the stuff from which will come an even better understanding of a very complex Thomas L. Kane and his important Utah War contributions awaits our discovery. All that is needed to find such material is energy, imagination, support, and persistence of the type that have created in such wonderful fashion BYU's Kane collection.

William P. MacKinnon (MacKBP@msn.com) earned a BA degree magna cum laude from Yale University and an MBA from Harvard Graduate School of Business Administration. As an independent historian, MacKinnon's articles, essays, and book reviews on the American West have appeared in more than thirty journals and encyclopedias. He was honored with the Mormon History Association's Thomas L. Kane Award in 2008, and he is president-elect of the Mormon History Association for 2009–2010.

1. "Verastus" (pseud.) to Editor, May 24, 1857, "Col. Thomas L. Kane on Mormonism," *New York Daily Times,* May 26, 1857, 1. Some Mormon contemporaries and historians believed that "Verastus" was former Utah judge W. W. Drummond.

2. James C. Van Dyke to James Buchanan, December 9, 1857, James Buchanan Papers, Historical Society of Pennsylvania, Philadelphia. Van Dyke was U.S. attorney in Philadelphia and was the president's closest political advisor there. Kane's military title sprang from his brief appointment in 1846 as a militia lieutenant colonel on the staff of Pennsylvania's governor.

3. David J. Whittaker with Darcee Barnes, Patrick Mason, David Paoule, Sterling Fluharty, and Michelle Stockman, comp., *Register to the Thomas L. Kane and Elizabeth W. Kane Collection, Vault MSS 792*, 2 vols. (Provo, Utah: L. Tom Perry Special Collections, Harold B. Lee Library, Brigham Young University, Provo, Utah, 2001). A third volume describes additional Kane materials (Vault MSS 3190) acquired in 2003.

4. William P. MacKinnon, "Loose in the Stacks: A Half-Century with the Utah War and Its Legacy," *Dialogue: A Journal of Mormon Thought* 40 (Spring 2007): 43–81; William P. MacKinnon, "Stranger in a Strange Land: My Forty-Five Years with the Utah War and What I Have Learned," *Yale University Library Gazette* 80 (October 2005): 17–22. The author is a long-serving member of the board of the Yale Library Associates and was its chairman during 2000–2004; he has also been a member of the board of governors of the Clarke Historical Library, Central Michigan University, Mt. Pleasant, Mich.

5. Albert L. Zobell Jr., *Sentinel in the East: A Biography of Thomas L. Kane* (Salt Lake City: Nicholas G. Morgan, 1965); Richard D. Poll, "Thomas L. Kane and the Utah War," *Utah Historical Quarterly* 61 (Spring 1993): 112–35; William P. MacKinnon, *At Sword's Point, Part 1: A Documentary History of the Utah War to 1858* (Norman, Okla.: Arthur H. Clark Co., 2008); William P. MacKinnon, *At Sword's Point, Part 2: A Documentary History of the Utah War, 1858 and After* (forthcoming); Matthew J. Grow, *"Liberty to the Downtrodden": Thomas L. Kane, Romantic Reformer* (New Haven, Conn.: Yale University Press, 2009); Richard E. Bennett, "'He Is Our Friend'—Thomas L. Kane and the Mormons in Exodus 1846–1850," Lecture, Perry Special Collections, October 8, 2008, copy in author's possession.

6. While twenty-five hundred men is the size of the Utah Expedition most frequently cited by historians (and was its originally intended strength), by the time the expedition had reached Fort Bridger in November 1857 massive desertions had reduced it to slightly under fifteen hundred. By early 1858, a total of more than five thousand troops were under orders for Utah. See MacKinnon, *At Sword's Point, Part 1*, 221 n. 52; Roger B. Nielsen, *Roll Call at Old Camp Floyd, Utah Territory: Soldiers of Johnston's Army at the Upper Camp July 8 to September 1858* (Springville, Utah: n.p., 2006), iii; Curtis E. Allen to William P. MacKinnon, January 18, 2009, copy in author's possession.

7. For a review of the nearly ten years of deteriorating Mormon-federal relations leading up to the Utah War, see David L. Bigler, "A Lion in the Path: Genesis of the Utah War, 1857–1858," *Utah Historical Quarterly* 76 (Winter 2008): 4–21; William P. MacKinnon, "And the War Came: James Buchanan, the Utah Expedition, and the Decision to Intervene," *Utah Historical Quarterly* 76 (Winter 2008): 24–25; MacKinnon, *At Sword's Point, Part 1*, 41–82. For more on Utah's quest for statehood, see Thomas Alexander's essay herein.

8. Although not a successful executive, James Buchanan was a competent lawyer and was careful to justify the Utah Expedition as a measure to maintain federal authority rather than to confront Mormon Utah on religious grounds. In 1859, he reprimanded Utah's chief justice Delana R. Eckels, his own appointee, for charging a federal grand jury on the subject of polygamy, a practice against which there was no federal prohibition until enactment of the Morrill Act in 1862 during the Lincoln administration.

9. For a review of this Utah-centric label's use and implications, see Gene A. Sessions, "The Legend of 'Johnston's Army': Myth and Reality among the Mormons," paper presented at Mormon History Association annual conference, Salt Lake City, May 26, 2007.

10. William P. MacKinnon, "'Who's in Charge Here?': Utah Expedition Command Ambiguity," *Dialogue: A Journal of Mormon Thought* 42 (Spring 2009): 30–64.

11. There have been two interrelated factors destructive to any positive assessment of Buchanan's handling of "the Mormon problem." First came a largely successful campaign—begun by Mormon leaders during the Civil War—to portray the entire Utah War as a blunder brought on by ineptness as well as proto-Confederates among Buchanan's cabinet officers covertly plotting disunion as early as 1857. Implicit in the depiction of the Utah War as "Buchanan's Blunder"—a label still used by Mormon commentators—was the notion that the entire confrontation, including the removal of Brigham Young as governor, was unnecessary as well as horribly expensive. (I have likened this image campaign by Mormon leaders to that by which, after the Civil War, former Confederate generals created the Myth of the Lost Cause to justify a War Between the States in defense of a chivalric, agrarian society rather than to perpetuate chattel slavery. See William P. MacKinnon, "Epilogue to the Utah War: Impact and Legacy," *Journal of Mormon History* 29 [Fall 2003]: 217. An example of the negative effect on James Buchanan's image is the title of Richard D. Poll and Ralph W. Hansen, "'Buchanan's Blunder': The Utah War, 1857–1858," *Military Affairs* 25 [Fall 1961]: 121–31.) Accompanying this thrust was a second factor—widespread revulsion over the Civil War's carnage that broke over Buchanan's reputation indiscriminately and with such corrosive force that no memorial would be erected to him in Washington until as recently as Herbert Hoover's administration. The impact of these twin forces over the past 150 years has been the degradation of Buchanan's historiographical image into one blending a cartoonish bumbler on barely understood Utah matters with a passive, if not pro-Southern, chief executive presiding over the national slide into disunion.

12. Boyd K. Packer, "The Test," *Ensign* 38 (November 2008): 91. For an assessment of Buchanan's presidential performance in dealing with "the Mormon problem," including discussion of the "blunder" label, see William P. MacKinnon, "Precursor to Armageddon: James Buchanan, Brigham Young and a President's Initiation to Bloodshed," in *Disrupted Democracy: James Buchanan and the Coming of the Civil War*, ed. Michael J. Birkner and John Quist (Gainesville: University of Florida Press, forthcoming).

13. Brigham Young to Thomas L. Kane, January 7, 1857, Church History Library, The Church of Jesus Christ of Latter-day Saints, Salt Lake City. Because President Pierce appointed no successor who accepted the position after Young's term expired, Young remained governor on a de facto basis under a continuance, an ambiguity left to Buchanan to resolve. See MacKinnon, *At Sword's Point, Part 1*, 223.

14. The somewhat awkward opening phrase of the January 7 letter implies noncommunication. On April 14, 1856, the governor had written to Kane seeking political counsel but with no apparent response to that letter or to Elder George A. Smith's unsuccessful follow-up visit to Philadelphia while Kane was absent. For that matter, there is no indication that Kane wrote to Young at any

time during 1856, although Elder Taylor visited Kane at his Philadelphia home on March 8, 1856, and undoubtedly discussed the statehood (Deseret) thrust. John Taylor to Brigham Young, April 16, 1856, Church History Library.

15. A summary description of these distractions appears in MacKinnon, *At Sword's Point, Part 1*, 61–63.

16. Young to Kane, January 7, 1857. The text of much of this letter appears in MacKinnon, *At Sword's Point, Part 1*, 74–76.

17. Young to Kane, January 7, 1857.

18. Brigham Young to Thomas L. Kane, January 31, 1857, Church History Library. Fillmore, upon Kane's recommendation, had appointed Young in September 1850.

19. Thomas L. Kane to James Buchanan, March 21, 1857, Kane Collection, Perry Special Collections; MacKinnon, *At Sword's Point, Part 1*, 114–15.

20. William I. Appleby to Brigham Young, April 1, 1857, Church History Library.

21. John Taylor to Brigham Young, April 18, 1857, Church History Library.

22. Thomas L. Kane to Brigham Young, ca. late March 1857, Thomas L. Kane Papers, Stanford University Libraries, Stanford, Calif.

23. MacKinnon, *At Sword's Point, Part 1*, 112, 406.

24. For Judge Drummond's newspaper attack on Kane and Kane's campaign, in league with Elders Smith and Taylor, to discredit Drummond, see MacKinnon, *At Sword's Point, Part 1*, 119–20.

25. MacKinnon, *At Sword's Point, Part 1*, 99–111; MacKinnon, "And the War Came," 23–31.

26. Thomas L. Kane to Brigham Young, May 21, 1857, Thomas L. Kane Papers, Yale Collection of Western Americana, Beinecke Rare Book and Manuscript Library, Yale University, New Haven, Conn.; MacKinnon, *At Sword's Point, Part 1*, 135.

27. Thomas L. Kane to U.S. Attorney General Jeremiah S. Black, April 27, 1857, Black Papers, Library of Congress, Washington; MacKinnon, *At Sword's Point, Part 1*, 119–21.

28. James C. Van Dyke, Memorandum for Thomas L. Kane, March 28, 1859, Kane Collection, Pennsylvania State Archives, Harrisburg, Pennsylvania; MacKinnon, *At Sword's Point, Part 1*, 121 n. 41, 496–99.

29. MacKinnon, *At Sword's Point, Part 1*, 283–85, 405–11, 480–81, 485–87, 494–509.

30. Thomas L. Kane to Elisha K. Kane, May 17, 1846, Thomas L. Kane Papers, American Philosophical Society, Philadelphia, transcription courtesy of Matthew J. Grow. Kane's 1846 letters to his family from Iowa at the William L. Clements Library, University of Michigan, Ann Arbor, also shed light on this political motive.

31. David Chapin, "'Science Weeps, Humanity Weeps, the World Weeps': America Mourns Elisha Kent Kane," *Pennsylvania Magazine of History and Biography* 123 (October 1999): 275–301.

32. Judge John K. Kane to Thomas L. Kane, January 4, 1858, Kane Collection, Perry Special Collections; MacKinnon, *At Sword's Point, Part 1*, 510–11.

33. James C. Van Dyke to James Buchanan, December 9, 1857, Historical Society of Pennsylvania; MacKinnon, *At Sword's Point, Part 1*, 485–87.

34. Thomas L. Kane to James Buchanan, January 3, 1858, Historical Society of Pennsylvania.

35. Elizabeth W. Kane, Journal, December 26, 1857, Perry Special Collections. "Papa" referred to Thomas, not to her father.

36. John M. Bernhisel to Brigham Young, December 11, 1858, Church History Library.

37. John K. Kane Jr. to family, January 21, 1858, John K. Kane Collection, American Philosophical Society, Philadelphia.

38. Van Dyke, Memorandum for Kane. Based on these concerns and Kane's secretive behavior while passing through southern Utah and even once in Salt Lake City, it appears that his use of the *nom de guerre* "Dr. Osborne" was intended as much to protect him from apprehensive Latter-day Saints as from angry, anti-Mormon Californians.

39. David J. Whittaker, "New Sources on Old Friends: The Thomas L. Kane and Elizabeth W. Kane Collection," *Journal of Mormon History* 27 (Spring 2001): 67–94.

40. Brigham Young to Thomas L. Kane, May 8, 1858, Church History Library; Grow, *"Liberty to the Downtrodden,"* 190.

41. Elizabeth W. Kane, Journal, May 21, 1858; "Col. Thomas L. Kane," Editorial, *Washington Union*, May 21, 1858, 2. Pat Kane's complaint to Buchanan about the *Union's* treatment of Thomas and Buchanan's immediate communication with the newspaper may have been prompted by the *Union's* publication of a letter a few days earlier asserting, "Mr. KANE, of Philadelphia, *is a Mormon, and not sent out by the President, or any authority of the Government.*" Union (pseud.) to *Washington Union*, May 15, 1858, reprinted in *New York Times*, May 21, 1858, 1.

42. Elizabeth W. Kane, Journal, June 20, 1858; Grow, *"Liberty to the Downtrodden,"* 193–94.

43. Van Dyke, Memorandum for Kane.

44. George A. Smith to Col. William H. Dame, February [March] 3, 1858, Church History Library, transcription courtesy of Will Bagley.

45. The assessments by Messrs. Plitt, Forney, and Pat Kane were recorded in Elizabeth W. Kane, Journal, April 16, 1858. For a discussion of Buchanan's letters, see MacKinnon, *At Sword's Point, Part 1*, 503–6.

46. "Rebellion Complaints of Bad Faith," Editorial, *Washington Union*, July 8, 1858, 2. This disavowal of any official role for Kane was followed by the same newspaper's denigration of Kane's influence over Cumming's decision making an assertion that reports of Kane's effectiveness in motivating Cumming to travel to Salt Lake without the army were "unture in every particular. Col. Kane admitted his mission was a failure." "Truth" (pseud.) to editor, July 2, 1858, *Washington Union*, August 1, 1858, 3.

47. James Buchanan, "Second Annual Message of the President," December 6, 1858, in *The Works of James Buchanan, Comprising His Speeches, State Papers, and Private Correspondence*, 12 vols., ed. John Bassett Moore (New York: Antiquarian Press, 1960), 10:245. This sentence later appeared in James Buchanan, *Mr. Buchanan's Administration on the Eve of the Rebellion* (New York: D. Appleton, 1866), 238.

48. MacKinnon, *At Sword's Point, Part 1*, 295–328.

49. The date of Kane's departure for Fort Bridger can be determined from Brigham Young to Thomas L. Kane, March 9, 1858, Perry Special Collections.

50. David L. Bigler, "Mormon Missionaries, the Utah War, and the 1858 Bannock Raid on Fort Limhi," *Montana: The Magazine of Western History* 53

(Autumn 2003): 30–53; David L. Bigler, *Fort Limhi: The Mormon Adventure in Oregon Territory, 1855–1858* (Spokane, Wash.: Arthur H. Clark Co., 1998); MacKinnon, *At Sword's Point, Part 1*, 423–27.

51. Brigham Young to Thomas L. Kane, March 9, 1858, Perry Special Collections.

52. For Kane's virtually unknown predeparture intent to discuss an exodus with Young, see MacKinnon, *At Sword's Point, Part 1*, 501–3.

53. Alfred Cumming to House Speaker James L. Orr, May 12, 1858, Historical Society of Pennsylvania; James L. Orr to James Buchanan, June 21, 1858, Historical Society of Pennsylvania.

54. William P. MacKinnon, "Epilogue to the Utah War: Impact and Legacy," *Journal of Mormon History* 29 (Fall 2003): 244–45; MacKinnon, "Precursor to Armageddon."

55. "The News from Utah," editorial, *New York Times*, May 24, 1858, 4; "The Utah Question," editorial, Washington, D.C. *National Era*, July 1, 1858, 102.

56. The Buchanan-Kane exchange was reported in Elizabeth W. Kane, Journal, June 20, 1858.

57. An example of the mixed feelings about Buchanan's motives and the reliability of his support for Kane appears in Elizabeth W. Kane, Journal, April 16, 1858. In contrast, Judge Kane found Buchanan to be extremely helpful to his son and was grateful to the president. Judge John K. Kane to James Buchanan, January 2, 1858, Historical Society of Pennsylvania.

58. Judge John K. Kane to James Buchanan, December 31, 1857, copy in author's possession, courtesy of its owner, the late Ms. Anne Richards Horton, San Marino, Calif.; MacKinnon, *At Sword's Point, Part 1*, 501–3.

59. Brigham Young to John M. Bernhisel, March 5, 1858, Church History Library; Brigham Young to Asa Calkin, March 5, 1858, Church History Library.

60. William P. MacKinnon, "Predicting the Past: The Utah War's Twenty-First-Century Future," Leonard J. Arrington Mormon History Lecture Series no. 14, Utah State University, Logan, Utah, September 25, 2008.

Of all the potential discoveries of Kane-related documents that I most anticipate, five items immediately come to mind:

• The long memo of instructions that Wilford Woodruff drafted on March 4, 1858 to prepare Kane for his visit to the army at Fort Bridger. Is there anyone who would not like to know what Apostle Woodruff wrote on six pages "giving a reason of our hope and faith and the cause of our defending ourselves"? Wilford Woodruff, Memorandum for Thomas L. Kane, described in Wilford Woodruff, *Wilford Woodruff's Journal, 1833–1898, Typescript*, ed. Scott G. Kenney, 9 vols. (Midvale, Utah: Signature Books, 1983–84), 5:173 (March 4, 1858).

• The daguerreotype that Elizabeth Kane took at her home in June 1858 to capture the handsome face of Maj. Howard Egan, the Mormon frontiersman, bodyguard, and executioner who mesmerized her while awaiting completion of a Kane memo to carry back to Brigham Young. Elizabeth W. Kane, Journal, July 17, 1858.

• The 1857–58 letters home of Lafayette Shaw (Fay) Worthen, the young Kimball relative from Illinois who accompanied Kane and Egan during their long journey east in May 1858. Fay Worthen's father, Amos Henry Worthen, was Illinois state geologist. As a distant relative of LDS first counselor Heber C. Kimball, courier between Salt Lake City and Fort Bridger during the late winter of 1857–1858, informal aide to Gov. Cumming, and long-distance escort for Kane, Worthen's missing papers are potentially rich sources about the war, especially its later stages.

• The papers of Capt. John Cleveland Robinson, Fifth U.S. Infantry, the Utah Expedition officer who carried an exhausted, frozen Kane to the warmth of his own tent upon his nocturnal arrival at Fort Bridger on March 12, 1858. Kane described Capt. Robinson's compassion and overnight hospitality to the president in Thomas L. Kane to James Buchanan, ca. March 15, 1858, Kane Collection, Perry Special Collections. Long after receiving the Medal of Honor and losing a leg as a Civil War major general and serving as New York's lieutenant governor, Robinson wrote a brief account of the Utah War. John Cleveland Robinson, "The Utah Expedition," *Magazine of American History* 11 (January–June 1884): 335–41. This study ignored Kane and most of the author's personal experiences in Utah as a company commander. Any surviving Robinson papers contemporary to the Utah War would potentially shed light on Kane's dramatic arrival at Fort Bridger, including their overnight discussions in Robinson's quarters, as well as life within the historiographically "silent" Fifth Infantry, a regiment from which virtually no insider accounts have surfaced.

• The text of the lecture that Kane delivered at the New-York Historical Society in March 1859 to describe the beneficial impact of Governor Cumming's April 1858 journey from Fort Bridger to Salt Lake City on the smoothness with which he assumed his gubernatorial role. It was a supportive lecture that helped to preserve Cumming's position at a crucial juncture when Buchanan was considering removing him. We have press accounts but not the text of this important speech. "The Executive of Utah, Lecture by Col. Thomas J. [sic] Kane," *New York Times*, March 23, 1859, 2. The author's belief is that the text of this lecture is missing from the otherwise voluminous files of Kane and the New-York Historical Society because he may have given this material to T. B. H. Stenhouse or Apostle George Q. Cannon. Both Mormons were present at the talk so as to obtain national publicity for Kane's remarks by immediately visiting the editors of New York newspapers and the Manhattan headquarters of the Associated Press.

61. Grow, "Liberty to the Downtrodden," 198–99.

62. For Kane's "fish" metaphor, see George A. Smith, "Historian's Office Journal," entry ca. April 13, 1858, Church History Library. In this entry Smith also noted: "G.A.S.'s first impression when he saw Cumming was that he was a toper [drinker], but on examining him with his glasses he concluded he was a moderate drinker and a hearty eater." Daniel H. Wells to Brigham Young, May 1, 1858, Church History Library. Other comments on Cumming's alcohol consumption appear in Thomas L. Kane to Brigham Young, July 24, 1859, Church History Library; and Brigham Young to Thomas L. Kane, December 15, 1859, Church History Library.

63. Kane to Young, c. late March 1857, Stanford University Libraries; Wells to Young, May 1, 1858.

64. See p. 96 above.

FIG. 1. Elizabeth Dennistoun Wood Kane. Wife of Thomas L. Kane and fourteen years his junior, Elizabeth, or "Bessie," was a deeply religious woman who shared her husband's zeal for reform. L. Tom Perry Special Collections, Harold B. Lee Library, Brigham Young University.

FIG. 2. Thomas L. Kane, photograph by Elizabeth W. Kane, who was an amateur photographer. L. Tom Perry Special Collections, Harold B. Lee Library, Brigham Young University.

Tom and Bessie Kane and the Mormons

Edward A. Geary

Thomas L. Kane and Elizabeth Dennistoun Wood—"Tom" and "Bessie" in their personal relationship—were united during their thirty years of marriage by intelligence, idealism, and deep mutual affection (figs. 1 and 2). However, they were divided by temperament and personal philosophy. Tom was ambitious yet burdened by a sickly constitution, resistant to religious and social orthodoxies yet preoccupied with his own social status and personal reputation; he was a compulsive risk-taker, indifferent to prudential considerations. Bessie was deeply religious, devoted to home and family, and hungry for emotional and social security. Tom wanted to change the world through heroic action and was driven to espouse the causes of oppressed or reviled groups, including women, the urban poor, slaves, juvenile offenders, and Mormons. Bessie shared Tom's interest in improving the world by elevating the status of women but sought to accomplish the goal through unostentatious Christian service and a reform of social and sexual mores.

Although differing in perspective and approach, Tom and Bessie left their imprint on the history of the Latter-day Saints. Tom did so through his many years of devoted service, while Bessie contributed, more reluctantly, through a landmark literary treatment of nineteenth-century Mormon society.

The Kanes' involvement with the Latter-day Saints is too extensive to examine in detail here. Instead, this article focuses on representative elements of key episodes in which they interacted with the Mormons. First I will briefly discuss Tom's visit with the exiled Saints in 1846 and his subsequent activities that culminated in the delivery and publication of his influential lecture that was published as *The Mormons* in 1850 as well as his reaction to plural marriage in 1851; then I will explore Tom's assistance during the Utah War in 1857 and 1858 and Bessie's journals from the Kanes' 1872–73 visit to Utah, published as *Twelve Mormon Homes* (1874) and *A Gentile Account of Life in Utah's Dixie* (1995).[1]

A Brief Overview of the Kane Family

Tom and Bessie Kane were second cousins. Their common great-grandfather, John O'Kane, emigrated from Ireland to New York in 1752; dropped the Irish "O" from his name; married Sybil Kent, the daughter of a prominent clergyman; became a prosperous farmer; and sired a large family. When the American Revolution broke out, John Kane remained loyal to the British Crown, with the result that his properties were confiscated and his family forced to spend the war years as refugees in Nova Scotia. Following the war, the family returned to New York, where the sons established a trading firm that prospered until the disruption of transatlantic commerce by the Napoleonic Wars and the War of 1812. Bessie's grandfather, John, managed the firm of Kane and Brothers in New York, while Tom's grandfather, Elisha, established a branch in Philadelphia. The sons and daughters married well, uniting the Kanes with such prominent American families as the Livingstons, Morrises, Schuylers, and Van Rensselaers.[2]

Tom's father, John, adopted his stepmother's family name, Kintzing, as his own middle name to distinguish himself from several cousins also named John. John Kintzing Kane (fig. 3) received a classical education in Philadelphia schools, added a degree at Yale, and then returned to Philadelphia for legal training. He was admitted to the bar in 1817 and began a determined and ultimately successful courtship

FIG. 3. John Kintzing Kane. Thomas's father, John K. Kane, was an influential lawyer and skillful political writer whose anonymous articles to newspapers across the country proved successful in swaying public opinion and securing John political appointments. Thomas modeled these activities for the Mormons. L. Tom Perry Special Collections, Harold B. Lee Library, Brigham Young University.

of Jane Duval Leiper, whose father, Thomas Leiper, was a prominent Philadelphia industrialist. The family into which Thomas Leiper Kane was born on January 27, 1822, has been aptly characterized as "politically powerful and socially aspiring."[3] The family did not possess great wealth, but they lived comfortably (though with periodic money worries) on John K. Kane's income from his law practice and from a series of political appointments.[4]

The chief instrument of John K. Kane's political influence was a skillful pen. The larger American cities had dozens of competing newspapers, most of them aligned with a political party, and all of them eager for material.[5] John K. Kane supplied the papers that supported the rising Democratic Party with numerous unsigned articles reflecting his capacity "to influence, inspire, and use public opinion."[6] In addition, he published an influential pamphlet during Andrew Jackson's 1828 presidential campaign titled *A Candid View of the Presidential Question* that portrayed Jackson in heroic terms while offering a much less flattering portrait of his opponent, John Quincy Adams.[7] In 1844, John Kane turned his talents to the service of James K. Polk and his running mate, George Dallas, who was a personal friend, publishing a campaign biography, helping to draft Polk's messages to Congress, and being rewarded, in 1846, with an appointment to the federal bench.[8] John Kane further extended his social influence as a prominent Freemason and for many years as secretary and finally president of the American Philosophical Society.[9]

Unlike his father, who followed a steady career path, Tom Kane was driven in his early years by a restless ambition, an intense idealism, and frustrating personal limitations that included an undersized frame, frequent bouts of incapacitating illness, and periods of depression that he characterized as "blue devils."[10] His formal education ended at age seventeen when he dropped out of Dickinson College following a student rebellion.[11] After leaving college, he traveled to England and France in 1840 and visited France again in 1842–43. While there he had one brief encounter with Auguste Comté.[12]

Even though it is doubtful Tom entered the philosopher's social circle, it does seem likely he discovered Comté's writings while in Paris, probably on the second visit, and it is certain that Comté's thought had an important influence on Tom's intellectual development. Even after his early disaffection from the family's Presbyterian faith, Tom retained a lifelong interest in religion. To his brother Elisha he confided an early aspiration

> that I should make to me fame by a religion. You often saw me at work upon it. By Jove it was a grand scheme:—a religion suited to the 19th century—a religion containing in itself all things and influencing all things—conduct of life—of man, nation & government—emancipating

women & slaves—industrial classes—a religion containing itself the principle of its own change and amelioration—finally a religion of movement.[13]

These early ideas must have resonated with Comté's concept of a "religion of humanity," not based on a belief in God or in universals, but on an application of scientific analysis to social problems. Comté coined the word "altruism" to express the obligation to serve others and place their interests above one's own. The opposite of egoism, which places the self at the center, altruism accurately describes Tom's particular brand of benevolence. Tom also found something appealing in the Catholic ascetic tradition as reflected in *The Imitation of Christ* by Thomas à Kempis. Later in life, Tom settled on his own version of nondenominational Christianity that included elements of these and other religious influences.

Tom's wife, Elizabeth "Bessie" Dennistoun Wood, was born in Bootle, a suburb of Liverpool, England, on May 12, 1836, making her fourteen years younger than her future husband. Her mother, Harriet Amelia Kane, was the youngest daughter of John Kane, who was the eldest and most influential of the Kane brothers. Her father, William Wood (fig. 4), a member of a family prominent in the Glasgow business community, was a merchant banker engaged in the cotton trade. Educated at St. Andrews and Glasgow universities, Wood was a free-trade liberal with wide intellectual interests and a trusted friend and confidant to Tom Kane long before he had any thought of becoming his father-in-law.

A biographical notice prepared by the family at Bessie's death in 1909 states, "When she was six years old, she found her ideal in the gallant young cousin who . . . found welcome and healing in her father's house. His kindnesses won her childish heart; and the French doll he gave her was never forgotten."[14] In fact, Tom probably first met

FIG. 4. William Wood, albumen print, carte-de-visite photograph, March 18, 1865, by M. Ormsbee, New York. Elizabeth's father, William Wood, was a close friend of Thomas L. Kane long before Thomas and Elizabeth began their courtship. L. Tom Perry Special Collections, Harold B. Lee Library, Brigham Young University.

Bessie during "a fortnight" he spent with the Wood family at Liverpool in July 1840. William Wood recalled him as an engaging young man, "full of mannerism, which, indeed, rarely left him even in after life."[15] Bessie would have been only four years old at the time of this meeting. Correspondence indicates that William and Harriet Wood did invite Tom to stay at their home while he recovered from his October 1840 foot injury.[16] However, he chose instead to spend his convalescence at the Norfolk estate of a more distant relative, Archibald Morrison, where he remained through the winter.[17] He probably visited the Woods before he returned home in spring 1841. Perhaps that is when he presented Bessie with the French doll. However, Bessie would have been scarcely five years old at this time, not six. On his second trip to Paris in 1843–44, Tom sailed directly from New York to Le Havre and did not visit England,[18] so he would not have met the Wood family again until they moved to New York in July 1844, when Bessie was eight.

First Involvement with the Mormons

The year 1846 found Tom at a loose end; he did not find his new legal career satisfying. He wanted to become engaged in meaningful activities and chafed at the limited means and opportunities that constrained his range of action. In January, Tom's father, who had been influential in President James K. Polk's election, had been in Washington assisting with the preparation of the president's message to Congress.[19] Therefore, Tom would have been well aware of the president's plans to extend the U.S. borders by settling the Oregon boundary dispute with Britain and compelling Mexico to cede California and New Mexico well in advance of the declaration of war with Mexico in May. The idea of going to California at such a momentous time appealed to Tom, who knew the Mormons had plans to relocate to the West. On May 13, he attended a Latter-day Saint meeting in Philadelphia, where he met Jesse C. Little, who oversaw Church affairs in the east.[20]

There was some ambiguity in Tom's motives, and this complexity was evident in his initial involvement with the Saints. Depending on the motivational strand selected, it is possible to construct a convincing account of his actions based on altruistic compassion for a persecuted and driven people. However, it is equally plausible to account for his actions as having been motivated by self-interest. Tom viewed the westward-bound Mormons as a means to achieve his own ambitions for power and prominence, perhaps resulting in a federal appointment in California.[21]

It appears, however, that the Mormons constituted only one portion of Tom's plans to achieve his ambitions. Having previously failed to secure a military commission,[22] he was no doubt gratified when the Polk administration entrusted him with dispatches for Colonel Stephen W. Kearney as well as additional dispatches for California.[23] Tom had wanted to travel directly to California from Fort Leavenworth. It was only after Kearney and William Gilpin advised Tom that he was too late to catch the season's California emigration and that it would be too dangerous to attempt to cross the plains alone that he redirected his course northward to the Mormon camps on the Missouri River, arriving at Council Bluffs on July 11.[24] He was disappointed when he learned the Mormons did not plan to go farther west in 1846 and that their ultimate destination was not the Sacramento Valley but the less politically vital Great Basin. At this point, he hoped he could establish a name for himself by writing a popular book about Mormonism.[25]

It is possible to construct yet a third version of Tom's motives, suggesting he went among the Mormons, not as a disinterested benefactor, but rather as a government agent. Following an interview with President Polk, Tom wrote a letter to his brother Elisha, his closest confidant, declaring, "You must know that it has weighed upon my mind for months past whether it was not my duty to go with the Mormons, and this increased as I began to see signs of something which even to my eyes looked like English tampering with their leaders." He then described his interview with the president, during which he told Polk "what I knew of the people and their leaders, and what I knew of H. B. [Her Britannic] Majesty's interference—also my own peculiar position and means of influence, and then said that, if he thought it of enough importance that I should expatriate myself for a time and expose myself to risk and hardship, I would do so."[26] This was similar to what he later confided to Bessie during their courtship:

> It was thus, after wasting no more time than was absolutely necessary to ingratiate myself with some Mormons in Philadelphia and procure my purposes to be misrepresented; invested with amusingly plenipotential powers civil and military, I "went among the Mormons."
>
> Bessie, this is a little State Secret. Mr. Polk knew it. General Kearney knew it. One Col. Allen detailed by Kearney to march off a Battalion knew it. But probably no one else.[27]

However duplicitous or self-promoting Tom's initial motives may have been, his experiences in the Mormon camps appear to have transformed him. He presented himself as "Colonel Kane"—an honorary title he had seldom, if ever, used before this time—and was greeted warmly. He found the Church leaders to be "men more open to reason and truth plainly stated" than any others he had met and reported to his family "the most delightful relations subsist between the Twelve and myself. They are without any exaggeration a body of highly worthy men and they give me their most unbroken & childlike confidence." To his parents he wrote, "I will devote much of time when I come home to the Mormons," particularly to the "main task" of reshaping their public image. "If public opinion be not revolutionized," he lamented, "the miserable dramas of [persecution against the Mormons in] Missouri and Illinois will be acted over again, with the alteration that there will be no country left to which the persecuted can fly."[28]

In a letter written four years later to Brigham Young and his other Mormon friends, Tom described his initial encounter with the Saints in terms suggestive of religious conversion:

> I believe there is a crisis in the life of every man, when he is called upon to decide seriously and permanently if he will die unto sin and live unto righteousness.... Such an event, I believe ..., was my visit to [you]....
> It was the spectacle of your noble self denial and suffering for conscience sake, [that] first made a truly serious and abiding impression upon my mind, commanding me to note that there was something higher and better than the pursuit of the interests of earthly life for the spirit made after the image of Deity.[29]

Although Tom never joined the Latter-day Saint faith, he clearly had an interest in the religion and the people.[30] He knew the Book of Mormon and Doctrine and Covenants well enough to quote from them and to employ religious symbolism from their pages.[31] Furthermore, he challenged his wife's Presbyterianism by describing "the exceedingly miraculous powers" he had observed among the Mormons. "He has seen instances, scores of them, of invalids restored to health and working capacity by the word of the Mormon priest."[32] And he cherished throughout his life the blessing he received from Patriarch John Smith on September 7, 1846. Even Bessie was compelled to admit, years later, that this blessing "has been curiously fulfilled so far, strange to say."[33]

Tom's labor and personal sacrifice in support of Latter-day Saints were different from his many other altruistic and reform projects both in their extent—beginning at age twenty-six and continuing throughout his entire adult life—and the intensity of his personal engagement. Typically, Tom adopted an attitude of aristocratic responsibility, extending benefits derived from his privileged and influential social position to those lower on the social scale, be they slaves, youthful offenders, or Mormons. That characteristic attitude appeared in his work with the Latter-day Saints; however, it was mixed with a deeper engagement. Matthew J. Grow noted that, "unlike the objects of his other reforms, Kane could not keep an emotional distance from the—Mormons."[34]

In its social dimensions, the Latter-day Saint religion exhibited some qualities Tom longed to promote. Mormonism was not just a ritualized Sunday religion: it involved all aspects of its members' lives; it expressed an ideal of government in the concept of the Kingdom of God on earth; it melded converts from different social backgrounds into one community; and it contained within itself "the principle of its own change and amelioration" through the concept of continuing revelation.[35] While he always viewed Mormons as his social and intellectual inferiors, Tom respected Brigham Young as a social genius, one of the great men of the age. Tom also developed a high personal regard for several other Latter-day Saint leaders, particularly George Q. Cannon (fig. 5). As Grow further declared, "Besides Kane's immediate family, no one influenced the direction of his own life more than Young." At the same time, Young relied on Tom as "his most trusted outside adviser" for three decades.[36]

FIG. 5. George Q. Cannon. Counselor to Brigham Young in the Church's First Presidency, Cannon served for ten years as the congressional delegate from Utah Territory, (1873–82). Thomas L. Kane tutored Cannon in navigating the waters of Congress and the media, and the two became close friends. L. Tom Perry Special Collections, Harold B. Lee Library, Brigham Young University.

The Mormons

When Tom returned home to Philadelphia in fall 1846, he continued his lobbying and public relations activities in support of the Saints. Employing the strategy his father had used so successfully in his political activities, Tom began by planting editorials favorable to Mormons in eastern newspapers. As he wrote to Brigham Young, "It was found next to impossible to do much for you before public opinion was corrected," and so "it became incumbent on me to manufacture public opinion as soon as possible."[37] This campaign culminated in a public lecture, presented to the Historical Society of Pennsylvania on March 26, 1850, titled "The Mormons." An expanded version of the lecture was published and then distributed to members of Congress and other public opinion makers.[38]

The Mormons, which Tom claimed to have written on his sickbed, reflected his strategic rhetorical skills. In his actual encounter with the Saints, he went first to the encampments near the Missouri River and then visited Nauvoo on his way home. However, *The Mormons* began with the visit to Nauvoo and suggested that he was a tourist with no prior knowledge of the Mormons. He described traveling up the Mississippi River through a dreary region. Suddenly, "a landscape in delightful contrast broke upon my view. Half encircled by a bend of the river, a beautiful city lay glittering in the fresh morning sun; its bright new dwellings, set in cool green gardens, ranging up around a stately dome-shaped hill, which was crowned by a noble marble edifice, whose high tapering spire was radiant with white and gold."[39]

These opening paragraphs established a contrast sustained throughout the work. The Mormon city, like the Saints, reflected a higher standard of civilization than was to be found elsewhere on the Western frontier. Nauvoo and its environs exhibited "the unmistakeable marks of industry, enterprise and educated wealth,"[40] but the homes, gardens, workshops, and fields had been abandoned, and the author found a drunken rabble in possession of the city. The last Mormon refugees were starving in camps on the Iowa shore while "those who had stopped their ploughs, who had silenced their hammers, their axes, their shuttles and their workshop wheels; those who had put out their fires, who had eaten their food, spoiled their orchards, and trampled under foot their thousands of acres of unharvested bread; these,—were the keepers of their dwellings, the carousers in their Temple,—whose drunken riot insulted the ears of their dying."[41]

Tom's image-making continued in the description of the Saints at Council Bluffs. The camps were "gay with bright white canvas, and alive with the busy stir of swarming occupants." Herd boys were "dozing upon the slopes" while great herds of livestock grazed in the meadows. Beside a small creek, "women in greater force than blanchisseuses upon the Seine" were "washing and rinsing all manner of white muslins, red flannels and parti-colored calicoes, and hanging them to bleach upon a greater area of grass and bushes than we can display in all our Washington Square."[42] As he mingled with "this vast body of pilgrims," hospitably received everywhere, the author declared, "I can scarcely describe the gratification I felt in associating again with persons who were almost all of Eastern American origin,—persons of refined and cleanly habits and decent language."[43] The message suggested the Mormons were very much like members of the author's own audience, and very unlike "the vile scume" who lived in "Western Missouri and Iowa."[44]

The author extolled the Mormons' "romantic devotional observances," their "admirable concert of purpose and action," their "maintenance of a high state of discipline,"[45] and the way in which their religion "mixed itself up fearlessly with the common transactions of their every-day life."[46] He also praised their patriotism for volunteering for the Mormon Battalion, as "the feeling of country triumphed" over a call that "could hardly have been more inconveniently timed."[47] In framing the enlistment in these terms, Tom contributed to the longstanding misconception among many Saints that the request for volunteers was one more unjust exaction by a society that had already subjected them to much suffering. Actually, the Mormon Battalion, as Kane well knew, was the government's response to the Saints' request for assistance in their journey west.

The final part of *The Mormons* described the journey to Utah and the establishment of a society there. Here, Tom's chief source of information was the epistles from Church leaders directed to the Saints who had not yet gathered to Utah. These epistles were themselves exercises in the manipulation of public opinion and painted early Utah society in the most favorable terms.

The Mormons was soon reprinted by Latter-day Saint periodicals, both in England and in the U.S. The pamphlet has been quoted or paraphrased by many who were unaware of their indebtedness to Thomas L. Kane for the enduring images of the City Beautiful and the camps of Israel. Written for the purpose of shaping national public opinion toward the Saints, *The Mormons* arguably had a more powerful and enduring effect on the Saints themselves.

Polygamy: "This Great Humiliation"

In a second edition of *The Mormons,* issued in July 1850, the author added a postscript answering criticisms that had been levied against the original publication. Responding to claims that he had portrayed the Saints in too positive a light, Tom reaffirmed his judgment that they did not "in any wise fall below our own standard of morals" and displayed a "purity of character above the average of ordinary communities."[48] In answering rumors about Mormon polygamy, he emphasized "their habitual purity of life" and quoted a passage from what was then Section 109 of the Doctrine and Covenants, which declared, "we believe, that one man should have one wife, and one woman but one husband."[49]

This was not the only occasion in which Tom vouched for the monogamy of Mormons. When his good friend and future father-in-law, William Wood, asked him pointedly "Do the Mormons allow polygamy, or do they not?"[50] Tom categorically replied in the negative. Wood wrote, "I am much pleased to have your testimony to the purity of the Mormons. I wanted to be able distinctly to contradict the accusations of their tolerance of Polygamy."[51]

Then, on December 27, 1851, Tom received a visit from Jedediah M. Grant, a member of the Twelve, who sought Tom's assistance in composing and placing newspaper articles to refute damaging allegations by non-Mormon Utah territorial officers. In the course of their discussions, Grant learned that Tom did not know the Saints had been practicing plural marriage. Even though he had been welcomed by the Saints on the Missouri as a trusted friend, they had not revealed to him their peculiar marital practices.[52]

Because of his emphatic denials of the polygamy rumors, this information was devastating to Tom. On December 27, he wrote, "Heard this day first time Polygamy at Salt Lake." The following day he added, "This I record as the date of this great humiliation, and I trust final experience of this sort of affliction.... Similar doubtless to discovery of wife's infidelity."[53]

Two days after learning of polygamy, Tom drafted a letter to John M. Bernhisel, the Utah territorial delegate to Congress, saying, in part:

> Mr. Grant has made me for the first time acquainted with a state of facts at the Salt Lake which puts it out of the power of the Mormon people any longer truthfully to refute the accusation of their enemies that they tolerate polygamy or a plurality of wives among them. It is not my place here to express the deep pain and humiliation given me by this communication for which I was indeed ill prepared.

Tom went on, however, to reaffirm "the relations of personal respect and friendship" toward Bernhisel, "the more so that I understand you have grieved with myself at this intelligence."[54]

Several months passed before Tom wrote to Brigham Young. In the interim, Tom continued to assist Jedediah Grant in his public relations campaign and also lobbied the government for the appointment of a new federal judge for Utah Territory. During this time, however, Tom seemed to be thinking of discontinuing his work for the Mormons. He wrote to William Wood in May 1852 declaring his recent efforts to be "my last labor of the kind" and expressing the hope that Bessie Wood (to whom he was by then engaged) would not see the newspaper articles he had helped Grant to prepare.[55]

Writing to Brigham Young in October 1852, Tom explained the delay in his communication by reporting the illness and death of his youngest brother, Willie. Tom broached the topic of polygamy in terms that expressed both a personal and an intellectual disappointment:

> I wish to thank you for making my old friend Grant the bearer to me of his tidings. I ought not to conceal from you that they gave me great pain. Independent of every other consideration, my Pride in you depends so much on your holding your position in the van of Human Progress, that I so grieve over your favor to a custom which belongs essentially, I think, to communities in other respects behind your own.

In other words, the Mormons had, in Tom's estimation, betrayed their potential as "a religion for the 19th century" by adopting a retrograde social model. He predicted an adverse impact on "female education, the concord of households, the distribution of family property, and the like," from the practice of polygamy. At the same time, he reaffirmed his personal regard for Young, a friendship that made his present frankness possible:

> I have not yet been disappointed in treating you as a <u>Man</u>, able and accustomed to look and speak to <u>Men</u> in the face. You understand me now as you have understood me hitherto, and have it in your power to accept understandingly the friendship of which I also understandingly offer you the full continuance. I think it my duty to give you thus distinctly my opinion that you err. I can now discharge you and myself from further notice of the subject.[56]

Notwithstanding these friendly assurances, it appears that Tom's labors in behalf of the Mormons were significantly reduced from 1852 to 1857. In December 1857, Bernhisel remarked to one of Tom's friends, "Of late years [Tom] has treated us very coldly; we think on account of our religion."[57] Bessie later noted that while her husband was rightly believed "to know more of the personal character of the Mormon leaders than any other Gentile," he was "completely deceived for years as to the practice of polygamy, and I can well remember his difficulty in believing that it did exist, or in keeping up his friendship for the Mormon leader when he realised it."[58]

Tom and Bessie's Courtship and Marriage

Tom's reduced involvement with the Saints corresponded with the period of his courtship and marriage. Tom had known Bessie from the time she was a young child, and family tradition holds that she had settled on him as her future husband by the time she was twelve.[59] Serious courtship began in early 1852, and they were married on April 21, 1853, when Tom was thirty-one and Bessie three weeks shy of seventeen.

Bessie's mother died in 1846, the year Bessie turned ten and the year Tom first worked among the Mormons. Thereafter, "for seven lonely years, she found comfort and companionship with her studies and poets, brightened by occasional glimpses of her idolized cousin. At twelve she said once to her sister, 'Why, I thought you all knew, I intend to marry Cousin Tom Kane!'"[60]

That intention was strengthened by an 1850 visit Bessie and her elder sister Charlotte paid to the Kane home in Philadelphia. In a love letter written two years later, she recalled listening to Tom playing the piano and singing, feeling "that though you were so very dear to me, you never would love me."[61] Sometime later, Tom joined the Wood family for several weeks at Newport. Bessie recalled an excursion to a teahouse where he "walked on the piazza with me, and spoke of the kind of husband I would marry," after which "I lingered behind [him] a step, that I might see the face of the one I had resolved to win!"[62]

Bessie and Tom arrived at a personal understanding in January 1852, when she was fifteen and he approaching thirty. They informed her father of their attachment in March 1852, but they did not tell Tom's parents until sometime later. William Wood wrote, "It is a pity that Bessie is so young, not that I think there would be the slightest chance of her changing her mind, if she had seen more of the world, nor in my opinion could she have chosen better had she been 32 instead of 16." He added, "Bessie from childhood has jumped into womanhood, instead of passing gradually from the one condition to the other."[63] Probably with the intention of slowing the advance of the couple's feelings, Bessie's father took her on an extended trip to England, Scotland, and France in summer 1852. Most of their courtship letters were written then.

Bessie was intellectually mature beyond her years (figs. 6 to 10), well read and articulate, but she displayed the intense emotional ups and downs of an adolescent.[64] She expressed the fear that her love for him amounted to idolatry "because you know we ought to have our treasure in Heaven, and I am afraid mine isn't there."[65] She wrote of her consciousness of "my inferiority to you" and begged him to take control of her education.[66]

Tom's letters were typically shorter and included reports on the condition of his dying brother, Willie, as well as more restrained declarations of love. When he did write at greater length it was to express his plans for the future: for a new country retreat, Fern Rock, to be built in an idyllic setting north of Philadelphia, or, more idealistically, for a lifetime of altruistic service.[67] In reply, Bessie wrote of visiting the poor districts in Glasgow to

Fig. 6.  Fig. 7.

Fig. 8.  Fig. 9.

Figs. 6–9. Elizabeth W. Kane at various ages. Figures 6, 7, and 8 are albumen prints, carte de visite photographs. Figure 7 was taken by Winderroth and Taylor, Philadelphia. Figure 8 was taken by W. Kurtz, New York. L. Tom Perry Special Collections, Harold B. Lee Library, Brigham Young University.

FIG. 10. Elizabeth W. Kane, May 1858. This photograph of a twenty-two-year-old Elizabeth was pasted in a diary and labeled "Only for Tom's eye." L. Tom Perry Special Collections, Harold B. Lee Library, Brigham Young University.

prepare herself for the career Tom envisioned. "I hope I shall get accustomed to seeing such people without feeling disgusted. . . . If you let me begin gradually, don't you think I could come to sympathise with them and love them?"[68] It seems likely that Bessie interpreted Tom's plan as a life of Christian service, while he was thinking along the lines of Comté's "religion of humanity."

Bessie's stepmother considered it improper for her to marry at such a young age.[69] However, William Wood gave his permission for the marriage on November 25, but stipulated, "I think it would sound better to the world in general if you allowed Bessie to pass her 17th birthday (12 May 1853) before she was married."[70] Tom and Bessie were married on April 21, 1853, three weeks before she turned seventeen.

The newlyweds initially lived in a rented house next door to the Kane family in Philadelphia. After a few months, the couple moved in with Tom's family, spending winters with them in the city and summers at the new country house, Fern Rock. They would not have a home of their own until they moved permanently to the Allegheny Mountains following the Civil War.

Bessie struggled to adjust during the first few years of marriage. Having grown up in a rather puritanical home, she was somewhat taken aback by the free-thinking and free-speaking Kanes, noting in her journal on one occasion, "Half the family [would] fly the dinner table in a passion—I supposed they were parted forever. But at the tea-table there they all were, cheerful and kind as if nothing whatever had happened to be forgotten or forgiven."[71]

Bessie's passionate devotion for Tom never wavered, but she was disappointed that he refused to attend church with her, and she was concerned that so large a portion of his earnings sustained his benevolent activities instead of building a financial foundation for his own family. She also believed the Kane family failed to appreciate Tom's qualities but instead dwelt on the failures of his grandiose plans.

After the birth of Harriet Amelia (named for Bessie's mother) and Elisha Kent (named for Tom's brother and his grandfather), Bessie settled more comfortably into family life, even though some tensions remained. Tom desired to make their marriage a model for reform and, ironically, tended to dominate his wife in the interests of gender equality. He pressed her to enroll in the Female Medical College of Pennsylvania (see fig. 11), for which he served as a "corporator" (trustee). She studied off and on for years, finally earning an MD degree in 1883.[72]

The year 1857 was an especially difficult time with the death of Tom's beloved elder brother, Elisha, and the business failure and nervous

FIG. 11. Female Medical College of Pennsylvania seal. Founded in 1850, this was the world's first school to offer medical training exclusively for women. Elizabeth W. Kane earned a medical degree from this institution in 1883. L. Tom Perry Special Collections, Harold B. Lee Library, Brigham Young University.

breakdown of Bessie's father.[73] It was during this period that Tom once again felt pressed to sacrifice his personal and family interests to give aid to the Mormons.

The Utah War

Tom's role in bringing the 1857–58 conflict between the federal government and the Latter-day Saints to a peaceful resolution has been extensively treated by other authors, including William MacKinnon's essay herein. My only intentions here are to emphasize the sacrifices required of Bessie by her husband's hazardous expedition and to highlight the importance of Tom's strategic rhetorical skills in his mediation efforts.

Tom's family was strongly opposed to his planned mission. On the eve of his departure, he resigned his position as clerk of the U.S. district court, leaving his wife without an income and with uncertain future prospects. The money he left was quickly exhausted as he had characteristically underestimated the amount of every obligation,[74] leaving her "to eat the bread of Dependence, bitterer than gall."[75] Her circumstances became even more difficult when Tom's father died in February 1858 following a short illness.

Bessie was sustained through all these trials by the information her husband had confided to her before his departure; he had expressed his readiness to become a Christian. When Bessie wrote of the "horrors we have passed through," she then added, "God has mercifully brought out of them one great blessing already, in uniting Tom and me in the bonds of a common faith." Strengthened by this assurance, she was willing to consign her husband into God's hands "to bring peace to those lost Sheep of Israel."[76]

The hope that had sustained Bessie during her husband's absence was abruptly terminated upon his return home on June 20, 1858: "Tom told me the first moment we were alone, like my dear honest darling, that the hope that had dawned on him of being a Christian is gone."[77] It was hardly surprising that Bessie should have blamed the Mormons for blighting Tom's budding faith, though there was no indication he made such an attribution. (It seems equally possible that his grief at his father's death could have been a decisive factor.) Still, these events intensified Bessie's longstanding grudge against the Mormons, especially Brigham Young.

Tom's skill at manipulative rhetoric appeared in the documents he prepared as part of his mediation efforts. While his actions were at times foolhardy, his writing was well calculated. He knew President Buchanan was firmly convinced the Mormons were in a state of active rebellion. Rather than attempting to refute that view directly, Tom constructed an image of the Mormons as divided between a war party and a peace party, with Brigham Young serving as the leader of the peace party. In a letter to the president, Tom asserted that it was of the greatest importance to "strengthen the hands of those—and they are not few here—who seek to do good and whose patriotism is as elevated as any which labors elsewhere to confirm the bands of the Union." He continued, "From the commencement nearly of the unhappy difficulties between Utah and the United States, [Brigham Young's] commanding influence has been exercised to assuage passion, to control imprudent zeal, and at all risks, either of his own person or that of others, to forbid and ensure a just condemnation for bloodshed."[78] After arriving at the army encampment, Tom sent another letter in which he described the previous one as "the joint composition of an eccentric great man and myself."[79]

Evidently, Tom enclosed the letter to the president in another letter to his father, in which he asked his parent to assist in this public relations campaign by publishing Tom's information in a suitable form in newspapers such as "the Episcopal Recorder, or the Observer of New York." This article was to emphasize the human suffering Mormon women and children would face if forced to flee from their homes into the wilderness. While the innocent would suffer, "the leading heresiarchs" would "instigate resistance as long as it was perfectly safe to do so, and then retire disguised at their pleasure toward any one of the points of the compass." The article also would pose the question, "What will be the fate of the real abominable thing which we ought to wish shd. perish.—the evil Religion itself—the Mormonism." He would argue that persecution would only increase the appeal of Mormon missionaries abroad: "What a clover of female approbation the Mormon lecturer will delight in who appears before his British audience 'in deep black' for his murdered family."[80]

Fortunately for the outcome of Tom's mission, he and the new territorial governor, Alfred Cumming, took a liking to each other, quite different from the mutual animosity between Tom and the military. He drafted several letters for the governor, some to federal officials and others to the citizens of Utah, in which he further consolidated his image-making of the conflict—and, not incidentally, he accomplished some self-promotion as well. However, in his aristocratic pride he refused to capitalize on his fame as a peacemaker by writing a book on his experiences, nor would he allow either the federal government or the Mormons to reimburse the expenses of his journey.[81]

The Kanes' Visit to Utah

There were relatively few contacts between Tom and the Mormons during the 1860s. When the Civil War began in 1861, Tom's idealism and impulsiveness drove him to volunteer for immediate service. At his own expense, he enlisted a regiment of volunteers from the Allegheny region (commonly known as the "Bucktail Regiment" because the soldiers affixed a deer tail to their hats).[82] Tom was shot in the face at Dranesville, wounded in the leg and captured at Harrisonburg, and commissioned as brigadier general for gallant service at Catlett's Station and the second Battle of Bull Run. He left his bed in a Baltimore hospital, where he was suffering from pneumonia, to take command of his brigade on Culps Hill at the Battle of Gettysburg, even though he was too weak to sit on his horse. Following a stern warning by his physician that his mental and physical constitution would not survive another battle, Tom resigned from service on November 7, 1863.[83]

Following Tom's resignation, the family returned to McKean County in the Allegheny Mountains where, despite the continuing effects of his war injuries, Tom developed the timber resources, recruited settlers, promoted railroad construction, and established the town of Kane. While the Kanes owned a substantial acreage and managed additional lands, the area's development went forward slowly and did not provide the family with financial security until near the end of Tom's life. After his death, the development of oil resources brought prosperity to Bessie and her family.[84]

Tom again initiated correspondence with Brigham Young in 1869[85] and resumed lobbying efforts for the Latter-day Saints, working against the series of antipolygamy bills that were being introduced in Congress. In response to Young's invitations to visit Utah for consultations, Tom replied, "I still persuade myself that I will come out before I die and complete the collection of my materials for the Life of Brigham Young. I often cheer myself with a vision of pleasant weeks to be spent in your company—when—our minds both free from the common cares which now compel our thoughts—our converse shall turn as of old on higher things."[86] In light of his personal aversion to polygamy, it is interesting that in advising the Church leader on strategies for achieving Utah statehood, Tom cautioned Young not to pretend to adopt any policy the Church was not willing to comply with in reality: "Duplicity, I see, without a shadow, will not be a good policy for you."[87]

Bessie did not share her husband's renewed interest in the Mormons, nor did she wish to travel to Utah. Adding to her longstanding resentment of the Mormon influence on Tom was her awareness that the developments at Kane were at a critical stage that required his full attention. She agreed to the trip only when the proposal of a visit during winter 1872–73 opened the prospect of Tom's escaping the rigors of the season in western Pennsylvania.[88]

At age thirty-six, Bessie was a more confident and independent woman than the vulnerable young wife who had seen her husband depart for Utah in 1858. Now the mother of four children (fig. 12), she assisted in the management of Tom's business affairs with a more practical head for business than he possessed. She had initially undertaken medical studies because Tom wanted her to be an example of what education could do for a woman. As she intermittently pursued work toward her degree, in addition to her family responsibilities, she discovered that her skills were both useful and empowering in the medically underserved region around Kane. Bessie also had developed an interest in women's rights and had begun the temperance work to which she would devote her later years. Most importantly, while she still loved Tom, she depended less on his judgment and had achieved a genuine

FIG. 12. Elizabeth W. Kane and son, c. 1860. The baby Elizabeth is holding is probably Elisha Kent Kane, named for Thomas's older brother. L. Tom Perry Special Collections, Harold B. Lee Library, Brigham Young University.

intellectual independence. These qualities shine through her writings on the Mormons.

Bessie's account of her experiences initially took the form of journal entries and letters to her family. After returning home, Tom encouraged and assisted her in publishing these in hopes a book would assist in his lobbying efforts against the antipolygamy Poland Act, which was then before Congress.[89] The result was a slender volume, published in 1874, titled *Twelve Mormon Homes Visited in Succession on a Journey through Utah to Arizona*, as discussed by Lowell C. Bennion and Thomas Carter's essay herein.

The book appeared with a secondary title page that read, "*Pandemonium or Arcadia: Which?*" Bessie also used this phrase, in inverted order, near the end of her St. George journal:

Farewell, Arcadia!
Or Pandemonium—Which?[90]

At the most obvious level, she used this phrase as a rhetorical device to emphasize paradoxical images of the Latter-day Saint religion and society. *Pandemonium* is the name coined by John Milton for the city built by Lucifer and his fallen angels in *Paradise Lost*. Bessie used it to reflect the demonizing of the polygamous and theocratic Mormons by much of the national political establishment, the press, and zealous Protestant religionists, including her fellow Presbyterians. This image was additionally reinforced by a line from John Bunyan's *Pilgrim's Progress*, which Bessie uses as an epigraph: "As I walked through the wilderness of this world, I lighted on a certain place where was a den."[91] The image of Mormondom as a den of iniquity is also reflected in the letters friends from home had written, urging her to hasten away from "those dreadful Mormons."[92] *Arcadia*, originally a pastoral district in ancient Greece, later became a literary figure for an idealized existence of rural seclusion, characterized by a natural virtue free from the contaminating influences of urban society. In Bessie's usage, *Arcadia* evoked the image of the western Zion as a refuge from worldliness, an image promulgated by nineteenth-century Latter-day Saint missionaries in the United States and Europe. The implicit answer offered in both *Twelve Mormon Homes* and the St. George journals is that Mormon country was *neither* Pandemonium nor Arcadia but, like any human society, contained a mixture of positive and negative aspects.

At a deeper level, Bessie's question reveals her unresolved ambivalence toward the Mormons. Secure in her own religious faith, she had little interest in Latter-day Saint doctrines and found their claims to religious authority offensive. She might have taken an interest in Mormon social experiments aimed at eliminating poverty and creating a more egalitarian community had those experiments not included plural marriage. She also felt the Mormons had claimed too much of her husband's life, had prevented him from attaining the social distinction he otherwise might have enjoyed, had drained resources that could have contributed to strengthening his own family's security, and—worst of all—had somehow prevented him from sharing her own devout Christian faith. And yet, because Tom was devoted to the Mormons, and Bessie was devoted to Tom, she could not dismiss a cause he valued.

Aside from the political strategy involved in the publication and distribution of *Twelve Mormon Homes* "with the design of commanding sympathy for the MORMONS, who are at this time threatened with hostile legislation by Congress,"[93] Bessie's rhetoric, unlike her husband's, was not essentially strategic. Where Tom's prose seemed always to be calculating the effect of his words upon a reader and to be primarily concerned with shaping a public image, Bessie's work was characterized by a sincere and steady effort to report the truth of her own impressions and judgments. The quest for honesty included a sustained attempt to record the thoughts and feelings of the Mormons—particularly the Mormon women—in their own voices. Bessie frankly acknowledged her own social missteps and the prejudiced views she was compelled by her experiences to renounce or revise, and she used a lively wit and a sense of irony to underscore her own weaknesses and those of others.

Bessie's attitudes toward the Mormons were softened, first, by the great affection and respect they displayed to Tom. In Utah, everyone seemed to hold him in the same high regard as she did. Thus, for Tom's sake, she tried to get to "know and appreciate his poor friends."[94] This was often easy to do, such as in the case of William Staines (fig. 13), who had been Tom's host in 1858 and who became a favorite with Bessie

FIG. 13. William C. Staines. Thomas Kane had stayed with Staines during his 1858 Utah War visit. It is likely that this preexisting relationship led to Staines being included in the St. George caravan in 1872–73. Used by permission, Utah State Historical Society, all rights reserved.

and her young sons. She described the man as "the deformed gentleman [Staines had a hunched back] whose earnest simplicity and sincerity have struck me, as much as his kindness has done the children. He is the only Mormon man with whom I have more than a passing acquaintance."[95]

Although Brigham Young treated her with great courtesy, Bessie could not overcome her resentment against him as the chief representative of all she found objectionable in Mormonism. And yet she tried to do him justice in her writings and ended up providing one of the best portraits of this man in action. Bessie remarked on the "characteristic look of shrewd and cunning insight" and noted, "His photographs, accurate enough in other respects, altogether fail to give the expression of his eyes."[96] She appreciated Young's generosity in giving the Kanes his luxurious city coach to travel in. When the driver of a heavy wagon from the Nevada mines deliberately drove into their coach, damaging a wheel hub, she acknowledged the calm dignity with which Young received the offender's apology, aware that her impetuous husband would not have shown such restraint.[97]

At each stop along the route to St. George, Bessie observed with interest the "informal audiences" during which Young received the "reports, complaints, and petitions" of local residents. In an incisive passage, she wrote:

> I think I gathered more of the actual working of Mormonism by listening to them than from any other source. They talked away to Brigham Young about every conceivable matter, from the fluxing of an ore to the advantages of the Navajo bit, and expected him to remember every child in every cotter's family. And he really seemed to do so, and to be at home, and be rightfully deemed infallible on every subject. I think he must make fewer mistakes than most popes, from his being in such constant intercourse with his people. I noticed that he never seemed uninterested, but gave an unforced attention to the person addressing him, which suggested a mind free from care. I used to fancy that he wasted a great deal of power in this way; but I soon saw that he was accumulating it.[98]

After hearing him speak at a meeting in St. George, Bessie reflected, "Poor Brigham Young. With *such* powers, what might he not be but for this Slough of Polygamy in which he is entangled!"[99] She also was critical of his economic policies, particularly the emphasis on "home industry" and self-sufficiency, which she believed had brought unnecessary suffering to the "saints who had been told off to Southern settlements where the desert had failed to blossom as the rose" and who were "expected to show their faith in Providence by flying in the face of Adam Smith."[100] And she remained startled when she realized Young, so full of practical wisdom, actually *believed* the incredible doctrines of Mormonism. Hearing reports in St. George of the rise of a Paiute "prophet" in Nevada, Bessie asked Young his opinion of the man. He replied:

> No, it was only tags and scraps of old Mormon teaching that the man had picked up. If he was genuinely inspired—of course he would have been inspired to come at once to him, Brigham Young.
>
> Brigham Young is so shrewd and full of common sense that I keep forgetting he is a Mormon himself, and this answer, so natural a one from his point of view took me completely aback. I felt as if I had asked one lunatic his opinion of another![101]

Clearly, Bessie's biggest problem with Young was his support of plural marriage. During the journey to St. George, she became well acquainted with "Delia," one of the leader's youngest wives, condemned (as Bessie saw it) to serve as a nurse to her husband in his declining years. She wrote, "I pitied Delia from the depths of my soul!"[102]

In *Twelve Mormon Homes*, Bessie made an effort to disguise the identity of most of the Mormons who practiced plural marriage. However, it is easy to penetrate the disguise as she made her sharpest indictment of Brigham Young. When "Delia" affirmed her faith in the divinity of plural marriage, Bessie reacted strongly:

> How I detested her husband as she spoke! I felt sure *he* could not believe that that was a divine ordinance which sacrificed those women's lives to his. I heard him say that when "Joseph" first promulgated the Revelation of Polygamy he "felt that the grave was sweet! All that winter, whenever a funeral passed,—'and it was a sickly season'—I would stand and look after the hearse, and wish I was in that coffin! But that went over!"
>
> I should think it *had* gone over! He has had more than half a dozen wives.[103]

Bessie had come to Utah in hopes that the polygamy problem might be solved by encouraging Congress to pass a law that would recognize the legitimacy of existing plural marriages while prohibiting the contraction of future polygamous unions. To her surprise and dismay, she found that every polygamous wife to whom she presented this idea vehemently rejected it as making a mockery of their faith and their personal sacrifices. To Bessie's suggestion that such a law would secure these women's social positions, "Delia" replied, "How can that satisfy me! I want to be assured of *my position in God's estimation*. If polygamy is the Lord's order, we must carry it out in spite of human laws and persecutions. If our marriages have been sins, Congress is no viceregent of God; it cannot forgive sins, nor make what was wrong, right."[104]

As Bessie's hopes for a legislative solution ran aground on the firm resistance of the Mormon women, her view of the Saints' future became more pessimistic. She envisioned a time when effective antipolygamy laws would either destroy the Mormon community entirely or send its members once again fleeing, with either result bringing immense suffering to the innocent. When the elderly Lucy Young fervently affirmed her faith that God would protect the Saints in their mountain sanctuary, Bessie reflected, "It is hard to set down this faith of hers that God *was* taking care of them as a fancy: especially as I want to believe that He watches over me in the same special sort of way."[105] Ultimately, Bessie fell back on the hope that "more than one Mormon woman sees that such an intimate friendship such communion of mind and heart as is possible between a man and his one wife, cannot subsist in polygamy. My happiness is a stronger missionary sermon than anything I could say by word of mouth."[106]

Despite her concerns, Bessie acknowledged that women enjoyed some advantages in Mormon society. After observing a highly professional inspection of the female-staffed telegraph office in Lehi by a female inspector from Salt Lake City, Bessie wrote, "It was an example of one of the contradictions of Mormonism. Thousands of years behind us in some of their customs; in others, you would think these people the most forward children of the age. They close no career on a woman in Utah by which she can earn a living."[107] Later, after going on a round of home visits with leaders of the St. George Relief Society, she noted:

> A curious difference between the Mormon women and those of an Eastern harem appears in their independence. So many of them seem to have the entire management, not only of their families, but of their households and even outside business affairs, as if they were widows; either because they have houses where their husbands only visit them instead of living day in and day out, or because the husbands are off on Missions and leave the guidance of their business affairs to them.[108]

As Bessie met more women, it became increasingly difficult for her to think of polygamy in abstract and doctrinal terms. Each individual had her own story. For example, Bessie pitied Eliza B. Young, her hostess in Provo, because her experiences seemed "much more solitary . . . when the evening of her life closed in. No 'John Anderson' to be her fireside companion, none of the comfort that even a lonely widow finds in the remembrance of former joys and sorrows shared with one to whom she has been best and nearest."[109] However, Bessie did not pity the "Steerforth" (Pitchforth) wives of Nephi, who lived happily together with their common husband in a single home. These, Bessie wrote, "were the first Mormon women who awakened sympathy in my breast, disassociated from an equally strong feeling of repulsion."[110]

She formed a close personal relationship with "Maggie McDiarmid" in St. George. Maggie was willing to admit she had struggled at times in her role as first wife in a plural family. In a sudden outburst, she declared, "I'd have slapped any one's face twenty years ago that dared to tell me I'd submit to what I have submitted to." Even so, Maggie insisted she hadn't "the least fault to find" with her husband and was dedicated to her polygamous marriage.[111]

Several other themes were skillfully woven into Bessie's narrative. While attending her first Latter-day Saint church service, she surveyed the Nephi congregation expecting to see "the 'hopeless, dissatisfied, worn' expression travelers' books had bidden me to read" on the women's faces. Instead, she discovered, they "wore very much the same countenances as the American women of any large rustic and village congregation." She also found "the irrepressible baby . . . present in greater force than with us, and the element young man wonderfully largely represented. This is always observable in Utah meetings."[112] The services, though less formal than those she was accustomed to, seemed dignified, and the sermons satisfactorily orthodox. Bessie and her young sons especially enjoyed the lively sermons of William Staines. His talk in Nephi "began like a Methodist 'experience'—became psychological: afterwards touched on the miraculous. A Mormon is never inconvenienced by his story turning on a miracle."[113] In St. George, she heard Erastus Snow deliver "a well reasoned doctrinal sermon, as dry and quite as orthodox as any that I have heard at home."[114] Later, she noted:

> The Mormon meetings for spiritual purposes are invaded by the concerns of their daily lives, as much as their daily lives are by their religion. I would not myself like to live either under Roman Catholic or Mormon or Quaker discipline, with either priests or brethren poking their noses into my concerns, but I must confess that it renders the Mormon meetings far more interesting to a stranger who sees their actual doings and intentions "laid before the Lord", than one of our own Presbyterian or Dutch Reformed or Episcopal services.[115]

Bessie also developed an appreciation for Mormon prayers and music. The prayers she described as being more specifically concerned with individual persons and events than the "prudent generalities" of Protestant prayers. She added, "I liked this when I became used to it, and could join in with some knowledge of the circumstances of those we prayed for."[116] She wrote, "I do not think they as often say, 'If it be Thy Will,' as we do, but simply pray for the blessings they want, expecting that they will be given or withheld, as God knows best." She also enjoyed the church music in St. George, where the choirmaster, John M. Macfarlane, was an accomplished musician. Of one meeting, Bessie noted, "If there is anything irreverent in the Mormon addresses there is nothing irreverent in their prayers.

... Nor was there anything irreverent in the hymn that ended our meeting, though there was no organ, and the trained voices of the choir were unpaid. All the congregation joined in the chorus. It went to my heart. I love to see people in earnest."[117]

Tom and Bessie met parties of Indians several times and observed them frequently in St. George. Bessie's distaste for them was explicit, but she admired the more tolerant attitude of her Mormon hosts. Of the Indians she wrote, "They have the appetites of poor relations, and the touchiness of rich ones with money to leave. They come in a swarm; their ponies eat down the golden grain-stacks to their very centres; the Mormon women are tired out baking for the masters, while the squaws hang about the kitchens watching for scraps like unpenned chickens."[118]

Tom, however, was very interested in the Indians and took advantage of every occasion to talk with and observe them. In St. George he called Bessie out to observe an arbitration of a dispute between a Paiute man and a Mormon boy over the ownership of a horse. Tom remarked, "It is the first time he ever saw an Indian treated fairly in a Court of Law."[119]

Bessie also related a lengthy discussion about the discovery of the gold plates and the translation of the Book of Mormon by Joseph Smith. This occurred in the home of Artemisia Beaman Snow, whose father reputedly assisted Smith as he concealed the Gold Plates. True to her usual approach, Bessie attempted to render the participants' views in their own words; however, she also inserted her own perceptions:

> Mrs. Snow sate knitting a stocking as she talked, like any other homely elderly woman. She certainly seemed to *think* she had actually gone through the scene she narrated. I know so little of the history of the Mormons that the stories that now followed by the flickering firelight were full of interest to me. I shall write down as much as I can remember, though there must be gaps where allusions were made to things I had never heard of and did not understand enough to remember accurately. The most curious thing was the air of perfect sincerity of all the speakers. I cannot feel doubtful that they believed what they said.[120]

The mild winter climate of St. George seemed to agree with Tom. Although he needed crutches to walk when they arrived, his strength grew until he was capable of making "a mountain climb of two miles, returning scarcely more fatigued than I was," and walking without using a cane, something he had been unable to do since the time he was wounded at Harrisonburg.[121] Sometime shortly after January 23, he took a turn for the worse, "some dreadful affection—perhaps from cold taken in his wounds. He endured frightful suffering, and lay long at the point of death" before rallying in early February.[122]

The Mormons' response to Tom's illness made a powerful impression on Bessie. She wrote, "I thought myself a pretty good nurse, but I have learned lessons from them."[123] Men were always at hand to lift Tom, "or bathe him with a tender handiness that my feeble strength could not imitate." A man Bessie referred to as "Elder Johns," whom she had earlier criticized for devoting too much time and too many resources for the service of others while his own family suffered, now "heaped coals of fire on my head" by his untiring service to Tom. The residents of the three settlements, St. George, Washington, and Santa Clara, assembled in the unfinished tabernacle to offer a special prayer meeting in Tom's behalf. When she resumed entries in her journal following a hiatus during Tom's illness, Bessie wrote, "before closing these leaves I write this Memorandum in red ink—

> If I had entries in this diary to make again,
> they would be written in a kindlier spirit.[124]

That "kindlier spirit" was evident in the draft of a letter Bessie wrote to her daughter Harriet. Bessie reported that a convalescent Tom had urged her to take the boys for a walk while Brigham Young sat with him. The three family members climbed a little way up the Black Mesa. There they sat while Bessie looked down on the town below and reflected on the good women there who had treated her family so kindly and for whom she could see "no prospect . . . but one of wretchedness." She concluded:

> You will not understand how I have come to pity this people; for you know how hard it was for me to make up my mind to come among them and associate with them, even for the sake of benefiting Fathers health by this climate. I have written to you as a sort of penance for the hard thoughts and contemptuous opinions I have myself instilled into you.
>
> When I came home, I stepped softly to the open door and peeped through. Father was lying in a sound sleep, and a bulky figure that I recognised knelt beside a chair, praying. I stole back and rejoined the children on the porch, and we re-entered the house with sufficient noise to make the watcher aware of our presence. He came out into the parlour to give me the good news that Father had slept almost ever since we left.
>
> Oh, dear H—, I find myself thinking kindly of this man, too![125]

To complete her penitential experience, Bessie consented to spend a week with Young's family in the Lion House (fig. 14) upon the return to Salt Lake City, "a step which I took as a public testimony to the little circle of those to whom my name is known, that my opinion of the Mormon women had so changed during the winter that I was willing to eat salt with them."[126]

FIG. 14. Brigham Young's Beehive and Lion houses, Salt Lake City. This sketch comes from the papers of Thomas L. Kane. L. Tom Perry Special Collections, Harold B. Lee Library, Brigham Young University.

Epilogue

Tom retained his interest in the welfare of the Latter-day Saints for the remainder of his life. Upon Brigham Young's death in 1877, Tom again traveled to Utah to reassure himself that the Church was still in capable hands. He also hosted George Q. Cannon at his expanding manorial estate at Kane in 1880.[127] In the final moments of his own life in December 1883, Tom instructed Bessie to "send the sweetest message you can make up to my Mormon friends—*to all, my dear Mormon friends.*"[128]

The warm feelings toward the Mormons with which Bessie left St. George in 1873 cooled somewhat in subsequent years. She lived to see the Church leaders announce the 1890 Manifesto ending plural marriage and the 1896 achievement of Utah statehood, a goal toward which her husband had tirelessly worked. When she learned that a travel writer was planning to publish a book in which he would renew the claim that Thomas L. Kane had secretly been a Mormon, she was stirred to a vigorous defense of her late husband's reputation in which she did not spare her Mormon friends. "General Kane was a highly educated man," she wrote. "It would have been as impossible for him as for yourself to accept the teachings or authority of the Book of Mormon or the Book of Doctrine and Covenants." His devotion to the Mormons arose solely from his recognition that he "owed his life to the tender care and nursing that he received from the Mormons" in 1846. "He was particularly grateful to Brigham Young; and throughout the rest of his life he showed his gratitude to the Mormons and his pity for that people at the cost of obloquy cast upon him by his dearest friends, and at the risk of his life. But gratitude and pity were his sole incentives to all he did." She continued, "As he saw the Mormon people, he felt that many of their detractors and enemies could not afford to throw a stone at them, and he believed that their <u>theory</u> was better than the <u>practice</u> of many of their enemies." Then she wrote and subsequently cancelled a more damning judgment: "It is of course true that their theory is as much below true Christianity as the practice of bad Mormons, or perhaps one may say of any Mormons is below that of good, ordinary citizens."[129]

Pandemonium or Arcadia?

Edward A. Geary (who can be reached via email at byustudies@byu.edu) earned his PhD in English literature from Stanford University. At Brigham Young University, he taught in the English Department, directed the Charles Redd Center for Western Studies, worked as editor in chief of *BYU Studies*, participated in London study abroad programs, and served as an associate dean in the College of Humanities and as chair of the English Department.

Appendix

A Brief Genealogical Guide to The Thomas L. and Elizabeth W. Kane Family[1]

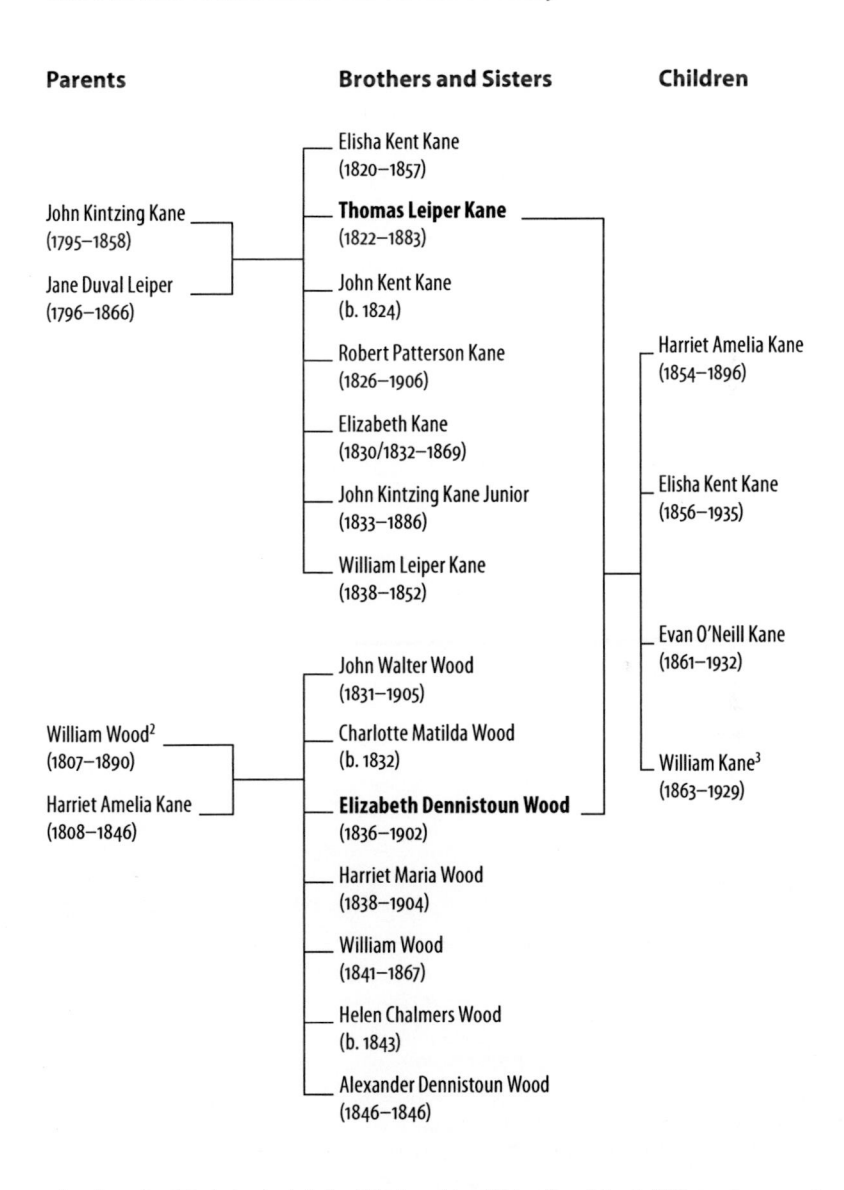

Parents

John Kintzing Kane
(1795–1858)

Jane Duval Leiper
(1796–1866)

William Wood[2]
(1807–1890)

Harriet Amelia Kane
(1808–1846)

Brothers and Sisters

Elisha Kent Kane
(1820–1857)

Thomas Leiper Kane
(1822–1883)

John Kent Kane
(b. 1824)

Robert Patterson Kane
(1826–1906)

Elizabeth Kane
(1830/1832–1869)

John Kintzing Kane Junior
(1833–1886)

William Leiper Kane
(1838–1852)

John Walter Wood
(1831–1905)

Charlotte Matilda Wood
(b. 1832)

Elizabeth Dennistoun Wood
(1836–1902)

Harriet Maria Wood
(1838–1904)

William Wood
(1841–1867)

Helen Chalmers Wood
(b. 1843)

Alexander Dennistoun Wood
(1846–1846)

Children

Harriet Amelia Kane
(1854–1896)

Elisha Kent Kane
(1856–1935)

Evan O'Neill Kane
(1861–1932)

William Kane[3]
(1863–1929)

---

1. An earlier version of this chart appears in the Kane Collection register at Brigham Young University, VMSS 792, volume 1, page 63.
2. William Wood married twice more in his life, both after losing his wife to death.
3. William Kane changed his name to Thomas Leiper Kane Jr. after his father's death in 1883.

1. Elizabeth Wood Kane, *Twelve Mormon Homes Visited in Succession on a Journey through Utah to Arizona*, ed. Everett L. Cooley (Philadelphia: William Wood, 1874; reprint, Salt Lake City: Tanner Trust Fund, University of Utah Library, 1974); Elizabeth Wood Kane, *A Gentile Account of Life in Utah's Dixie, 1872–73*, ed. Norman R. Bowen (Salt Lake City: Tanner Trust Fund, University of Utah Library, 1995).

2. "Autobiography of John K. Kane," typescript, 1–8, Thomas L. Kane and Elizabeth W. Kane Collection, L. Tom Perry Special Collections, Harold B. Lee Library, Brigham Young University, Provo, Utah, (hereafter cited as Perry Special Collections). References to family connections occur in John K. Kane's autobiography as well as in numerous family letters in the Kane Collection, Perry Special Collections. See also Elizabeth D. Kane, "Memorandum of E. D. Kane relating to Gen Washington's occupation of John Kane's house as Headquarters in 1778," Kane Collection, Perry Special Collections.

3. Mark Metzler Sawin, "Heroic Ambition: The Early Life of Dr. Elisha Kent Kane," *American Philosophical Society Library Bulletin* 2 (Fall 2002): 2, www.amphilsoc.org/library/bulletin/2002/Kane.htm.

4. He served as a federal commissioner to settle war claims with France, as Philadelphia city solicitor, as attorney general of the Commonwealth of Pennsylvania, and from 1846 to the end of his life in 1858 as United States district judge. Sawin, "Heroic Ambition," 4.

5. Daniel Walker Howe, *What Hath God Wrought: The Transformation of America, 1815–1848* (New York: Oxford University Press, 2007), 227–29.

6. Sawin, "Heroic Ambition," 5.

7. Sawin, "Heroic Ambition," 3–4. During the Jackson administration, Kane reportedly served occasionally as a speechwriter and as an adviser to the president.

8. John K. Kane to Elisha Kent Kane, June 14, 1844, Kane Collection, Perry Special Collections.

9. Sawin, "Heroic Ambition," 4, 5; Matthew J. Grow, *"Liberty to the Downtrodden": Thomas L. Kane, Romantic Reformer* (New Haven, Conn.: Yale University Press, 2009), 6, 7, 19, 21.

10. Thomas L. Kane to John K. Kane, July 28, 1840, Kane Collection, Perry Special Collections.

11. John K. Kane to Thomas L. Kane, July 1, 1839, Kane Collection, Perry Special Collections.

12. See Grow, *"Liberty to the Downtrodden,"* 22–23. There is no mention in the letters he wrote from Paris of any kind of personal association with Comté, beyond one brief meeting. BYU's Kane Collection includes a later letter from Comté that bears a notation in Tom's handwriting as coming from one of his "two best friends." However, there is nothing of a personal nature in the letter itself. It is a perfunctory letter of thanks for a contribution Tom had sent anonymously to the French philosopher. Auguste Comté to Thomas L. Kane, October 27, 1851, Kane Collection, Perry Special Collections.

13. Thomas L. Kane to Elisha Kent Kane, June 8, 1845, Kane Collection, Perry Special Collections.

14. "Elizabeth Dennistoun Kane, the Mother of Kane," Kane Collection, Perry Special Collections.

15. William Wood, *Autobiography of William Wood*, 2 vols., ed. Elizabeth Wood Kane (New York: J. S. Babcock, 1895), 1:119.

16. William Wood to Thomas L. Kane, October 2, 1840, Kane Collection, Perry Special Collections.

17. Thomas L. Kane to John K. Kane and Jane D. Leiper Kane, October 3, 1840, Kane Collection, Perry Special Collections.

18. Thomas L. Kane to John K. Kane and Jane D. L. Kane, October 28, 1843, Kane Collection, Perry Special Collections; Thomas L. Kane to John K. Kane and Jane D. L. Kane, March 28, 1844, Kane Collection, Perry Special Collections.

19. John K. Kane to Thomas L. Kane, January 3, 1846, Kane Collection, Perry Special Collections.

20. Albert L. Zobell Jr., *Sentinel in the East: A Biography of Thomas L. Kane* (Salt Lake City: Nicolas G. Morgan, 1965), 2–3. For more on Jesse C. Little, see Richard Bennett's essay herein.

21. Thomas L. Kane to Elisha K. Kane, May 16–17, 1846, American Philosophical Society, Philadelphia, Penn.; quoted in David L. Bigler and Will Bagley, *Army of Israel: Mormon Battalion Narratives* (Logan: Utah State University Press, 2000), 55–56. In letters to his brother Elisha, Tom reported that with "a little tact and patience and a little maneouvring" in Philadelphia he had gained the trust of Jesse C. Little, who had provided him with letters to Church leaders. Tom envisioned the advance party of Mormons carrying "to California the first news of War with Mexico." With California falling into U.S. control, "at one time or other a government representative may be wanting. Who so fit for one as I?—above all if on the journey I shall have ingratiated myself with the disaffected Mormon army before it descends upon the plains. I could carry my commission in my money belt, and according to the promptings of occasion, be or be not the first U.S. Governor of the new territory of California." Thomas L. Kane to Elisha K. Kane, May 16–17, 1846, American Philosophical Society.

22. Sawin, "Heroic Ambition," 26.

23. Thomas L. Kane to George Bancroft, July 11, 1846, original in Bancroft Papers, Massachusetts Historical Society, Boston, Mass., typescript copy in Kane Collection, Perry Special Collections.

24. Colonel Kearney to Thomas L. Kane, June 25, 1846, Kane Collection, Perry Special Collections; W. Gilpin to Thomas L. Kane, June 29, 1846, Kane Collection, Perry Special Collections.

25. Thomas L. Kane to "My Own Dear Father and Mother," July 18–22, 1846, The Papers of Thomas Leiper Kane, Marriott Library, University of Utah, Salt Lake City (original in American Philosophical Society library); quoted in Bigler and Bagley, *Army of Israel*, 58.

26. Thomas L. Kane to Elisha Kent Kane, May 29, 1846, Kane Collection, Perry Special Collections.

27. Thomas L. Kane to Elizabeth D. Wood, May 19, 1852, Kane Collection, Perry Special Collections.

28. Thomas L. Kane to "My Own Dear Father and Mother," July 18–22, 1846, The Papers of Thomas Leiper Kane, Marriott Library, University of Utah, Salt Lake City, quoted in Bigler and Bagley, *Army of Israel*, 58, 60, 61.

29. Thomas L. Kane to "My dear friends, all of you," July 11, 1850, Church History Library, The Church of Jesus Christ of Latter-day Saints, Salt Lake City,

quoted in Leonard J. Arrington, "'In Honorable Remembrance': Thomas L. Kane's Services to the Mormons," *BYU Studies* 21, no. 4 (1981): 392.

30. For a longer discussion of this topic see William McKinnon's essay herein.

31. Thomas L. Kane alludes to Book of Mormon teachings on the Native American Indians in *The Mormons*, 70; he also quotes what were then Sections 109 and 110 of the Doctrine and Covenants in the Postscript to the Second Edition, 88, 89. There is also a letter to Brigham Young in which Kane describes the signet rings he has had made for Church leaders from some California gold they had sent to him. The rings bore symbols from the Book of Mormon. Thomas L. Kane to Brigham Young, February 19, 1851, quoted in Zobell, *Sentinel in the East*, 50–52.

32. Elizabeth D. Kane, 1858–1860 Journal, July 11, 1859, typescript, Kane Collection, Perry Special Collections.

33. Kane, *Gentile Account*, 164.

34. Grow, *"Liberty to the Downtrodden,"* 278.

35. Thomas L. Kane to Elisha K. Kane, June 8, 1845, Kane Collection, Perry Special Collections.

36. Grow, *"Liberty to the Downtrodden,"* 278.

37. Thomas L. Kane to Brigham Young, December 2, 1846, quoted in Zobell, *Sentinel in the East*, 29–30.

38. Thomas L. Kane, *The Mormons: A Discourse Delivered before the Historical Society of Pennsylvania: March 26, 1850* (Philadelphia: King and Baird, 1850). For more on this lecture, see Richard Bennett's essay herein.

39. Kane, *The Mormons*, 3.

40. Kane, *The Mormons*, 4.

41. Kane, *The Mormons*, 10.

42. Kane, *The Mormons*, 25–26.

43. Kane, *The Mormons*, 26, 27.

44. Kane, *The Mormons*, 27.

45. Kane, *The Mormons*, 34.

46. Kane, *The Mormons*, 47.

47. Kane, *The Mormons*, 29, 28.

48. Kane, *The Mormons*, 85.

49. Kane, *The Mormons*, 88 n. The "Postscript to the Second Edition" is reproduced in full as an appendix to Zobell, *Sentinel in the East*.

50. William Wood to Thomas L. Kane, April 25, 1851, Kane Collection, Perry Special Collections.

51. William Wood to Thomas L. Kane, June 14, 1851, Kane Collection, Perry Special Collections.

52. See Gene A. Sessions, *Mormon Thunder: A Documentary History of Jedediah Morgan Grant* (Urbana: University of Illinois Press, 1982); Grow, *"Liberty to the Downtrodden,"* 88.

53. Thomas L. Kane, Journal/Notebook, November 11, 1851–September 27, 1852, Kane Collection, Perry Special Collections.

54. Thomas L. Kane to John M. Bernhisel, December 29, 1851, draft, Kane Collection, Perry Special Collections.

55. Thomas L. Kane to William Wood, May 21, 1852, Kane Collection, Perry Special Collections.

56. Thomas L. Kane to Brigham Young, October 17, 1852, quoted in Zobell, *Sentinel in the East,* 71–72.

57. Remarks of Dr. John M. Bernhisel to C. VanDyke, quoted in Zobell, *Sentinel in the East,* 104.

58. Elizabeth D. Kane to Rev. Dr. Buckley, March 6, 1906, draft, Kane Collection, Perry Special Collections.

59. "Elizabeth Dennistoun Kane, the Mother of Kane," Kane Collection, Perry Special Collections.

60. "Elizabeth Dennistoun Kane, the Mother of Kane," Kane Collection, Perry Special Collections.

61. Elizabeth D. Wood to Thomas L. Kane, July 18, 1852, Kane Collection, Perry Special Collections.

62. Wood to Kane, July 18, 1852.

63. William Wood to Thomas L. Kane, March 18, 1852, Kane Collection, Perry Special Collections.

64. Elizabeth D. Wood to Thomas L. Kane, September 19, 1852, Kane Collection, Perry Special Collections.

65. Elizabeth D. Wood to Thomas L. Kane, August 8, 1852, Kane Collection, Perry Special Collections.

66. Elizabeth D. Wood to Thomas L. Kane, August 8, September 2, 1852, Kane Collection, Perry Special Collections.

67. Thomas L. Kane to Elizabeth D. Wood, August 6, 1852, Kane Collection, Perry Special Collections.

68. Elizabeth D. Wood to Thomas L. Kane, September 23, 1852, Kane Collection, Perry Special Collections.

69. Elizabeth D. Wood to Thomas L. Kane, September 30, 1852, Kane Collection, Perry Special Collections.

70. William Wood to Thomas L. Kane, November 25, 1852, Kane Collection, Perry Special Collections.

71. Grow, *"Liberty to the Downtrodden,"* 133.

72. See Darcee D. Barnes, "A Biographical Study of Elizabeth D. Kane" (master's thesis, Brigham Young University, 2002).

73. Grow, *"Liberty to the Downtrodden,"* 155, 160.

74. Elizabeth D. Kane, 1857–58 Journal, February 2, 1858, typescript, Kane Collection, Perry Special Collections.

75. Kane, 1857–58 Journal, June 20, 1858, Kane Collection, Perry Special Collections.

76. Kane, 1857–58 Journal, December 26, 1857, December 28, 1857, Kane Collection, Perry Special Collections.

77. Kane, 1857–58 Journal, June 20, 1858, Kane Collection, Perry Special Collections.

78. Thomas L. Kane to [President Buchanan?], March 4, 1858, Kane Collection, Perry Special Collections.

79. Thomas L. Kane to [President Buchanan?], c. March 15, 1858, Kane Collection, Perry Special Collections.

80. Thomas L. Kane to John K. Kane, n.d., Kane Collection, Perry Special Collections.

81. See, for example, Thomas L. Kane to John K. Kane, April 4, 1858, Kane Collection, Perry Special Collections; A. Cumming to Lewis Cass, May 2, 1858, draft in Thomas L. Kane's handwriting with corrections by Cumming, Kane Collection, Perry Special Collections; John M. Bernhisel to Robert Patterson Kane, June 29, 1858, Kane Collection, Perry Special Collections; Eli K. Price to Thomas L. Kane, July 8, 1858, and Thomas L. Kane's reply to Price, July 1858, Kane Collection, Perry Special Collections; Elizabeth W. Kane to John M. Bernhisel, June 22, 1880, Kane Collection, Perry Special Collections; and Elizabeth D. Kane to Dr. Buckley, March 6, 1906 (draft letter), Kane Collection, Perry Special Collections.

82. Grow, *Liberty to the Downtrodden,* 212–13.

83. Elizabeth W. Kane to Elizabeth Kane Shields, August 23, 1863, Kane Family Papers, William Clements Library, University of Michigan, Ann Arbor, Mich.; "Dates of T. L. K.'s Military Record," Kane Collection, Perry Special Collections.

84. Elizabeth D. Kane to Dr. Buckley, March 6, 1906 (draft letter), Kane Collection, Perry Special Collections; see also T. L. Kane, "Son of Kane's Founder Recalls Early History" (1926), Kane (Penn.) Chamber of Commerce, www.kanepa.com/history%201.htm.

85. Brigham Young to Thomas L. Kane, October 26, 1869, Kane Collection, Perry Special Collections.

86. Thomas L. Kane to Brigham Young, October 12, 1871, Kane Collection, Perry Special Collections.

87. Thomas L. Kane to Brigham Young, November 30, 1871, Kane Collection, Perry Special Collections.

88. Elizabeth Kane, *Gentile Account,* 170; "Elizabeth Dennistoun Kane, the Mother of Kane," Kane Collection, Perry Special Collections.

89. For an account of the preparation of Bessie's book, see Grow, *"Liberty to the Downtrodden,"* 267–70.

90. Kane, *Gentile Account of Life in Utah's Dixie,* 177.

91. Kane, *Twelve Mormon Homes,* 1 (page numbers refer to the 1974 edition).

92. Kane, *Gentile Account,* 177.

93. William Wood, prefatory note, in Kane, *Twelve Mormon Homes,* xxi.

94. Kane, *Gentile Account,* 168.

95. Kane, *Gentile Account,* 173. Staines was "Elder Potto" in *Twelve Mormon Homes.*

96. Kane, *Twelve Mormon Homes,* 5–6.

97. Kane, *Twelve Mormon Homes,* 24.

98. Kane, *Twelve Mormon Homes,* 101.

99. Kane, *Gentile Account,* 118, italics in original.

100. Kane, *Twelve Mormon Homes,* 108.

101. Kane, *Gentile Account,* 95–96.

102. Kane, *Twelve Mormon Homes,* 105.

103. Kane, *Twelve Mormon Homes,* 106, italics in original.

104. Kane, *Twelve Mormon Homes,* 105, italics in original.

105. Kane, *Gentile Account,* 108, italics in original.

106. Kane, *Gentile Account,* 21.

107. Kane, *Twelve Mormon Homes,* 5.

108. Kane, *Gentile Account,* 39.

109. Kane, *Twelve Mormon Homes*, 11. The editorial comment in the 1974 edition says the Kanes' host in Provo was likely Margaret Thompson McMeans Atkinson, the first wife of Abraham Smoot. However, this is incorrect. Lowell "Ben" Bennion and Thomas Carter have correctly identified the Provo hostess in their presentation in this lecture series.

110. Kane, *Twelve Mormon Homes*, 48.
111. Kane, *Gentile Account*, 121.
112. Kane, *Twelve Mormon Homes*, 42, 43.
113. Kane, *Twelve Mormon Homes*, 45.
114. Kane, *Gentile Account*, 31. My attribution here to Snow is based on an impression that she would not have characterized Staines as "dry."
115. Kane, *Gentile Account*, 160.
116. Kane, *Twelve Mormon Homes*, 18.
117. Kane, *Gentile Account*, 161.
118. Kane, *Twelve Mormon Homes*, 33.
119. Kane, *Gentile Account*, 35.
120. Kane, *Gentile Account*, 70, italics in original.
121. Kane, *Gentile Account*, 173.
122. Kane, *Gentile Account*, 167.
123. Kane, *Gentile Account*, 168.
124. Kane, *Gentile Account*, 167–68.
125. Kane, *Gentile Account*, 169–70.
126. Kane, *Gentile Account*, 177.
127. Zobell, *Sentinel in the East*, 218–22.
128. Elizabeth W. Kane to George Q. Cannon, December 30, 1883, quoted in Grow, *"Liberty to the Downtrodden,"* 282.
129. Elizabeth D. Kane to Rev. Dr. Buckley, March 6, 1906, draft, Kane Collection, Perry Special Collections. Underlining in the original.

FIG. 1. Elizabeth W. Kane in Salt Lake City, winter 1872–73. Photo by C. R. Savage. L. Tom Perry Special Collections, Harold B. Lee Library, Brigham Young University.

Touring Polygamous Utah with Elizabeth W. Kane, Winter 1872–1873

Lowell C. (Ben) Bennion and Thomas R. Carter

Thomas L. Kane was an influential general and politician from Pennsylvania. He had helped the Mormons so much at two earlier junctures in their history (first in 1846 and then in 1858) that in 1872 Brigham Young invited him to visit Salt Lake City again, this time via train, with his wife and children. Based on his own experience in Utah's St. George (capital of "Utah's Dixie"), Young assured Kane that spending the winter there together would improve each other's health. Kane accepted the invitation, not just to benefit his ailing body but also to advise his close friend on legal matters and to take notes for a planned biography of him.

Tom never got around to writing such a book, but his wife, Elizabeth Wood Kane (fig. 1), who came to Utah with no manuscript in mind, kept journals and penned letters to family members in Pennsylvania. These materials became the basis for a curious little book "printed for private circulation" in 1874 in Philadelphia with an awkward title: *Twelve Mormon Homes Visited in Succession on a Journey through Utah to Arizona*.[1] Promoted by Elizabeth's husband and published by her father, this small volume set forth a lively account of the Kanes' 330-mile trip from Salt Lake City to St. George during winter 1872–73[2] (fig. 2). This essay combines her curiosity about plural living with our interest in Mormon architecture and historical geography through an examination of one of the homes included in *Twelve Mormons Homes* and by trying to better understand the everyday lives of Latter-day Saints participating in plural marriage.

FIG. 2. Thirteen Mormon towns visited by the Kanes, 1872–73. Prepared by Eric Harker. International Daughters of Utah Pioneers Museum, Salt Lake City.

The Kanes Visit Utah

After taking the train from Salt Lake City as far as they could (thirty-five miles to Lehi), the Kane family traveled by carriage in the company of their host and an entourage that included two of Brigham Young's wives and several close associates (fig. 3). The group stopped overnight in twelve different towns and stayed in thirteen separate homes (two in Fillmore). In all but two instances, the Kanes and their youngest children (both boys, ages eleven and nine) lodged with a polygamous family.[3] These encounters proved fortuitous, for they gave Elizabeth, a thirty-six-year-old mother of four, an unprecedented opportunity to view firsthand the vagaries of Mormon domestic life under what she perceived as the un-American system of plural marriage. Elizabeth, whom Tom called "Bess," had agreed to accompany her ailing husband only with "great reluctance." Her hesitation came not because she feared two long rides over rough roads in wintry weather might worsen Tom's condition; instead, she dreaded the prospect of finding herself "in a sink of corruption, among a set of Pecksniffs and silly women their dupes."[4]

As with many of her contemporaries, Elizabeth Kane was bothered by Mormon polygamy and concerned about the subservient position in which it seemed to place women. How was such a repulsive marital practice

FIG. 3. The greeting Brigham Young's party received when touring Utah settlements. This image captures the kind of welcoming procession that Young's group encountered when it entered a Mormon settlement. Illustration from T. B. H. Stenhouse, *The Rocky Mountain Saints* (D. Appleton, New York: 1873).

Kane Calendar for December 12–24, 1872

Twelve Mormon Homes Itinerary:
The Kanes' Journey from Salt Lake City to St. George

12. After their two-week stay in Jesse C. Little's American Hotel, the Kane-Young caravan took the train thirty-five miles from Salt Lake City via Sandy Station to Lehi, then the terminus of the Utah Southern Railroad. They traveled by carriage about fourteen miles to Provo and spent the night in Brigham and Eliza Burgess Young's home (not with President Abraham O. Smoot, as editor Everett L. Cooley had assumed).
13. After touring the Provo Woolen Mills, the caravan journeyed eighteen miles to Payson, where the Kanes lodged with William and Agnes Douglass, a monogamous couple (not with Bishop Joseph S. Tanner and his wife).
14. Their first full day of travel (twenty-five miles) brought the Kanes to Nephi, where they stayed with Samuel Pitchforth and his wives Mary and Sarah Ann.
15. The Kanes spent the Sabbath in Nephi with the Pitchforths, giving them a chance to attend their first Latter-day Saint worship service.
16. A thirty-eight-mile journey brought the Kanes to Scipio, where they stayed in the one-room cabin of Bishop Daniel Thompson's plural wife Lydia. On the return trip, the Kanes lodged in first wife Lorinda's two-room cabin.
17. From Scipio the caravan traveled about twenty-five miles to the Millard County seat of Fillmore. On the way south, the Kanes stayed with a monogamous couple, Thomas R. and Matilda King. On the return trip, the Kanes lodged with Mary Phelps, third wife of Bishop Thomas Callister.
18. From Fillmore the party journeyed thirty-six miles to Cove Creek Fort, where the entire party spent the night as guests of one of Ira N. Hinckley's two wives. He and the other wife (a sister of their hostess) had gone to Salt Lake City.
19. From Cove Fort the caravan traveled twenty-five miles to Beaver, where the Kanes lodged in the large home of Bishop John R. Murdock and his three wives.
20. The thirty-five-mile trip to Parowan took the Kanes to the house of Bishop William H. Dame and his three childless wives.
21. This day the caravan traveled about eighteen miles to Cedar City, where nearly blind Bishop Henry Lunt and two of his three wives—Ellen and Mary Ann (not Sarah Ann)—hosted the Kanes.
22. The even shorter distance from Cedar City to Kannarra, fifteen miles, gave three of the Kanes a chance to attend church services with their hosts, Bishop Lorenzo W. Roundy and perhaps one or both of his wives. Mrs. Kane chose not to attend the service.
23. The next day's journey was equally short (fifteen miles) but terribly rough and steep. The women in the party voted to stop in Bellevue (Pintura), where Jacob Gates's third wife, Mary Ware, took care of the Kanes. Gates and his other two wives lived in St. George.
24. The last thirty miles of the Kanes' thirteen-day journey brought them to their winter destination—Erastus Snow's "Big House" in St. George, where Elizabeth Ashby, the third of his four wives, served as their main hostess.

possible in the United States? Were these women victims or willing partners? As a self-styled "anti-polygamist questioner,"[5] Elizabeth initially recorded her impressions of plural living in diaries and letters. The more wives she watched and interviewed, the more inclined she was to portray them with sympathy as they carried out their household tasks under the trying conditions they and their families faced in colonizing the desertlike "Deseret" territory. She never became an apologist for polygamy in spite of her increasing sympathy for the many women trying to live the "Principle." Elizabeth let her father publish *Twelve Mormon Homes* only because she hoped it would help the Saints avoid more persecution as the national campaign against polygamy intensified in the early 1870s.[6]

As an amateur ethnographer who realized she was probably "the only 'Gentile' woman of respectability who [had] been admitted freely into the [Mormon] homes, and to the society of the women,"[7] Elizabeth Kane produced an account of Mormon life that tantalizes as much as it satisfies. One cannot read it without wanting to know more about the towns, buildings, and people she introduces but never fully embodies. Who were these Mormons? What kinds of houses and towns did they live in? This essay (and the forthcoming book from which it is drawn[8]) attempts to address these and other questions by placing the families the Kanes visited within the broader framework of community history.

Polygamy in Utah Territory

Two major themes emerge from our research. First in importance is simply the surprising prevalence of polygamy (fig. 4). Elizabeth Kane apparently never asked the challenging question posed by other contemporary outsiders: What proportion of the Mormon population practiced polygamy? But in both *Twelve Mormon Homes* and in her St. George journal (not published until 1995),[9] she expressed amazement upon learning that someone, supposedly a monogamist, actually lived in "plurality."[10] Wherever the Kane family went, they found themselves in the company of polygamists—both in the party that accompanied them to St. George and in the homes in which they stopped overnight. Those frequent "plural" encounters might have been a natural, if unintentional, result of Young's inclination to place the Kanes in the homes of leading Latter-day Saints, presumably those most likely to practice polygamy. But in Utah's Dixie, where Thomas and Elizabeth mingled for eight weeks with a broad cross section of residents, the Kanes became acquainted with numerous plural families, not just those of the so-called elite.

FIG. 4. A house in Fillmore, Utah, c. 1900–4, owned in turn by three different plural families: Callister, Hinckley, and Anderson. The Christian Anderson family stands in front of the dwelling. This elegant Gothic Revival style house, under construction when the Kanes passed through town, reflected a Mormon desire to keep abreast of architectural trends in the eastern U.S. Church History Library.

Seldom did Elizabeth Kane hesitate to ask the women she met questions about Mormonism's most vexing practice. While polygamy, even for most twenty-first-century Latter-day Saints, remains a mystery half-hidden in the closet of history, we concluded from our own (and others') research that it was prevalent enough to label Utah *polygamous* in spite of its monogamous majority. Consider for a moment the impact of polygamy on a given town: married Saints with only one spouse were expected to accept plural marriage as a valid principle and were warned time and again not to oppose its practice openly at the risk of being "cut off" from the Church.[11] Moreover, many members of the monogamous majority who steered clear of "Polly Gamy" (a future plural wife's pun) were indirectly tied to her through polygamous relatives—their own parents, siblings, children, or in-laws. Plural households were known and accepted as part of the local social topography—the townscape that people walked through as part of their daily routine. These factors made early Mormon settlements undeniably polygamous, a social reality we think historians should acknowledge.

The second theme resulting from our study centers on what we like to call "the ordinary architecture of an extraordinary practice" (fig. 5).[12] As already indicated, most of the houses visited by Elizabeth Kane were residences of plural wives. Although polygamous housing constituted a distinctive aspect of the Mormon cultural landscape, it is also apparent that such architecture, like the practice of polygamy itself, while widespread, was also virtually invisible, lost in its ordinariness. For the few historians interested in the housing of plural families, several well-known but unique examples have stood for the whole corpus of multiwife architecture. Most notable are the large houses built for Brigham Young and his counselor Heber C. Kimball in Salt Lake City, yet nearly all the buildings associated with the practice are less—much less—spectacular; in fact, they are so normal that most have gone unnoticed.[13]

In Mormon settlements, the solution to the problem of accommodating multiple families was found in what the Saints already knew, in the

FIG. 5. Jacob and Mary Ware Gates's I-house in Bellevue, Utah, c. 1890. The photo postdates the Kanes' visit, for the spindled porch was an obvious later addition. Church History Library.

traditional and popular housing of the time. Most plural families adapted their new marital status to houses that from the outside appear to be single-family residences. In this sense, the architecture sustains our general perception that life in the Principle was so commonplace and tacitly accepted by the monogamous majority that it should be viewed not as an exception, but as an ordinary, integral part of the Saints' social life.[14]

The Pitchforths of Nephi

The Samuel Pitchforth family lived in Nephi, the Juab County seat in central Utah. This was the town that Elizabeth seemed to favor most. She gave it and her three Nephite hosts (poorly disguised as "Steerforths") twice as many pages as any other place or family in the book, perhaps because "we stayed longer at their house than at any other on [the] tour."[15] The Kanes spent three nights there instead of the usual two, stopping for the Sabbath (December 15, 1872) and attending their first Latter-day Saint church service. Here, in this small town at the foot of towering Mount Nebo, we begin our own journey expressly designed to "revisit" *Twelve Mormon Homes.*

Nephi, as Elizabeth Kane surmised, was smaller than Provo and Payson, with fewer than thirteen hundred inhabitants in 1870. The town, which was informally called Salt Creek after the salty stream running through it, lay along the main road between Salt Lake and Southern California, providing horse-powered travelers with a convenient place to stop, rest, and refit. Nephi also stood strategically at the mouth of Salt Creek Canyon, which led to the colonies emerging eastward in Sanpete County; the city later supplied salt and timber to the Tintic mines to the west. As with most early Mormon towns, Nephi was laid out on the grid plan favored by Church leaders, in this case with four lots to the block (fig. 6). The main occupations of Nephi were farming, milling, and mining, with most families living within the town and commuting to the surrounding fields and mountains that sustained them.[16]

Upon entering Nephi, Young's party separated into "squads," each carriage apparently assigned to a different house. The Kanes presumably could have stayed with any of the town's better-known families—the Biglers, Bryans, Caziers, Footes, McCunes, or Udalls. Instead, Young steered them to the "plain adobe [two-story] house" of Samuel Pitchforth (fig. 7) on Center Street—close to the town's Social Hall and just a block away from the Tabernacle on Main Street (fig. 8). No family treated the Kanes more cordially than the Pitchforths, who prepared a "bountiful lunch" for them when they left for Scipio, their next town, and gave them two books

Samuel Pitchforth's Nephi
c. 1870

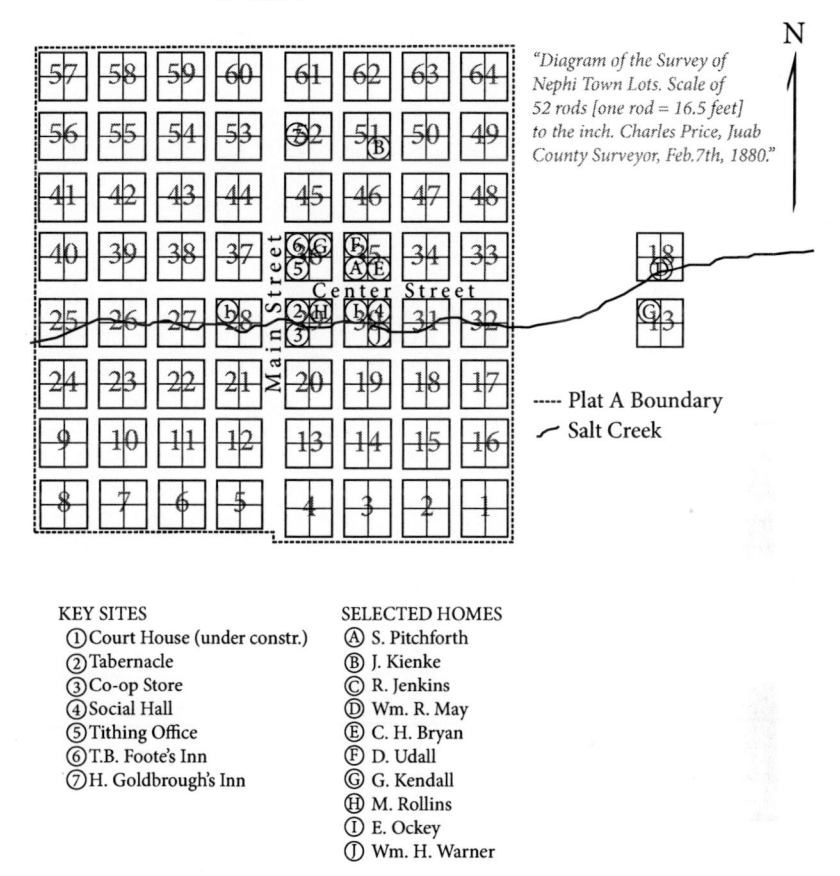

"Diagram of the Survey of Nephi Town Lots. Scale of 52 rods [one rod = 16.5 feet] to the inch. Charles Price, Juab County Surveyor, Feb.7th, 1880."

----- Plat A Boundary
⌒ Salt Creek

KEY SITES
① Court House (under constr.)
② Tabernacle
③ Co-op Store
④ Social Hall
⑤ Tithing Office
⑥ T.B. Foote's Inn
⑦ H. Goldbrough's Inn

SELECTED HOMES
Ⓐ S. Pitchforth
Ⓑ J. Kienke
Ⓒ R. Jenkins
Ⓓ Wm. R. May
Ⓔ C. H. Bryan
Ⓕ D. Udall
Ⓖ G. Kendall
Ⓗ M. Rollins
Ⓘ E. Ockey
Ⓙ Wm. H. Warner

FIG. 6. Samuel Pitchforth's Nephi, c. 1870. Cartography by Eric Harker.

of poetry (one by Eliza R. Snow) on their return trip. Besides, as Elizabeth Kane noted, Samuel's two sister-wives, Mary and Sarah Ann, "were the first Mormon women who awakened sympathy in my breast" through their "tender intimacy."[17]

Samuel Pitchforth became acquainted with polygamy five years before taking a second wife late in 1851 at the rather young age of twenty-five. His mother, Ann Hughlings, grew up in a family of Welsh extraction and married Solomon Pitchforth, a wealthy West Yorkshire businessman. When his wire mill burned down, the couple moved to Douglas on the Isle of Man. There they managed an inn and in 1840 boarded a pair of Mormon

FIG. 7. Pitchforth family house in Nephi, 1896. This image, taken from an old newspaper clipping in Doris Ann Cloward Clark's collection, is the only known photo of this dwelling. L. Tom Perry Special Collections, Harold B. Lee Library, Brigham Young University.

FIG. 8. East side of Main Street, Nephi, with Tabernacle (and tower) visible in the distance, 1886. Photo by C. R. Savage. International Daughters of Utah Pioneers Museum, Salt Lake City.

missionaries named Joseph Cain and John Taylor, one of the Church's twelve Apostles. The family heard the missionaries' message and, in the case of Ann and Samuel, they heeded it. Solomon permitted their baptism, but he opposed his young son's desire to preach the Mormon gospel in Douglas. Ann responded by leaving Solomon and taking their only son and three younger daughters back to England to live with her father.[18]

Then, with funds provided by Mr. Hughlings, Ann and the four children soon boarded a ship in Liverpool bound for New Orleans. On the same day they set sail, Samuel married Mary Mitchell of Herefordshire. She was the woman whom Elizabeth Kane characterized as "the chief speaker" of the Pitchforth wives, "tall rosy, brown-haired, and blue-eyed."[19] Upon reaching Nauvoo in March 1845, the Pitchforths were warmly welcomed by the same elders who had converted them. Once settled, Ann gave piano lessons to some of Elder Taylor's daughters while Samuel became his apprentice in the Church's *Times and Seasons* print shop. Early the next year, perhaps not so surprisingly, Ann was sealed as a plural wife to Elder Taylor just before the Saints began their exodus from Nauvoo. Sadly, the slow crossing of muddy Iowa proved too much of an ordeal for Ann, who died near Winter Quarters in late 1846. The next summer, the surviving Pitchforths joined the second company of Saints bound for the Salt Lake Valley, one led by the oft-married Taylor and fellow Apostle Parley P. Pratt.[20]

A few months before moving to the year-old settlement of Nephi in 1852, Samuel and Mary decided to join the growing number of Mormons inclined to try the plural life. Perhaps by then Mary's apparent inability to bear children also had influenced Samuel's decision to court Sarah Ann Goldsbrough, a young woman from South Yorkshire whom he married on December 20, 1851, two months after her arrival in Salt Lake City with her brother Henry. Elizabeth Kane viewed this second Mrs. Pitchforth as a quiet and "pale little lady, dark-haired and black-eyed," and "exceedingly unlike" the first wife, Mary (figs. 9 and 10).[21]

When the Pitchforths arrived in Juab County, they found most of the Nephi residents living within the walls of a fort being built for protection against the local Sanpete Ute Indians.[22] Central Utah was one of the few Great Basin areas with a large indigenous population, and it was here that hostilities, twice breaking out into warfare, were the greatest. No known record of the first Pitchforth house exists, but it was probably a temporary one- or two-room dwelling that resembled those described the previous year by a newspaper reporter. He noted the presence in Nephi of twelve houses: "three were built of adobe, two of willows plastered both inside

FIGS. 9 AND 10. Photographs of Samuel Pitchforth (*left*), and Mary M. Pitchforth (*right*), n.d. Courtesy Mary Nosack.

and outside, one two-story house built of four-inch plank, and the remaining houses of logs."[23]

By the end of the Black Hawk War in 1869, most of the Utes in the Juab area had been killed or removed to reservations, and Mormon settlements in central Utah—like Nephi—began to blossom. A correspondent informed the *Deseret Evening News* in January 1874 that "Nephi has been built up and improved surprisingly within the past seven years, a large number of public and private buildings having been erected in that time." A month earlier, the same paper reported that "Bishop Grover and W[m.] F[T]olley [two of the town's newcomers] have erected, each, a good and well finished dwelling-house, which serves to incite their neighbors to do likewise, for many such buildings are needed in Nephi."[24]

This late 1860s and early 1870s building boom probably saw the construction of the Pitchforths' two-story adobe abode (fig. 11).[25] It was not a grand house by any means, but it was comfortably large and well-fitted, having two rooms and a passage on each of the front levels. It also had a kitchen wing or ell, a one- or two-room wing placed on the back of the house (most often as a part of the original construction rather than a later addition) perpendicular to the main front section. The rear ell generally contained service rooms such as kitchens, pantries, and a servant's quarters. The range of housing options for polygamous families like the Pitchforths was always rather limited: each wife could have her own house, however small, or else some kind of cohabitation arrangement could be worked out. The ingenuity required in a "cohab" house design depended largely on the number of wives and children who needed accommodation. The more persons in the family, the more traditional design options were stretched. Large numbers called for dormitory or boarding house structures, like Brigham Young's Lion House or Aaron Johnson's sprawling compound in Springville.²⁶ The Pitchforth sister-wives, as Elizabeth Kane observed, were apparently a compatible pair in spite of their different appearances and personalities.²⁷ For them, a shared domestic space in the form of the common American two-story I-house probably proved to be a satisfactory choice.

The I-House

One of the most popular houses in the United States during the mid-nineteenth century was two stories high, two rooms wide, with a kitchen ell at the back and often a hallway separating the front rooms. Room use varied with the owners, but usually one of the downstairs front rooms served as a parlor or living room, the other as a parents' bedroom. Children frequently slept in the upstairs bedrooms. In the rear were the service areas, including a kitchen, dining room, pantry, and bedrooms for servants or boarders. Researchers named these homes I-houses because they were so common in the central Midwest (Indiana, Illinois, Iowa), and the name, while arbitrary, has stuck. Such houses were known in England and began to appear in colonial America in the eighteenth century, but they achieved their greatest popularity in the first half of the nineteenth, being found from Maine to South Carolina and from the Atlantic Coast into the Upland South and Ohio River Valley.²⁸ Mormon converts knew them from

FRONT ELEVATION

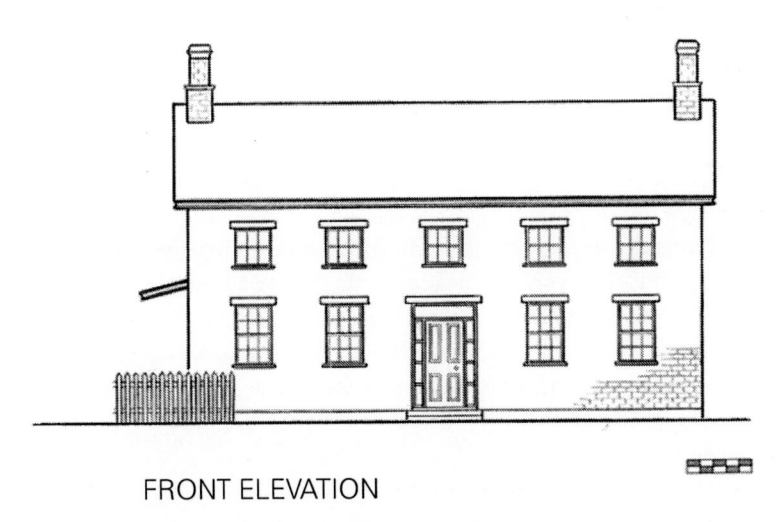

FIG. 11. Reconstructed drawing of the south front elevation of the Pitchforth family house, illustrating the rigid symmetry and classic proportioning of the I-house form. Drawing by David Henderson.

their home districts and built them in both Missouri and Illinois. I-houses could bear any number of decorative exterior treatments. In Nauvoo, for example, they appeared with stepped parapets on the gable ends, an upper Midwest fashion trend in the 1830s and 1840s.[29]

I-houses are notable not only for their numbers but also for their function as status symbols. Geographer Fred Kniffen found that "early in its movement southward the I-house became symbolic of economic attainment by agriculturists and remained so . . . throughout the Upland South and its peripheral extensions."[30] As carriers of style and prestige, such houses met the needs of Mormons eager to project an image of refinement and respectability to the outside world. They also served to clarify class distinctions within Mormon as well as American society, for these were the houses favored by Church leaders and prominent businessmen. Middle- and lower-class Saints built smaller one- or one-and-a-half-story houses with only one, two, or three rooms. Whenever Brigham Young and other authorities spoke of building good or better homes, I-houses were most likely the kind they had in mind.[31]

A diagram of the thirteen houses the Kanes slept in suggests the degree to which the I-house dominated Mormon domestic architecture, particularly in the postpioneering years (fig. 12). During the 1847–57 decade of Mormon colonization, housing styles were often quite diverse, reflecting the immediate background of the newcomers and the exigencies of first settlement. Elizabeth stayed in several of these first-period houses: the William Douglass house in Payson, "which had grown with his prosperity, for it had been added to three times";[32] Bishop Daniel Thompson's two tiny houses in Scipio, the first "a little, one-roomed log-cabin, with a lean-to behind";[33] the fortified dwelling of Ira Hinckley at Cove Creek;[34] and William Dame's central-chimney house in Parowan, a reminder of many such homes in his native Massachusetts.[35] These houses reflected the immediacy of frontier life, but they were frequently replaced during the second stage of settlement, when time and resources allowed fuller attention to building larger and more fashionable dwellings. Often, as figure 13 reveals, Mormons relied on an I-type house to convey their sense of style, permanence, and status. Of the thirteen houses in which the Kanes lodged, seven were variants of this popular form. Erastus Snow's house in St. George was a larger and even more prestigious four-room two-story cousin of the I-house type.[36]

The Pitchforth house, then, is typical of second-period, upper-middle-class houses in Mormon country, both monogamous and polygamous. An important caveat in examining such structures is to beware of the "double doors" prescription. For years almost everyone in Utah has assumed that

PHASE I

DANIEL THOMPSON, SCIPIO

DAME, PAROWAN

COVE FORT, MILLARD COUNTY

W. DOUGLASS, PAYSON

CALLISTER COTTAGES, FILLMORE (CONJECTURAL)

PHASE II

PITCHFORTH, NEPHI

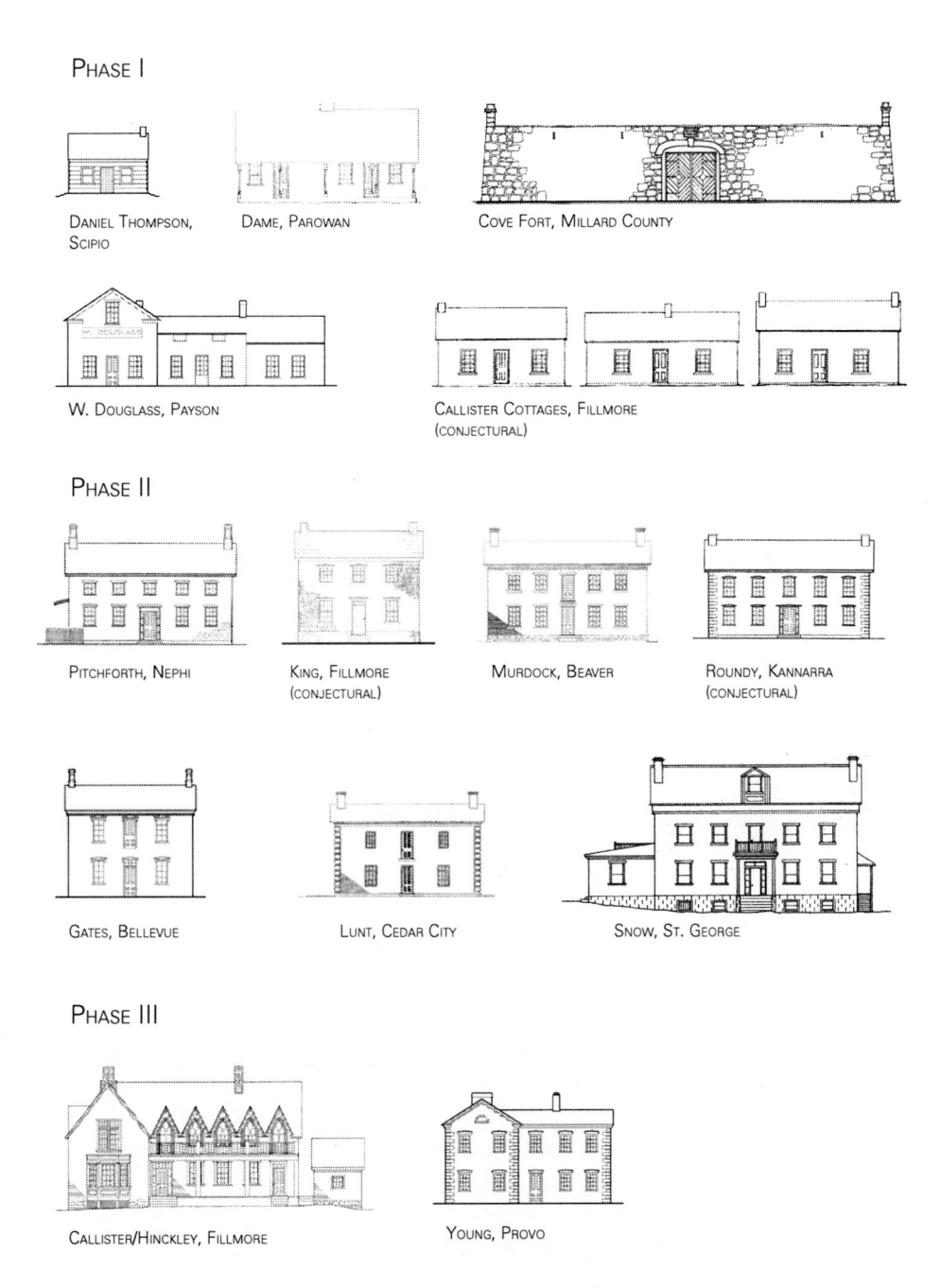

KING, FILLMORE (CONJECTURAL)

MURDOCK, BEAVER

ROUNDY, KANNARRA (CONJECTURAL)

GATES, BELLEVUE

LUNT, CEDAR CITY

SNOW, ST. GEORGE

PHASE III

CALLISTER/HINCKLEY, FILLMORE

YOUNG, PROVO

FIG. 12. Diagrammatic representation of the three main phases of nineteenth-century Mormon architecture: (I) settlement period marked by diversity of design; (II) contraction of designs around the classically styled I-house; (III) acceptance of irregular Victorian designs after 1880. Drafted by Thomas Carter, drawing by James Gosney.

a polygamous house needed to have two front doors—the double entry denoting two wives inside. This was simply not the case. Double front door houses, whether of the I-house type or smaller dwellings, were found throughout the United States in the nineteenth century. Double doors allowed the inside front rooms to be of equal size and gave the house a bilateral symmetry valued at the time. In Mormon country, to be sure, the two-front-door-home lent itself to cohab living, but there are many examples of houses with two doors and only one wife.[37]

The same caution holds as well for very large structures, such as Brigham Young's Beehive House and Erastus Snow's "Big House" in St. George. Despite their association with polygamists, both were single-wife dwellings at the time of the Kanes' visit.[38] In studying the architecture of polygamy, since exterior evidence remains ambiguous and households were so fluid, with wives often moving in or out, the best rule is to take nothing at face value. It is best to stick to the census and land deed records, which, although imperfect, are still the most reliable sources for knowing who lived where and when.

For the Pitchforths, an I-house was a convenient solution to their housing needs, giving them ample room and a central hallway for privacy (fig. 13). We cannot know for certain how the rooms were used. Elizabeth Kane mentions "a large bedroom on the ground floor" as well as a "cozy dining-room," a "great kitchen," and a "breakfast room."[39] Conventional usage of such houses suggests that one of the front rooms served as the bedroom and the other for dining, while the kitchen was located in the rear ell. What we do know, however, is that the house was full.

The Pitchforths had eight children, and to Elizabeth Kane's surprise, all except an adopted Native American, renamed Lehi, belonged to plural wife Sarah Ann. The children ranged in age from eighteen to one, with a noticeable gap among the youngest ones. The mother, whose first child died at birth, had four babies during the late 1860s, all of whom passed away within three years. At the time of the 1870 census, Samuel's youngest sister, Annie, also lived in the house with two sons, ages ten and seven, all three bearing the name Pitchforth. By then, Annie had divorced husband Robert Rollins and reverted to her maiden name. She and her children may have lived in the small rooms just off the kitchen.[40]

Polygamous Households Related to the Pitchforths

Life in a polygamous household could be, as Nephi's leading official, Jacob G. Bigler, told a gathering of the local women's Relief Society, "a great trial." In fact, he admitted, "if many of you were to give way to your

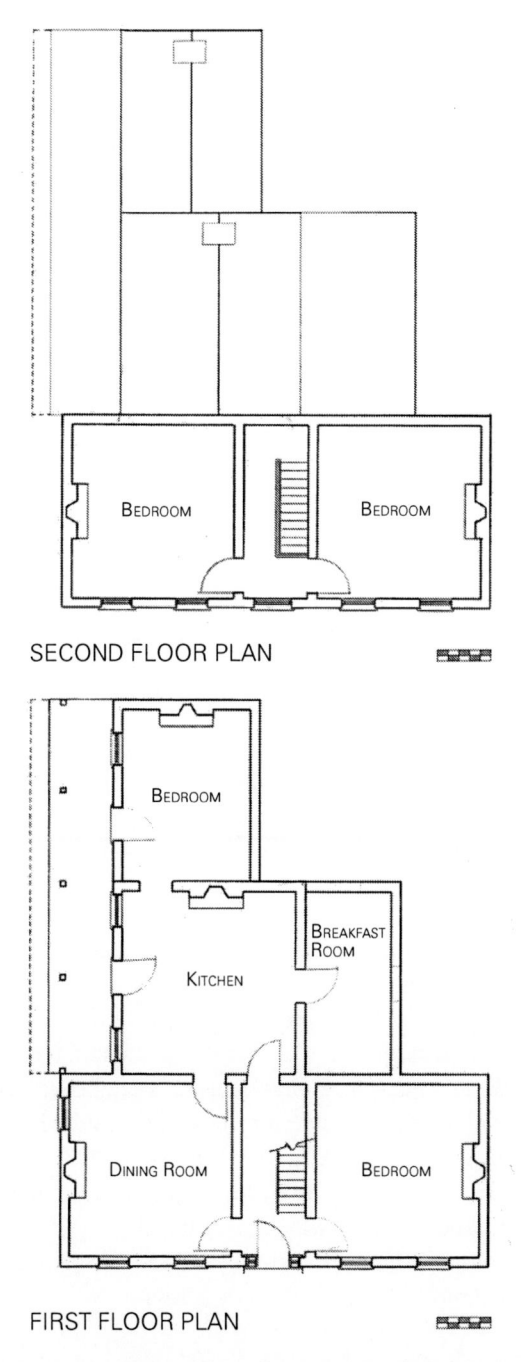

FIG. 13. Conjectural ground- and upper-story floor plans of the Pitchforth family house. The Pitchforths may have opted for a central passage to create more privacy, allowing people to move through the house without passing through any bedrooms. Drawing by David Henderson.

feelings, you [would] do as Jobs wife counciled him to do[,] curse God and die."[41] Certainly he could have cited some examples of conflict, remorse, and divorce from his experience as a stake president and probate judge. But the Pitchforths, Elizabeth Kane discovered, were different; their plural marriage had worked well. For one thing, childless Mary had embraced Sarah and Samuel's children as if they were her own—"our girls," she called them.[42] Furthermore, there was common purpose: the women "pointed out to me the comfort, to a simple family, that there was in having two wives to lighten the labors and duties of the household." And Mary "spoke of the friendship that existed between such sister-wives, as a closer tie than could be maintained between the most intimate friends living in different circumstances." Elizabeth was stunned. "Can you imagine anything sober—more insane?" she asked.[43] But she became sympathetic toward, and even fond of, these two Pitchforth women who had found much more than a silver lining in the cloud of plurality.

The practice of plural marriage spread in spite of its challenges, at least among the Pitchforths. A year before Samuel's death in 1877, two of his daughters married the same man on the same day, apparently convinced, after growing up in a happy home, that polygamy, as their father believed, was the preferred form of matrimony. They were Sarah Ann's two oldest girls, Mary Amelia and Sarah Alice, each named for one of their "joint mothers." The girls' husband, William Robert May, was a rancher (and onetime public notary) who, at age thirty-three, was more than ten years older than they when the trio married. His literal sister-wives seemed as inseparable as Samuel's widows, still living in the same house with Mr. May as late as 1900.[44]

What would Elizabeth Kane have thought had she met Samuel's two oldest sisters and learned that they, too, had embraced polygamy, albeit as first wives? Writing about an unhappy marriage of his sister Mercy, Samuel opined, "I believe the Lord is letting her see some Trouble [from her husband] to show her that if a Woman marries a man that has no wife that she can have Trouble and sorrow[,] for her spirit must be humbled till she seeks to find life eternal for she has not felt well to the celestial Law of marriage."[45] On December 7, 1861, Mercy married Richard Jenkins, but not until 1870 did he take a second wife, a decision that may have pleased Samuel more than Mercy, although as late as 1880 the two Jenkins women lived next door to one another, each with six children.[46]

Samuel's second sister, Sarah Barbara, married a jovial German-born brick mason and farmer named John Kienke (figs. 14 and 15) as early as 1854.[47] They waited even longer than the Jenkins before entering polygamy by adding British-born Elizabeth Harvey to the family. The two wives initially lived in town as near neighbors, two blocks north of the Pitchforths. But by 1878, when John left for a two-year mission to German-speaking Europe, Elizabeth alone had moved to the family farm four miles north of Nephi.[48] Six years after his mission, John became bishop of Mona, a small settlement a few miles north of his farm. U.S. deputy marshals arrested him for unlawful cohabitation in 1888, but he was never brought to trial, perhaps thanks to the leniency of newly appointed U.S. Judge John W. Judd in Provo.[49]

Henry Goldsbrough became even more entangled in the "Slough of Polygamy"[50] than his brother-in-law Samuel. As with Mary Pitchforth, Amelia Hallam, Henry's first wife, had no children. Henry took a second wife in December 1851 on the same day that his sister Sarah married Samuel and almost a year before the Church publicly acknowledged its practice of plurality. After attending the Church's April 1857 general conference in Salt Lake City, the two brothers-in-law had their wives sealed to them at the same time in the Salt Lake Endowment House. Brother Pitchforth then bade goodbye to "Bro Goldsbrough and his wives. . . . He has 3 having got [another] one lately."[51] In 1858, Henry added a fourth wife, Ellen Jackson, to his family. By the time of the 1870 census, three of his four spouses occupied adjoining houses with ten children (and two servants). A decade later,

FIGS. 14 and 15. Photographs of John and Sarah B. Kienke, n.d. Courtesy Mary Nosack.

FIG. 16. The Goldsbrough Inn, after 1900. The evolution of Goldsbrough's property from house to inn to inn with a livery stable follows a common pattern of architectural change in Utah. The one-or one-and-a-half-story Period I house (*left*) was enlarged by adding a Period II I-house to serve as an inn (*center*). Then a gable-front addition (*right*) was added to stable horses and house carriages. Used by permission, Utah State Historical Society, all rights reserved.

the second wife, Susannah Spencer, no longer lived with the family, having apparently opted for a divorce after bearing Henry ten children.[52]

By 1865, the Goldsbroughs had moved from Davis County to join their Pitchforth and Kienke relatives in Juab County, whom they soon outnumbered. As Samuel said of Henry at an earlier date, "Bro G. is increaseing in Cattle and Sheep and children."[53] The 1870 census listed both men as farmers, but Goldsbrough's property was appraised at more than twice the value of Pitchforth's (and ten times that of Kienke's). Henry acquired a house on Main Street that he gradually expanded into an inn (fig. 16) and a livery stable to supplement his farm income. In the 1880 census he appears as a "hotel keeper" and in the 1900 census as a "livery stable proprietor." By the latter date he lived alone; his five wives had either divorced him or died, and all of their children had left home.[54]

Gentile visitors to Utah, like Elizabeth Kane, often remarked on "the great Mormon crop" of children.[55] But when Brigham Young decided in September 1868 to create a Juab Stake of Zion, a member of his traveling party exclaimed,

> The number of children [in the huge crowd that welcomed "Zion's Chieftain"] was something astonishing for a place no larger than Nephi. Accustomed as we [Mormons] are to seeing children in great abundance their numbers here surprised us. Probably the explanation is found in the inscription which we noticed on one of the banners which the

children carried, 'Monogamy at a Discount.' A monogamist in the company remarked that the only fault he could find with the sight was, "he had no hand in producing it."[56]

According to a biography of John Muir, the naturalist came to Nephi four years after the Kanes' tour, not to study polygamy but to climb Mount Nebo (fig. 17) in late May 1877. En route to Nephi, Muir lodged with David Evans, bishop of Lehi and the husband of five wives and father of forty-one children. Muir asserted, "The production of babies is the darling pursuit industry of Mormons." And he naturally used mountain metaphors to record his impressions of Mormon "baby farming." Wherever deltas developed at the mouths of canyon streams, there formed "a delta of babies[,] ... as if like the boulders they had been washed down in floods." He also observed that "the height of the baby line in Utah" lay at roughly six thousand feet. Above that line only "babyless, barren ... gold seekers" lived.[57]

Thanks to polygamy, Utah's cradles carried more babies per capita than any other American state or territory as of 1870. By then, close to 20 percent of the territory's population was under five years of age and nearly 60 percent under twenty (fig. 18).[58] Closer inspection of this population pyramid reveals that males barely outnumbered women in each age group between twenty and fifty-four—a result of the influx of Gentiles, mostly single men, with the railroad's arrival in 1869 and the fact that

FIG. 17. View of Mount Nebo from the southwest, with Nephi at its base, n.d. Used by permission, Utah State Historical Society, all rights reserved.

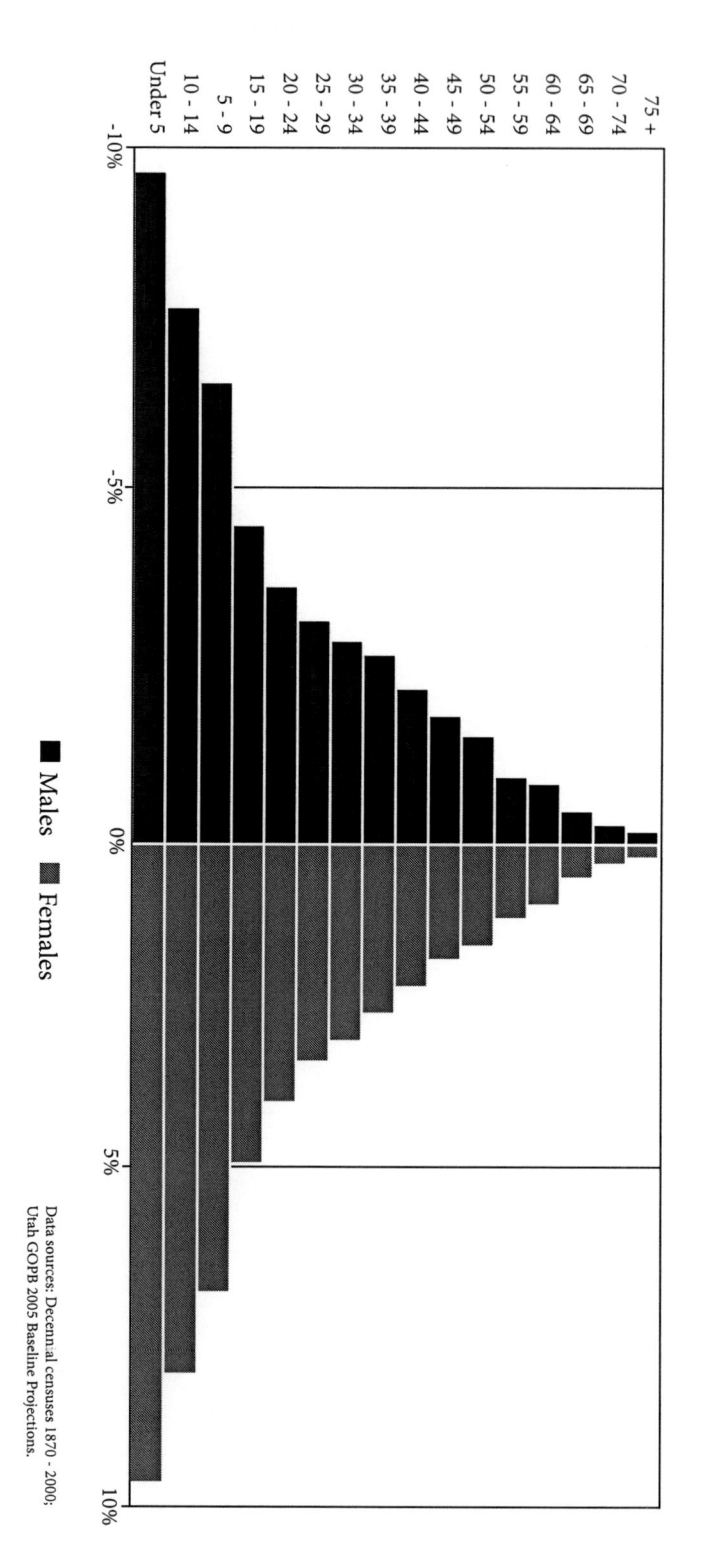

Utah Age Structure: 1870

■ Males ■ Females

Data sources: Decennial censuses 1870 - 2000;
Utah GOPB 2005 Baseline Projections.

FIG. 18. Utah age structure, 1870. Courtesy Pamela S. Perlich, Bureau of Economic and Business Research, University of Utah, July, 2007. Graphic prepared by Eric Harker.

some polygamists, notably those with wives living in different towns, were counted twice. One case in point is that of a Dane named Canute Brown and his two young sons, who were recorded in both Nephi and Ephraim, in each city with a different one of Canute's wives.[59]

If we accept demographers' assumption of a fairly even ratio of males to females among Mormons of marriageable age by 1870, a rarely asked question arises: how many men like Samuel Pitchforth, who firmly believed in plurality, could have secured a second wife? Some who wanted more than one had to wait quite a while before finally finding a second spouse. Homer Brown, an early Nephi polygamist, recorded that "John Cazier got home from the City and brought another wife with him he has now accomplished . . . [what] he has been trying to [do] for a year or two but he has been very unsuccessful heretofore."[60] A recent unpublished study concludes that in any stable society "polygyny by more than 20% of husbands and 30% of wives is on the high end of what is mathematically plausible, unless the difference in marriageable ages is very large."[61] Latter-day Saint believers like Henry Goldsbrough who "caught" anywhere from three to thirteen wives would further lessen the chances of aspiring polygamists, like John Cazier, to attract even a second spouse.

Having used the Pitchforths as a point of entry into Nephite society, we can begin to see to what degree polygamy pervaded local life. A scan of the two pages where they appear in the 1870 census schedule suggests that they lived in a centrally located neighborhood occupied by several other unrelated plural families. By combining census and genealogical records,[62] we have identified at least fifty-three polygamous households, twenty of them headed by one of the wives (see appendix). They are scattered across the town's four plats, but with a pronounced concentration in Nephi's original Plat A, surveyed in 1862 (fig. 19). To what extent polygamists tended to cluster in certain areas is difficult to determine because many, including Samuel Pitchforth and his three brothers-in-law, owned several lots. But the appendix does demonstrate that Nephi's plural households represented a broad range of family sizes, occupations, incomes, and national origins.

Altogether these households accounted for close to 15 percent of the married men, 28 percent of the married women, and about 23 percent of the town's total population as of July 1870.[63] The last figure includes the spouses, their children, and six family servants. However, these numbers exclude a few plural families that had either moved away or dropped out of polygamy due to death or divorce by the time the census was taken. The data also omit several men such as Pitchforths' aforementioned future son-in-law, William R. May, who entered into plurality after 1870. Nor have we counted those older children who grew up in a plural family but

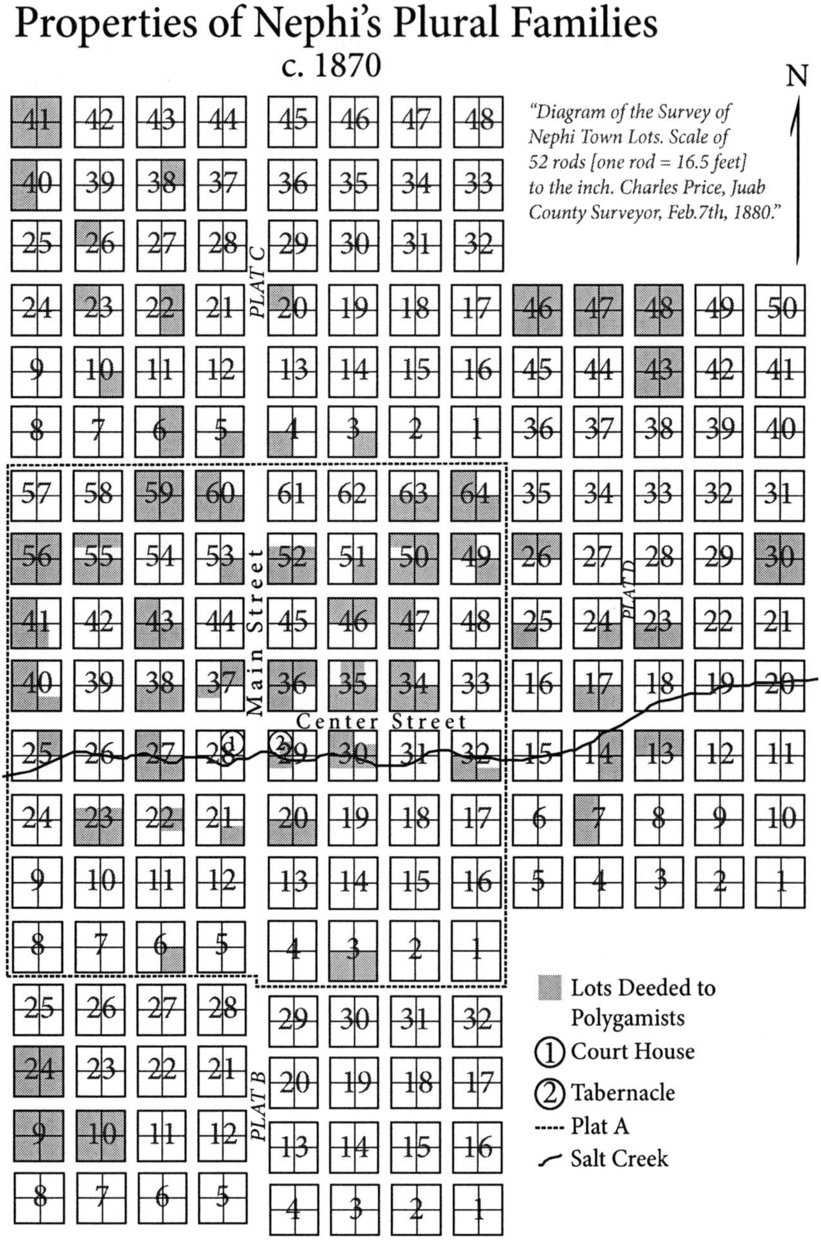

FIG. 19. Properties of Nephi's plural families, c. 1870. Cartography by Eric Harker.

who by 1870 had established monogamous households of their own in Nephi. These key variables—marriages, migration, births, deaths, and divorces—kept changing the incidence of polygamy in every Latter-day Saint settlement.

Were we to subtract from Nephi's 1870 census population any Gentiles, apostates (including those who joined break-off groups such as the members of the Reorganized Church of Jesus Christ of Latter Day Saints), or even lukewarm Latter-day Saints, the plural percentage would increase at least a little. By 1880, when either Church or government officials noted individuals' religious standing on the left-hand margin of the census, Nephi had about one hundred and thirty residents classified as disaffected members or Gentiles. This group included William Warwood, who joined the RLDS "Josephites" in 1869 partly because by then he shared their opposition to the Principle, but only after he was "cut off" from the Church for allegedly breaking up the marriage match of a polygamist's daughter and the suitor whom her parents favored.[64]

Polygamy cast a net broad enough to catch many members of monogamous households. A fair number of traditional couples sooner or later witnessed the marriage of a daughter (or even a son) into a polygamous family. For example, Edwin Harley had four daughters, two of whom married polygamists. In 1878, the father recorded that "Mary Emily started for St. George with [an already married] Edward Sparks contrary to my wishes." They were sealed in Utah's newly completed first temple.[65] Six years later, Edwin simply noted, "My Daughter Margaret started to Salt Lake City to Conference this morning," a trip that culminated in her marriage to Ira N. Hinckley, founder of Cove Fort, as his third living wife.[66] To reemphasize an important point, Nephi's monogamous majority could claim a large number of close relatives among its polygamous minority—children, parents, siblings, in-laws, not to mention first cousins, nephews, and nieces. If the two groups were combined, they probably comprised a majority among the residents of Nephi in 1870.

Prevalence of Polygamy Elsewhere in Utah

How did the incidence of polygamy in Nephi compare with that of the other places where the Kanes stopped on their journey through Utah?[67] Juab's county seat falls in the same 20 to 25 percent range calculated for most of the twelve towns with a population of more than five hundred. Fillmore barely reaches 20 percent even with the inclusion of Ira Hinckley's plural clan at Cove Fort. The figure for St. George, about 45 percent, stands well above that of all but one small settlement, Bellevue (later renamed Pintura). Even with her strong aversion to plural marriage (and Brigham Young, its principal proponent), Elizabeth Kane could not have asked for a place better suited to observe the often tangled lives of plural wives and their husbands. Only Bellevue (68 percent), with fewer than fifty people, exceeded St. George's percentage. In such hamlets, one or two polygamous families—like those of John D. Lee or Dudley Leavitt—could skew (or leaven) the numbers in polygamy greatly. Even more surprising than the figures found in "Dixie" is Scipio's rather high rank (30 percent), since Elizabeth saw it as "the poorest and newest of the settlements."[68] Ordinarily, one would expect to find fewer polygamists among a relatively poor and young population.

In whichever town the Kanes stayed—old or new, poor or well-to-do—they never escaped the presence of polygamy. Had they traveled up Salt Creek Canyon into Sanpete County, or past Salt Lake and Ogden into Brigham City, or through Sardine Canyon into Cache Valley, the Kanes would have found plurality even more prevalent than along the southern route they took.[69] By this time in the 1870s, all Latter-day Saints knew of the practice and were expected to accept and support it if they wanted to be in good standing with Church leaders. While the architecture of polygamy did not stand out and proclaim its identity, it was undoubtedly recognized by town residents. As people walked to their fields, to church, to the store, or to social gatherings, they frequently passed the houses of plural families. The mere presence of these dwellings, implicit reminders of the unique marriage system that distinguished the Saints from other Americans, cannot be discounted. Seemingly invisible and always fluid, the landscape of plurality remains vitally important to a fuller understanding of early Mormon history.[70] Just as the American North in the 1860s saw the South as a slave society that needed to be reconstructed, so it viewed Utah as a polygamous society that had to be changed. The families of slave owners probably constituted an even smaller minority of Southerners than polygamous households did among the Mormons.[71] But in each region a controlling minority tended to rule the population's majority. About twenty years after the United States went to war over slavery, it launched a ten-year campaign to abolish polygamy that finally enabled the Territory of Utah, after fifty years of waiting, to become a state. During the 1880s, a decade strongly marked by federal raids on those practicing plural marriage, the Church understandably sought to minimize the importance of its polygamous past.

In Nephi, as in most other nineteenth-century Mormon towns, plural marriage, directly and indirectly, had become so prevalent that Elizabeth Kane concluded federal persecution would make the Saints all the more determined to maintain their system of "Celestial Marriage."[72] Consequently, soon after arriving in St. George, she wrote that long letter to

Senator Simon Cameron of Pennsylvania, already cited, pleading with him to use his influence to stop the national antipolygamy campaign.[73] When that plea proved fruitless, she received encouragement from her husband and her father and agreed to have her impressions of Mormonism's plural society published and distributed, mainly to influential Easterners whose negative opinions the Kanes hoped to change.[74] What did Mormons themselves think of the book this perceptive gentile lady wrote about them? Most never saw it, and no known record exists of what Brigham Young might have thought. But one of his counselors in the First Presidency, George Q. Cannon, read the manuscript and gave Elizabeth Kane's "felicitous narrative" his approval in a letter he wrote to Thomas shortly before its publication. "Such a journal as this, ... cannot fail to ... dissipate many prejudices and misconceptions which prevail in relation to the people of Utah." Cannon also thought

> not one of the persons alluded to ... will take the least exception to the manner in which their households are described. To make contrasts vivid and striking there must be shadows. The people of Utah fully understand that rose-colored notices of them are viewed with distrust, and that a journal written as this is will be more acceptable to a large number of readers than one which should contain only kind and flattering descriptions.[75]

Perhaps not only Elizabeth Kane but also Elder Cannon would approve of our attempt to revisit and reconstruct Mormonism's polygamous landscape with its fascinating combination of rosy scenes and striking shadows.

Lowell C. (Ben) Bennion (lcbscb@q.com) earned his PhD from Syracuse University and spent his academic career teaching geography at Indiana University, Bloomington, and Humboldt State University, Arcata, California. His publications have examined California's Trinity Highway and Mormon historical geography, with a particular interest in the historical demography and dynamics of plural marriage between 1840 and 1904.

Thomas R. Carter (tcarter@arch.utah.edu) received his PhD from Indiana University, Bloomington. He is currently a professor in the College of Architecture and Planning and the director of the Western Regional Architecture Program at the University of Utah. His research has centered on the vernacular architecture of Utah and the American West.

Appendix

Nephi's Plural Households from the 1870 Census

Census #	Name	Age	(Family Members)	Occup.	Property Values	Birthplace
170	ANDREWS	58	John (2 wives, 1 child, 1 svt)	Sawmill Propr.	$6000/3000	England
234/35	BAKER	35	William G. (2 wives, 8 children)	Laborer	$550/400	England
246/47/48	BIGLER	57	Jacob G. Sr. (4 wives, 10 children)	Farmer	$3350/2350	VA
179	BROADHEAD	40	David (2 wives, 12 children)	Farmer	$100/400	England
95	BROWN	49	Canute (1 wife, 2 children, 1 svt)	Retail Merchant	$1500/2000	Denmark
47	BRYAN	62	Charles H. (3 wives, 1 child)	Farmer	$3000/3500	KY
67	CAZIER	36	David (2 wives, 4 children)	Farmer	$700/400	KY
187/245	CAZIER	49	John (2 wives, 4 children)	Teamster	$600/700	VA
13	EDGHILL	30	James (2 wives, 5 children)	Brick Mason	$500/300	England
35/36	FOOTE	70	Timothy B. (2 wives, 6 children)	Farmer	$2500/3000	NY
231/32/33	GOLDSBROUGH	47	Henry (3 wives, 10 children, 2 svts)	Farmer	$10300/2375	England
57/58	HAWKINS	52	John (3 wives, 3 children)	Shoemaker	$1150/300	England
212/13	HAYWARD	53	William (2 wives, 2 children)	Laborer	$200/550	England
63/97	JENKINS	35	Richard (2 wives, 9 children, 1 svt)	Farmer	$1500/1200	Wales
4	JONES	37	Edward (2 wives, 10 children, 1 svt)		$600/900	Wales
33/34	KENDALL	51	George (2 wives, 10 children)	Farmer	$1700/775	England
5/6	KIENKE	40	John (2 wives, 5 children)	Brick Mason	$450/400	Germany
123/27	LUNT	54	Edward (2 wives, 5 children)	Farmer	$800/550	England
189	McCUNE	59	Mathew (2 wives, 1 child)	Physician	$1000/400	Isle of Man
244	MECHAM	70	Elam (2 wives, 3 children)	no occupation	$250/300	NH
252	NORTON	37	Jacob W. (2 wives, 1 child)	Farmer	$300/200	AL
21/43	OCKEY	55	Edward (2 wives, 12 children)	Farmer	$4000/3400	England
176/78	PEXTON	59	James (2 wives, 7 children)	Blacksmith	$800/600	England
42	PITCHFORTH	43	Samuel (2 wives, 7 children, 3 relatives)	Farmer	$3000/2500	England
28/29	RICHES	40	Benjamin (2 wives, 6 children)	Farmer	$1100/950,	England
40/41	ROLLINS	38	Martin (2 wives, 2 children)	Farmer	$1900/3150	IL
18	SAPP	34	Alphies (2 wives, 1 child)	Farmer	$400/250	NC
117/18	TIDWELL	44	Thomas (2 wives, 14 children)	Farmer	$4400/6200	IL
3	TOLLEY	20	Sarah (pl. wife of Wm. F.*, 2 ch, 2 rel's)	Keeping House	$300/250	England
44/45	UDALL	46	David (3 wives, 9 children)	Farmer	$1500/1750	England
48/49	WARNER	43	William (2 wives, 9 children)	Farmer	$500/800	MA
196	WINN	38	Dennis (2 wives, 6 children)	Works in Grist Mill	$650/400	England

*Tolley, his first wife, and 9 children are listed in the Salt Lake City Sixteenth Ward on the 1870 Census.
The 1870 population of Nephi was 1,285; 294 (22.9 percent) lived in a plural household.

1. William Wood, "Introductory Note" in Elizabeth Wood Kane, *Twelve Mormon Homes Visited in Succession on a Journey through Utah to Arizona,* ed. Everett L. Cooley (Philadelphia: William Wood, 1874; reprint, Salt Lake City: Tanner Trust Fund, University of Utah Library, 1974), xxi (all page numbers refer to the 1974 edition). For an invaluable guide to Brigham Young University's Kane Collection, see David J. Whittaker, "New Sources on Old Friends: The Thomas L. Kane and Elizabeth W. Kane Collection," *Journal of Mormon History* 27 (Spring 2001): 67–94.

2. Matthew J. Grow, *"Liberty to the Downtrodden": Thomas L. Kane, Romantic Reformer* (New Haven: Yale University Press, 2009), especially ch. 13, provides indispensable background for the Kanes' visit to Utah.

3. The Kane Calendar, based on our reexamination of editor Everett L. Cooley's footnotes in the 1974 reprint of *Twelve Mormon Homes,* identifies the families with whom the Kanes stayed while in Utah. The idea of tying the Kanes' December 1872 journey to a day-by-day calendar originated with David J. Whittaker, curator of BYU's Kane Collection; we thank him for his assistance in compiling it and for the invitation to participate in BYU's 2008–9 Kane Lecture Series. We also want to thank Eric Harker, an exhibition designer and a senior at BYU, for processing this and the other graphics in our essay.

4. Elizabeth W. Kane to Pennsylvania Senator Simon Cameron, December/January 1873, Kane Collection, L. Tom Perry Special Collections, Harold B. Lee Library, Brigham Young University, Provo, Utah (hereafter cited as Perry Special Collections). "Pecksniff" is the name of a sanctimonious character in Charles Dickens's novel *Martin Chuzzlewit.*

5. Kane, *Twelve Mormon Homes,* 129.

6. Grow, *"Liberty to the Downtrodden,"* 265–70.

7. Elizabeth W. Kane to Senator Cameron, December/January 1873.

8. Lowell Bennion, Thomas Carter, and Alan Morrell, *Twelve Mormon Homes Revisited: New Views of Elizabeth Kane's 1872–73 Journey to Polygamous Utah,* forthcoming.

9. See Elizabeth W. Kane, *A Gentile Account of Life in Utah's Dixie, 1872–73: Elizabeth Kane's St. George Journal,* ed. Norman R. Bowen (Salt Lake City: Tanner Trust Fund, University of Utah Library, 1995). This book is an essential complement to *Twelve Mormon Homes.* The original journal is in the Kane Collection, Perry Special Collections.

10. See, for example, Kane, *Twelve Mormon Homes,* 83; and Kane, *A Gentile Account,* 119.

11. During the so-called Mormon Reformation of 1856–57, Nephi's Samuel Pitchforth witnessed the departure of ten apostates, most of them "honorable men," but "all the wives of theas men have opposed the Law of Celestial marri(a)ge." He seemed to imply that the women's opposition to the "Principle" led to the families' excommunication and exodus. See Samuel Pitchforth, Diary, March 5, 1857 [9–10], typescript, Church History Library, The Church of Jesus Christ of Latter-day Saints, Salt Lake City, copy in Perry Special Collections, Samuel Pitchforth, *Diary of Samuel Pitchforth, 1857–1868,* typescript copy, 1961.

12. For this phrase we are indebted to both David Lloyd Henderson, who titled his spring 2004 Vernacular Architecture Seminar paper "The Ordinary Appearance of an Unusual Lifestyle," and architectural historian Dell Upton, who

stresses the importance of the "ordinariness of architecture" in his *Architecture in the United States* (New York: Oxford University Press, 1998), 21–24.

13. The invisibility of plural-wife housing practices is discussed in Lowell C. Bennion, Alan L. Morrell, and Thomas Carter, *Polygamy in Lorenzo Snow's Brigham City: An Architectural Tour* (Salt Lake City: College of Architecture and Planning, University of Utah, 2005), 3–4.

14. The most comprehensive survey of polygamous housing practices in Utah is Thomas Carter, "Living the Principle: Mormon Polygamous Housing in Nineteenth-Century Utah," *Winterthur Portfolio* 35, no. 4 (2000): 223–51.

15. Kane, *Twelve Mormon Homes*, 26.

16. Several sources contain valuable information and insights on the evolution of Nephi. At the time this essay was published, the most recent one had been written by Pearl D. Wilson, *A History of Juab County* (Salt Lake City: Utah State Historical Society and Juab County Commission, 1999), 13–30. However, no one has yet written a comprehensive history of Nephi.

17. Kane, *Twelve Mormon Homes*, 25, 48, 50, 54.

18. The only known history of the Pitchforths was written by Englishman Keith Pitchforth, *A Family Remembered: A History of the Pitchforth Family thru Six Centuries* (Sheffield, Eng.: Pickard Communication, 2005), but only ch. 6, "Joining the Saints," focuses on Ann and her children.

19. Kane, *Twelve Mormon Homes*, 27. We are indebted to Marcus L. Smith for the photos of the Pitchforths and the Kienkes and for sharing with us his copy of the Pitchforth family history cited in the previous footnote. Mary's qualities must have impressed priesthood leaders as much as they did Elizabeth Kane, for after Samuel died, Mary served terms as Juab Stake Relief Society President and as a member of the Relief Society General Board.

20. For an account of the Pitchforth–Taylor connection, see Samuel W. Taylor's biography of John Taylor, *The Kingdom or Nothing: The Life of John Taylor, Militant Mormon* (New York: Macmillan, 1976), 72–76. This book and *A Family Remembered* do not always provide adequate documentation and should therefore be used with caution. One should also read the long letter Ann H. Pitchforth wrote to her parents soon after her family's arrival in Nauvoo. It appears in Carol Cornwall Madsen, ed., *In Their Own Words: Women and the Story of Nauvoo* (Salt Lake City: Deseret Book, 1994), 146–54.

21. Kane, *Twelve Mormon Homes*, 27. For the date of Samuel's second marriage, see Ancestry File No. 17ZD-L8 (hereafter abbreviated as AFN), located online at familysearch.org. Regrettably we could not find a photo of wife Sarah Ann.

22. Elizabeth Kane discussed the local Indian situation at length with the Pitchforth women and confessed that "Mrs. Mary's Indian stories made me nervous." Kane, *Twelve Mormon Homes*, 31–40.

23. J. L. Heywood, "Mr. Editor—Sir:—I left the city of Nephi . . . ," *Deseret News*, December 13, 1851, [3], as quoted in Alice P. McCune, *History of Juab County* (Springville, Utah: Juab County Company of the Daughters of Utah Pioneers, 1947), 58.

24. "Correspondence," *Deseret News*, January 21, 1874, 814; "Progress in Juab," *Deseret News*, December 17, 1873, 736. See also Journal History of The Church of Jesus Christ of Latter-day Saints, January 10, 1874, 2, and December 5, 1873, 1, Church History Library, also available on *Selected Collections from the Archives*

of *The Church of Jesus Christ of Latter-day Saints*, 2 vols. (Provo, Utah: Brigham Young University Press, 2002), vol. 2. A microfilm copy exists in Harold B. Lee Library, Brigham Young University.

25. The 1960 newspaper article from which we took this 1896 photo of the Pitchforth house asserts that it was built in 1860, but we found no way to document this claim, since the only copy we know of is in the family papers of Marcus L. Smith, who has tried in vain to find the original.

26. See Carter, "Living the Principle," 225–28.

27. Kane, *Twelve Mormon Homes*, 47–48.

28. See Henry Glassie, *Pattern in the Material Folk Culture of the Eastern United States* (Philadelphia: University of Pennsylvania Press, 1968), 49–69; and Alan Gowans, *Styles and Types of North American Architecture* (New York: HarperCollins, 1992), 55–57.

29. See Richard N. Holzapfel and T. Jeffery Cottle, *Old Mormon Nauvoo, 1839–1846* (Provo, Utah: Grandin Book Co., 1990), 76–77.

30. Fred B. Kniffen, "Folk Housing: Key to Diffusion," in *Common Places: Readings in American Vernacular Architecture*, ed. Dell Upton and John Michael Vlach (Athens: University of Georgia Press, 1985), 8–9.

31. For Brigham Young's advice on housing, see Dolores Hayden, *Seven American Utopias: The Architecture of Communitarian Socialism, 1790–1975* (Cambridge, Mass.: MIT Press, 1976), 142. A more general discussion of the values found in early Mormon architecture is found in Thomas Carter, "Folk Design in Utah Architecture, 1849–1890," in *Images of an American Land: Vernacular Architecture in the Western United States*, ed. Thomas Carter (Albuquerque: University of New Mexico Press, 1997), 41–60.

32. Kane, *Twelve Mormon Homes*, 17.

33. Kane, *Twelve Mormon Homes*, 55.

34. Kane, *Twelve Mormon Homes*, 74–75.

35. Kane, *Twelve Mormon Homes*, 99–100.

36. To date, the two best studies of Mormon housing are unpublished dissertations. See Leon S. Pitman, "A Survey of Nineteenth-Century Folk Housing in the Mormon Culture Region" (PhD diss., Louisiana State University, 1973); and Thomas Carter, "Building Zion: Folk Architecture in the Mormon Settlements of Utah's Sanpete Valley, 1849–1890" (PhD diss., Indiana University, 1984).

37. See Thomas Carter, "Living the Principle," 227; and Thomas Carter and Peter Goss, *Utah's Historic Architecture, 1847–1940: A Guide* (Salt Lake City: University of Utah Press, 1988), 18–20.

38. See Carter and Goss, *Utah's Historic Architecture*, 26; and W. Randall Dixon, "The Beehive and Lion Houses," in *Brigham Young's Homes*, ed. Colleen Whitley (Logan: Utah State University Press, 2002), 124–28.

39. Kane, *Twelve Mormon Homes*, 25–26, 47.

40. U.S. Bureau of the Census, "Population Schedules of the Ninth Census of the United States, 1870," Nephi City, Utah, prepared by the National Archives and Records Service (Washington, D.C., 196[?]). Elizabeth Kane makes no mention of meeting Annie. The 1880 federal census lists her as a divorced dressmaker, living without either son in the large family of Charles Price, Juab County's longtime surveyor. U.S. Bureau of the Census, "Population Schedules of the Tenth Census

of the United States, 1880," Nephi City, Utah, prepared by the National Archives and Records Service (Washington, D. C., 196[?]).

41. Nephi Ward, Juab Stake, Relief Society Minutes, February 20, 1869, Church History Library. The Nephi Relief Society minutes throughout the 1870s suggest that polygamy was a fairly common subject among the sisters.

42. Kane, *Twelve Mormon Homes*, 47–48.

43. Kane, *Twelve Mormon Homes*, 48.

44. See AFN 17ZB-HG for the William Robert May family and the "Population Schedules of the Twelfth Census of the United States, 1900," Nephi City, Utah, prepared by the National Archives and Records Service (Washington, D.C., 196[?]). In 1880, it appears that the two wives lived some distance apart, one of them next door to Samuel's two widows.

45. Samuel Pitchforth, Diary, July 1, 1857, [36–37]. Samuel's diary entry for May 5, 1857, notes that Mercy had been sealed to another man a few years before but left him soon afterward. Pitchforth, Diary, May 5, 1857, [18]. Mercy's marital history prior to her marriage to Richard Jenkins is unclear. Richard Jenkins's AFN 2S8T-15 mentions Mercy's marriage to a Samuel Marble, but gives no date and lists two children born before (1856 and 1858) her marriage to Richard (in 1861).

46. See "Population Schedules of the Tenth Census, 1880," and the Richard Jenkins's AFN 2S8T-15.

47. If anyone ever writes a John Kienke family history, it will be Marcus L. Smith, who has already roughed out a few chapters that he graciously allowed us to read and on which this paragraph is based.

48. John sold part of his 160-acre farm and two of his three town lots to help finance his mission.

49. Based on a list we have compiled of twelve Nephi men who were arrested for unlawful cohabitation, only four apparently served prison terms. Bishops Kienke, Udall, and Warner even avoided paying a fine. Andrew Jenson, *LDS Church Chronology: A Record of Important Events Pertaining to the History of the Church of Jesus Christ of Latter-day Saints*, revised by J. R. C. Nebeker (Orem, Utah: Quick and Easy Publishing, 2002), 164, records Bishop Kienke's arrest on August 24, 1888, but makes no later mention of his being fined or sentenced for "u.c." or unlawful cohabitation.

50. Kane, *Gentile Account*, 118.

51. Pitchforth, Diary April 11, 1857, [15].

52. See Henry Goldsbrough's AFN 1GTG-0H and also that of James H. Mynders, AFN 1GTG-1N, whom Susannah Spencer may have remarried ca. 1880. See also "Population Schedules of the Ninth Census of the United States, 1870," Nephi City, Utah; and "Population Schedules of the Tenth Census of the United States, 1880," Nephi City, Utah.

53. Pitchforth, Diary April 6, 1858, [101].

54. Compare the three separate population schedules of the ninth, tenth, and twelfth censuses taken by the federal government in 1870, 1880, and 1900. The manuscript schedules are available on microfilm in major libraries. But to locate more readily a particular individual, such as Henry Goldsbrough, one can use either of two subscription sites: Ancestry Family History Library Edition or Heritage Quest Online, both available in the Family History Library of The Church of Jesus Christ of Latter-day Saints in Salt Lake City.

55. Kane, *Twelve Mormon Homes*, 77.

56. Journal History, September 19, 1868, 4.

57. Donald Worster, *A Passion for Nature: The Life of John Muir* (Oxford: Oxford University Press, 2008), 229–32. We thank David Hall, California State University–Fullerton history instructor, for alerting us to Worster's biography and its mention of Nephi, whose name Muir apparently confused with that of the Utah County town of Lehi.

58. We acknowledge the generosity of Pamela S. Perlich, Senior Research Economist in the Bureau of Economic and Business Research, University of Utah, for sharing with us this population pyramid and the data she used to create it.

59. See "Population Schedules of the Ninth Census, 1870," for both Ephraim and Nephi cities, and Canute Brown's AFN 28KQ-NJ.

60. Homer Brown, Diary, October 29, 1856, Church History Library, Church of Jesus Christ of Latter-day Saints, Salt Lake City.

61. Davis Bitton and Val Lambson, "Demographic Limits of Polygyny," June 2008, unpublished manuscript in possession of Ben Bennion.

62. See "Population Schedules of the Ninth Census of the United States, 1870," Nephi City, Utah. Since the 1870 federal census did not ask for an individual's marital status or relationship to the head of a household, we had to check census names against sundry genealogical records found in the Family History Library in Salt Lake City to compile the Appendix.

63. We did not count the family of farmer Abraham Boswell, which the census-taker somehow missed. He had two wives, Gerusha L. Hambleton and Matilda Betts, each of whom gave birth in 1870. The family numbered nine living children at the time of the census, judging by the Family Group Record Collection, 1962–77, in the LDS Church's Family History Library. See also Abraham Boswell's Ancestral File, AFN 5D6M-53. The comparable file for Nephi Resident Thomas Wright, AFN 4SKK-4K, indicates that he took two plural wives on the same day in 1867, one of them a sister of his first wife, Sarah. The Wright household numbered five sons and one servant in 1870, but we left it out of the Appendix because the census failed to count Thomas's other two wives. Perhaps they had died or moved elsewhere by then, although Sarah Wright told her Relief Society sisters during that census year: "I am thankful for my experience in polygamy. I know that I am obliged to live humble if I enjoy the spirit of the Lord." Nephi Ward, Relief Society Minutes, January 15, 1870.

64. Robert D. Warwood, *Warwood Family Genealogy*, 2 vols. (St. Paul, Minn.: Richard Warwood Family Corporation, 1979), 2:141–61. 66. See Edwin Harley's AFN 29K7-HO.

65. Edwin Harley, Diaries, January 7, 1878, Church History Library, The Church of Jesus Christ of Latter-day Saints, Salt Lake City. See also Harley's AFN 29K7-HO.

66. Harley, Diaries, October 5, 1884. See also Clyde R. Carter, "Life History of Margaret Harley Hinckley," in *The Life and Family of Ira Nathaniel Hinckley*, comp. Arden and Lorraine Ashton (Salt Lake City: The Alonzo A. Hinckley Family Organization, 2000), 138–46.

67. This is a question that will be answered much more fully in our forthcoming book, *Twelve Mormon Homes Revisited: New Views of Elizabeth Kane's 1872–73 Journey through Polygamous Utah*. In addition, Bennion has prepared for a forthcoming atlas of Mormon history, to be published by BYU Studies, a

four-page map-essay that depicts and analyzes the incidence of plural marriage in fifty Mormon towns between the Bear Lake region and the Utah–Nevada border. All of the Kanes' twelve Mormon towns appear on that map. The figures given for Fillmore, Bellevue, St. George, and Scipio are taken from that map-essay and were calculated in the same way we compiled the appendix for Nephi. For a more detailed analysis of plural marriage in St. George, see Lowell C. Bennion, "A Bird's-eye View of Erastus Snow's St. George, Utah," Juanita Brooks Lecture Series (St. George, Utah: Dixie State College, 2006).

68. Kane, *Twelve Mormon Homes*, 54.

69. See the case studies of two particular towns, Kathryn M. Daynes, *More Wives Than One: Transformation of the Mormon Marriage System, 1840–1910* (Urbana: University of Illinois Press, 2001), 91–137; and Bennion, Carter, and Morrell, *Polygamy in Lorenzo Snow's Brigham City*.

70. For an illustration of how the prevalence of polygamy helped create and maintain power relations in a Mormon community, see Bennion, Carter, and Morrell, *Polygamy in Lorenzo Snow's Brigham City*, 17–31.

71. See Eugene D. Genovese, *The World the Slaveholders Made* (New York: Pantheon Books, 1969); and William R. Taylor, *Cavalier and Yankee: The Old South and American National Character* (New York: George Braziller, 1961).

72. Kane, *Gentile Account*, 177–79.

73. Elizabeth W. Kane to Senator Cameron, December/January 1873.

74. For the best analysis of the Kanes' "Anti-Anti-Polygamy" efforts, see Grow, "*Liberty to the Downtrodden*," 257–81.

75. George Q. Cannon to Thomas L. Kane, March 9, 1874, Kane Collection.

"My Dear Friend"
The Friendship and Correspondence of Brigham Young and Thomas L. Kane

David J. Whittaker

Living as we do in an age of electronic communications, with text messaging, emails, and cell phones, it may be difficult for us to imagine a world of personal relationships that required careful attention to the realities of time and space in the creation and sharing of public as well as private information. During much of the nineteenth century, it could take weeks or months for a letter to travel to its intended recipient—and there was the chance it might not get there at all or that it might be read by persons other than the addressee. Even those living in peaceful times and in stable communities could experience these problems; and if we consider the effects of religious and political tensions, mass movements of populations, and the roughness of the western frontier compounded by such factors as the level of the relationship between those communicating, the state of the postal service in the area, and the cost of mailing a letter, we can begin to sense the problems of communication. Unlike emailing today, the speed of which can easily trivialize the message being sent, correspondence in earlier times was more focused and thus generally more thoughtful.

Not all letters are of the same value, of course. But how much poorer would we be if we lacked the treasure trove of the John Adams–Thomas Jefferson correspondence? By reading their letters, thoughtful essays by those who were present "at the creation" of the United States, we are invited into a conversation between two great minds who contributed to its founding. Their correspondence constitutes a journal of their lives and reveals their concerns, their friendship (even under stress), and their great love for their lives' work. In a letter to Robert Walsh in 1823, Jefferson wrote, "The letters of a person, especially of one whose business has been chiefly transacted by letters, form the only full and genuine journal of his life."[1]

One could just as easily think of William W. Phelps and his wife Sally, neither of whom seems to have kept a journal, but whose letters, published in 1993 in *BYU Studies,* give us an important window into the formative years of Mormonism. William seems to have sensed this, counseling his wife to keep his letters safe, as he planned "to make a book of them." Presumably, this book would constitute a published record of his life.[2] Likewise, several years ago, Dean Jessee gathered the letters sent between Brigham Young and his sons and published them—these letters are some of the few documents that reveal the more private side of President Young in his role as a father, a role he considered the most important of all his many responsibilities. These letters allow us to see Young counseling his sons on their missionary work, their reading choices, and their schooling experiences, and the documents also reveal the sons' expressions of love and appreciation to their father. To read such letters is to be invited into a personal conversation that continues to teach us many years after they were written.[3]

When Joseph Smith was murdered in June 1844, it was Brigham Young and the Quorum of the Twelve Apostles who directed the Latter-day Saint exodus from Nauvoo and then their westward journey to the Salt Lake Valley. Until his death in August 1877, President Young served as the prophet and president of the Church, guiding its growth and development through colonization, immigration, and settlement in the American West, as well as the expansion of missionary work throughout the world.[4] Much of Young's leadership was directed through his extensive correspondence, surviving today in a large number of letter books maintained by his scribes and clerks. While most of the correspondence was with Church leaders and members, there are also letters to non-Mormons. Particularly valuable are the letters he exchanged with Thomas Leiper Kane, a man who became a close friend and confidant of President Young.

It was during the critical time when the Mormon exiles were temporarily settled in the Missouri River Valley that Thomas L. Kane first met Brigham Young. In January and February 1846, Kane had read accounts in the Philadelphia newspapers of the forced exile of the Mormons from their homes in western Illinois. Shortly after the United States declared war against Mexico in May, Kane sought out Mormon leaders in Philadelphia, first meeting Jesse C. Little, who gave Kane the latest information on the Mormons and their plight. Kane obtained letters of introduction to Mormon leaders from Little, met with President James K. Polk to obtain his counsel and assurances, and then headed west, where he eventually assisted with the call of the Mormon Battalion, helped the Mormons obtain governmental permission to reside temporarily on Indian lands, and began his lifelong friendship with Young and other Mormon leaders.

FIG. 1. Thomas L. Kane in his Civil War uniform, c. 1861–64. Because of the disruptions of the Civil War and Kane's military activities, almost no letters were exchanged between Brigham Young and Thomas Kane during this time. L. Tom Perry Special Collections, Harold B. Lee Library, Brigham Young University.

During his life, Kane was active in the antislavery movement, worked with the Underground Railroad, and fought for the Union Army in the American Civil War (fig. 1), leading a group of western Pennsylvania sharpshooters called the "Bucktails" and fighting at Gettysburg (fig. 2). After the war, he became involved in land development in northwestern Pennsylvania and was a developer of Kane, Pennsylvania (fig. 3). He also involved himself in prison and education reforms, helped establish a medical school, served as the first president of the Pennsylvania Board of State Charities, and had a role in organizing the New York, Lake Erie, and Western Coal Railroad Company among other social and economic institutions.[5] But it was the Mormon connection that was the major thread that ran through his life—and his friendship with Brigham Young was a significant part of that tapestry.

When they first met in 1846, Young was forty-five and Kane was twenty-two. Kane was single and determined to remain a bachelor; Young had already entered into plural marriage—at the time of Joseph Smith's death in June 1844, Young had married four plural wives (in addition to his original wife, Mary Ann), and the number had increased to at least twelve (and in addition he had already been "sealed" to about eighteen

FIG. 2. Members of the Bucktail regiment at a reunion, c. 1884. These men and their wives gathered outside the Kane chapel in Kane, Pennsylvania. Even though Kane had passed away, the group included his bust located under the flag in this photograph. Elizabeth is standing to the left of Thomas's bust. Thomas is buried beneath the flag. L. Tom Perry Special Collections, Harold B. Lee Library, Brigham Young University.

other women) by February 1846, when the Mormons began their exodus from Nauvoo.[6] Both Kane and Young stood about 5′6″ tall; Kane was more frail and thin (weighing at most 110 pounds), but both would struggle with various health problems throughout their lives.[7]

The Young–Kane Correspondence

The Brigham Young–Thomas L. Kane letters are an important source for understanding both men, as well as various aspects of early Latter-day Saint and American history. They also provide a window into one of those rare, enduring friendships that help reveal the times in which the writers lived.[8] There are about 125 known letters exchanged between them, beginning the year they met in 1846 and extending to 1877, the year Young died.[9] The number of letters averaged three or four per year, with a few spikes, usually during times of crisis: for example, twenty-two letters were exchanged in 1858; eleven in 1861; and nine in 1871. The letters vary in length, from short, one-page notes to letters of nine or more pages of detailed information. Kane's letters could be addressed to the First Presidency or to Brigham Young alone, and Young's could be from the First Presidency or just from himself. Not all of the letters are extant;

FIG. 3. The Kanes' large home in Kane, Pennsylvania, constructed 1863–65, burned, in March 1896. L. Tom Perry Special Collections, Harold B. Lee Library, Brigham Young University.

existing letters refer to other letters (some in cipher) that have been lost. Sometimes information was conveyed orally between Kane and Young by various individual Mormons who were going on trips east or west. No complete records were kept of the times Young and Kane met privately to talk in 1846, 1858, and 1872–73; for these meetings we have to use collateral sources. Both men used scribes (Young more than Kane), and Young was more careful in keeping copies of the correspondence he sent, even preserving the drafts of some of his letters. Kane also sent letters to other Mormon leaders and received correspondence from them, revealing the depth and breadth of his friendship with the Mormons.

Both Young and Kane lived through some of the most critical times in both American and Mormon history. They experienced the political and economic convulsions of Jacksonian democracy, a war with Mexico, the movement of the American population into the West (impelled even farther by the discovery of gold in what would become the state of California), and the growing division of the country into factions over slavery and western expansion that led to a cataclysmic civil war in 1861. Neither individual sat on the sidelines of history but, rather, chose to lead and influence the course of events. Kane found his calling in social reform and in defending the underdog, although he could and did mix his Christian charity with personal aggrandizement; Young found in Mormonism all he wanted and by the 1840s was emerging as a major leader in The Church of Jesus Christ of Latter-day Saints.[10]

Meeting the Mormons in 1846

In July 1846, before Thomas Kane had met Brigham Young, Kane and Henry G. Boyle took a walkabout near some temporary Mormon settlements in Iowa. Through an experience that occurred during this walk and that was recounted in 1882 by Boyle, we are given a glimpse into the deeper feelings Kane would develop for the Latter-day Saints, feelings that he seems to have carried throughout his life and that permeated his correspondence with President Young.

Boyle recalled the two of them

> following a narrow path through a thicket of undergrowth, [when] we came suddenly within a few feet of a man who had just commenced to pray. As we wore on our feet Indian moccasins, we made no perceptible noise, and the man evidently thought himself alone and praying in secret. At the time, I was in the path just in the rear of the Colonel, who, on hearing the beginning of the man's supplication, halted, and, in doing so, turned half around, with his face in the bright light of the full moon, and in such a position that every feature was plain to my view.

Boyle went on:

> I never listened to such a prayer, so contrite, so earnest and fervent, and so full of inspiration. We had involuntarily taken off our hats as though we were in a sacred presence. I never can forget my feelings on that occasion. Neither can I describe them, and yet the Colonel was more deeply affected than I was. As he stood there I could see the tears falling fast from his face, while his bosom swelled with the fullness of his emotions. And for some time after the man had arisen from his knees and walked away towards his encampment, the Colonel sobbed like a child and could not trust himself to utter a word. When, finally, he did get control of his feelings, his first words were, "I am satisfied; your people are solemnly and terribly in earnest."[11]

Within a week, Kane was introduced to Young. Three years later, Kane would remind his Mormon friends how powerful an impact his first few weeks with the Mormons had on him:

> I believe that there is a crisis in the life of every man, when he is called upon to decide seriously and permanently if he will die unto sin [or] live unto righteousness, and that, till he has gone through this, he cannot fit himself for the inheritance of his higher humanity, and become truly pure and truly strong, "to do the work of God persevering unto the end" without endorsing the cant of preachers either. I believe that Providence brings about these crises for all of us, by events in our lives which are the evangelists to us of preparation and admonition. Such an event, I believe too, was my visit to you. I had had many disregarded hints and warnings before, but it was the spectacle of your noble self denial and suffering for conscience sake, first made a truly serious and abiding impression upon my mind, commanding me to note that there was something higher and better than the pursuit of the interests of earthly life.[12]

Young was also impressed with their first interactions. In a letter of recommendation of Kane for Almon Babbitt and others on the East Coast in September 1846, Young recalled Kane's visit to the Mormon camps:

> You will receive this from the hand of Colonel Thomas L. Kane, whom we would introduce to you, as a solder, a gentleman, a philanthropist, personal friend of President Polk, and the son of Judge Kane of Philadelphia. Colonel Kane came among us at the time Mr. Little was here, whose acquaintance he formed in Washington, and by whom he became enlisting in the sufferings of the Saints, and came on to form their acquaintance & learn their prospects. Not long after his arrival he was seized with a fever, and has mostly been confined to the present time. We are happy to say to you that our acquaintance with Col Kane has been very pleasant, and interesting, and we trust an endless friendship exists between us.[13]

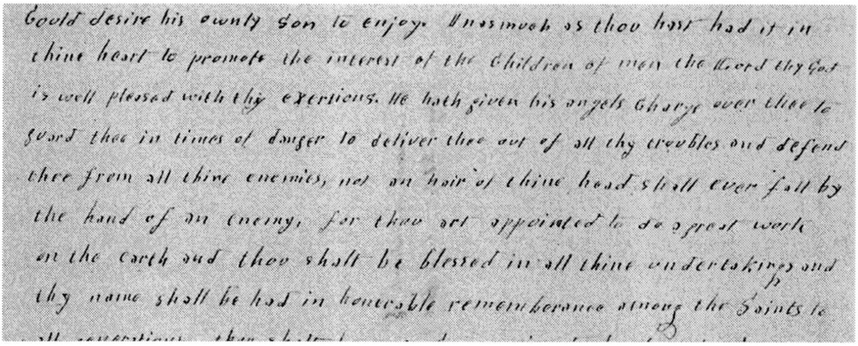
Gould desire his ownly son to enjoy. Inasmuch as thou hast had it in
thine heart to promote the interest of the Children of men the Lord thy God
is well pleased with thy exertions. He hath given his angels Charge over thee to
guard thee in times of danger to deliver thee out of all thy troubles and defend
thee from all thine enemies, not an hair of thine head shall ever fall by
the hand of an enemy, for thou art appointed to do a great work
on the earth and thou shalt be blessed in all thine undertakings and
thy name shall be had in honorable rememberance among the Saints to

FIG. 4. Detail of Thomas L. Kane's patriarchal blessing, given by John Smith, on September 7, 1846, and recorded by Wilford Woodruff. L. Tom Perry Special Collections, Harold B. Lee Library, Brigham Young University.

On the same day this letter was written, Church Patriarch John Smith pronounced a patriarchal blessing (fig. 4) upon Kane. It was given at Cutler's Park, Council Bluffs, and read, in part:

> Inasmuch as thou hast had it in thine heart to promote the interest of the children of men[,] the Lord thy God is well pleased with thy exertions. He hath given his angels charge over thee to guard thee in times of danger to deliver thee out of all thy troubles and defend thee from all thine enemies, not an hair of thine head shall ever fall by the hand of an enemy, for thou art appointed to do a great work on the earth and thou shalt be blessed in all thine undertakings and thy name shall be had in honorable rememberance [*sic*] among the Saints to all generations; thou shalt have a companion to comfort thy heart, to sustain thee under all thy trials. Thou shalt raise up sons and daughters that shall be esteemed as the excellent of the earth.[14]

It is hard to know what Kane thought about the blessing at the time it was pronounced, but the fact that he preserved a copy in his papers and referred to it in a number of letters suggests its importance to him. In fall 1850, Kane wrote to Young, "If I can lighten my tasks, a little ease and attention to health, I am sure, will very probably restore me permanently, and may even invite for me all the Blessings my good old friend the Patriarch invoked upon my head."[15] In another letter dated February 19, 1851, Kane recalled, "My valued ancient friend Mr. Smith gave me a blessing at the Omaha Camp that was full of kind and hopeful meaning," and then he asked if the blessing was "still to hold?"[16] Young conferred with Patriarch Smith and assured Kane that "it shall hold."[17] Kane had a special place in his heart for the old Patriarch, and Young reported in January 1854, "Your old friend the Patriarch, is also slowly sinking away."[18] He would die in

May. In July 1855, Kane wrote to President Young, expressing his feelings of sadness at the death of John Smith, but announcing that he had just become the father of a new baby daughter, as the Patriarch had promised him in the blessing.[19]

Years later, while in St. George with Brigham Young in 1873, William G. Perkins, the local patriarch, pronounced another blessing on Thomas Kane. At the same time, Thomas's wife, Elizabeth Wood Kane, received her own blessing. She remained skeptical about Mormonism and recorded in her journal her thoughts about the blessings: "The blessing was somewhat prophetical, and so far as it was did not coincide with one given K. long ago by the old patriarch John Smith, which has been curiously fulfilled so far, strange to say."[20]

In addition to assisting the Mormons in getting permission to settle on Indian lands for winter 1846–47 and obtaining certificates of the Mormon's good behavior when dealing with the Native Americans, Kane helped convince Mormon leaders they could trust President Polk's offer of financial help for those men (and thus the larger Church) who enlisted in the U.S. Army for service in the Mexican War. Kane worked with Captain James Allen in the recruitment efforts, even staying in Allen's tent for a short time. Here was the beginning of what would become a familiar pattern: Kane would play the role of the middleman—softening perceptions, defusing tense situations, and helping the Mormons defend themselves before a growing national audience. These would also be the major themes in his correspondence with Young.

Kane would return regularly in his memory and in his written letters to the events of 1846 and the care the Latter-day Saints gave him during his illness. By 1850, he had so identified the Mormon cause as his own that he wrote to Mormon leaders assuring them that he was their friend and that he would stand as their metaphorical second in any "affair of honor":

> It happened that the personal assaults upon myself made your cause become so indentified with my own that your vindication became my own defence and as "partners in iniquity" (to quote one particular blackguard of those times) we had to stand or fall together. This probation it is, that has made me _feel_ our brotherhood, and taught me, in the nearly four years, that have elapsed since I left the Camp where your kind nursing saved my life, to know from the heart, that I Iove you, and that you love me in turn.[21]

Kane further reported that he had altered his will, requesting that upon his death (figs. 5 and 6), the Mormons would "receive my heart to be deposited in the Temple of your Salt Lake City, that, after death, it may

Death of General Thos. L. Kane

[*Obituary printed in the* Deseret News, *January 2, 1884, page 6, likely written by George Q. Cannon.*]

THE very large majority of Utah's people will be pained to learn of the death of their esteemed and valiant friend, General Thomas L. Kane, which took place this morning at his home in Philadelphia. The sad news came by telegram to Hon. Geo. Q. Cannon. Yesterday he received a dispatch stating the General was "ill with pneumonia; very little hope, to morrow will decide." To-day the following was received:
PHILADELPHIA, Pa.,
8:29 a. m. Dec. 26, 1882.
Hon. George Q. Cannon:
Your friend died quietly at half past three, this morning.
ELISHA K. KANE [son of Thomas and Elizabeth].

To this the annexed reply was telegraphed at once:
I am stunned by this sad event so unexpected. President Taylor joins me in expressing the profoundest sympathy for your mother and the family in your bereavement. Thousands of hearts in this Territory will be filled with grief at the news of the departure of so devoted and steadfast a friend. At what time will the funeral take place?
GEORGE Q. CANNON.

There is no man outside of Utah who holds a warmer place in the hearts of the "Mormon" people than the hero who has just departed. The exact date of his birth we are not able to give at present. He was about sixty years of age, and was born in Philadelphia. His father was the celebrated Judge John Kent Kane, and his ancestors on both sides were illustrous [sic]. The family name of Kent came from Chancellor Kent, notable in the annals of jurisprudence, and the Van Renssellaers, to whom he was related on the mother's side, are well known to fame and cut a prominent figure in American history. His brother Dr. Elisha Kent Kane, after whom his son is named, stands prominent among the great men of the age now departed; as an explorer, a surgeon and a scientist he occupies a proud position in the estimation of the well informed in all the civilized world.

Our esteemed friend partook in an eminent degree of the qualities which shone so brightly in his illustrious relatives. His early days were spent in Philadelphia under the influence of the learned judge, his father, and to complete his education he was sent to England and France, where he spent several years, and the latter part of that time served as Secretary of the Legation at Paris. He then returned home and acted as clerk of the court in which his father presided, took an active part in politics, but declined the official career which was often opened to him. He was a prominent worker in the charitable associations of his state, and was noted for his kindness of heart and moral and physical courage.

His sympathies were powerfully enlisted in the "Mormon" cause when the news of the expulsion from Nauvoo became a subject of public interest. How he interested himself with President Polk and the Administration in company with Colonel Jesse C. Little, when the "Mormons" were seeking aid to cross the Great American Desert to the Pacific slope; how he folowed [sic] them to the frontier when the Mormon Battalion was mustered into service—taking the very strength out of the "Mormon" camp that was needed on the journey across the great plains—how he championed the cause of the afflicted people in the lecture halls and assemblies of the chief cities; how he interposed on behalf of this maligned people when, through false representations, an army was sent here to destroy them, how he crossed the isthmus and came up from the south at the solicitation of Prest. Buchanan, traveling incognito and passing through great perils and privations and many dangers; how he explained the facts to the General Government and procured the Commission which came here and found that the reports on which the army were sent here were groundless; how in many ways he befriended an unpopular people and manfully stood up against immense odds for their rights, are incidents in his career which are familiar to all who are acquainted with "Mormon" history.

When the war of the rebellion broke out he enlisted on the side of the Union, and commanded the Pennsylvania "Bucktails," performing deeds of valor which proved him as brave in the battlefield as in fighting for the right by tongue and pen. He was dangerously wounded, and for some time after his partial recovery went about on crutches, but in a subsequent visit to Utah recovered his health and threw away his wooden supports. For his prowess in the war he was breveted Major General, a

FIG. 5. Thomas L. Kane, postmortem photograph, December 1883. It was common in the late nineteenth century to take photographs of the deceased. L. Tom Perry Special Collections, Harold B. Lee Library, Brigham Young University.

promotion which he richly deserved. He was practically without fear, and in the disputes that arose over the so-called "Mormon war" he challenged General Albert Sydney Johnson [sic] to mortal combat.

Gen. Kane was small in stature but possessed a great and magnanimous soul. He was a brilliant writer and an impressive speaker. His views of all public matters and religious and philosophical principles were broad and strongly marked, and the qualities of the statesman, the warrior, the independent thinker, the poetic writer and the generous philanthropist were thoroughly established in his character.

In his labors of love for the unfortunate he has been ably supported by his talented and benevolent wife, who still figures prominently in the great charitable institutions of the country, and whom he has left with three sons and a daughter to honor his name and revere his memory. We condole with the bereaved, and express the sentiments of the people of Utah in imploring the divine influence for the comfort of those who mourn, and in saying, blest be the name of Thomas L. Kane through all generations, and may the flowers of peace bloom over his grave, and the rest of the righteous be his for ever!

FIG. 6. Thomas L. Kane's tombstone, outside Kane Chapel, Kane, Pennsylvania. L. Tom Perry Special Collections, Harold B. Lee Library, Brigham Young University.

repose, where in metaphor at least it often was when living."²² Kane wrote in February 1851:

> For you—I need not name you—who met me on the Prairie, you all of you who helped me, nursed me, and I know loved me as much as I bore you love in return—I avow I must always entertain a different kind of attachment than for others; but all the rest of you I wish to regard also as friends entitled to my best wishes and efforts always and always to be presumed by me united and worthy until the contrary be intrusively shown. I wish to work with you and for you, with all of you, and for <u>all</u> of you.²³

On his way home to Philadelphia from the Mormon camps in 1846, he visited Nauvoo, Illinois, which by then was almost a ghost town. Kane wrote to Brigham Young from Nauvoo on September 22, 1846; "I am getting to believe more and more every day as my strength returns that I am spared by God for the labour of doing you justice; but, if I am deceived, comfort yourself and your people, with the knowledge that my sickness in your midst has touched the chords of noble feeling in a brave heart."²⁴

After Kane returned home to continue his defense of the Mormons, he realized it was "next to impossible to do much for you before the public opinion was corrected" and concluded, "Outcasts you may be; but if I should turn the tide at last, believe me, nothing will give me more honest gratification than my right thereout [sic] to know myself your friend."²⁵

Kane's haunting description of Nauvoo was an important part of his 1850 address to the Historical Society of Pennsylvania. Published as *The Mormons: A Discourse Delivered before the Historical Society of Pennsylvania, March 26, 1850* (fig. 7), the address was distributed to members of Congress, various newspaper editors, and to other influential people in the country. When it raised questions about Mormon beliefs, Kane soon reissued it with some supplementary material that attempted to address these questions. Mormons also reprinted the discourse in their newspapers, first in the *Frontier Guardian* and then in other venues. The work was the first short history of the Latter-day Saints read by either Mormons or non-Mormons, and it helped shape Mormon self-understanding. For literary effect, the work reversed the actual chronology of Kane's visit to Nauvoo, beginning first with his visit to the vacant city and then moving west to meet the Mormons, when, in fact, he visited Nauvoo on his way home from assisting them.²⁶

Through *The Mormons* and in his many other public relations efforts, Kane was helping to create the image of the Mormons as a suffering and downtrodden people, an image that remains a powerful factor in Mormon historiography even into the twenty-first century. Kane also was the first to publicly tell the story of the miracle of the seagulls in early Utah history,

FIG. 7. Title page from Thomas L. Kane's 1850 pamphlet, *The Mormons*. On March 26, 1850, Kane gave an address on the Mormons to the Historical Society of Pennsylvania. An expanded version was published in pamphlet form and soon sold out, requiring a second printing in July 1850. The second printing contained a postscript in which Kane further defended the beliefs and character of the Latter-day Saints. This publication was an effective part of Kane's public relations efforts on behalf of the Mormons. L. Tom Perry Special Collections, Harold B. Lee Library, Brigham Young University.

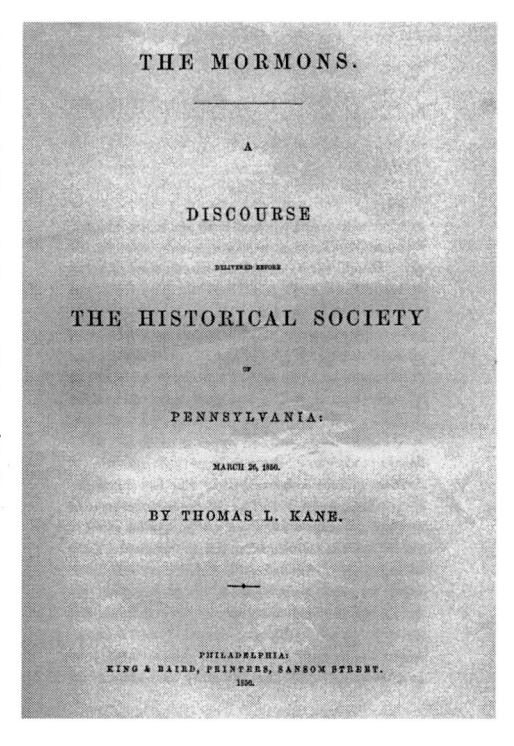

a story he received secondhand, probably from Joseph Young via a letter from William Appleby (fig. 8).

Because of Kane's genuine affection for the Mormons, his home in Philadelphia was a welcome stop for Mormons traveling in the area, including the regular visits of the Utah territorial delegates, with whom Kane would counsel on various matters relating to the Mormons. Many of Kane's Mormon visitors would hand-deliver letters to Kane from Young and also take notes for Young back with them to Utah.[27]

All of his activities in behalf of the Mormons, and especially his close friendship with Brigham Young, led a number of writers to wonder if Thomas Kane was indeed a secret member of The Church of Jesus Christ of Latter-day Saints. Had Thomas, they suggested, been baptized into the Church in 1846? In a 1906 letter to a Reverend Buckley, Elizabeth Kane responded to Buckley's discussion of her husband's relationship to the Mormons in a forthcoming book. She told of her husband's visit to the Mormon camps in 1846 in western Iowa and his serious illness there:

> He broke down while they were still on the Platte in "Misery Bottom," with the malarial fever, and "black canker," from whose consequences

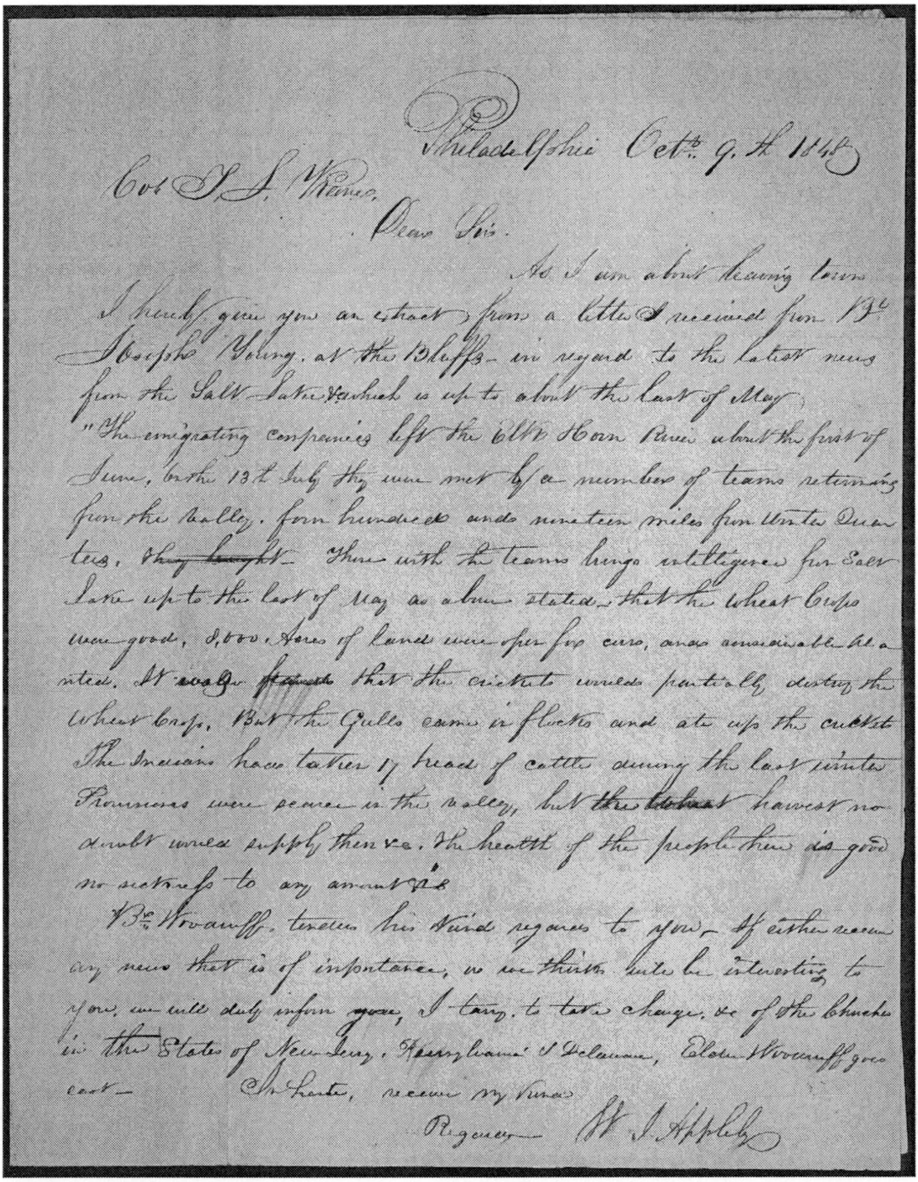

Philadelphia Oct. 9th 1848

Col T. L. Kane

Dear Sir.

As I am about leaving town I hereby give you an extract from a letter I received from Br. Joseph Young at the Bluffs in regard to the latest news from the Salt Lake & which is up to about the last of May

"The emigrating companies left the Elk Horn River about the first of June, on the 13th July they were met by a number of teams returning from the Valley, four hundred and nineteen miles from Winter Quarters. ~~they brought~~ These with the teams brings intelligence from Salt Lake up to the last of May as above stated, that the Wheat Crops were good, 5,000 Acres of land were open for corn, and considerable cultivated. It was ~~feared~~ that the crickets would partially destroy the Wheat Crops, But the Gulls came in flocks and ate up the crickets The Indians have taken 17 head of cattle during the last winter Provisions were scarce in the valley, but the ~~wheat~~ harvest no doubt would supply them &c. The health of the people there is good no sickness to any amount &c"

Br. Woodruff tenders his kind regards to you. If either receive any news that is of importance, or we think would be interesting to you, we will duly inform ~~you~~, I tarry to take charge &c of the Churches in the States of New Jersey, Pennsylvania & Delaware, Elder Woodruff goes east —

In haste, receive my kind

Regards — W. I. Appleby

Fig. 8. William I. Appleby to Thomas L. Kane, October 9, 1848. Here, Appleby, then the leading Church official on the East Coast, reports information obtained from Joseph Young (who was reporting it from a third party) regarding seagulls attacking crickets that had been threatening the Mormons' crops in the Salt Lake Valley. This information, probably combined with other sources, encouraged Kane to discuss this famous episode with great literary flare in his 1850 publication titled *The Mormons.* For many readers, it was their first knowledge of what came to be understood as a miracle in Mormon pioneering history. L. Tom Perry Special Collections, Harold B. Lee Library, Brigham Young University.

he never wholly recovered. He owed his life to the tender care and nursing that he received from the Mormons. He was particularly grateful to Brigham Young; and throughout the rest of his life he showed his gratitude to the Mormons and his pity for that people at the cost of obloquy [disgrace or shame] cast upon him by his dearest friends, and at the risk of his life. But gratitude and pity were his sole incentives to all he did. It is perfectly true, as stated by Linn, that Colonel Kane was baptised [sic], but it was when he was believed to be dying. He was delirious and entirely unconscious of what they were about. They hollowed out a log, filled it with water from the Platte and put him in. The shock aroused him, and cooled the fever. Probably it did him good physically, but I never heard any Mormon claim that it did him spiritual good to his own knowledge. I have no doubt that they deemed it efficacious to salvation, however, and did it from the purest motives.[28]

Since Elizabeth was not there, she must have heard some of the details from Thomas. The details are good enough to suggest a basic accuracy of the account. But what she seems to be describing is not the normal Mormon priesthood ordinance, or ritual, of baptism by immersion for entrance into Church membership. It is not the practice of Latter-day Saints to baptize "delirious" or "unconscious" people. But it is possible that she is describing the early Mormon practice of baptism for the restoration of health.[29]

If Kane had been secretly baptized, Young, of all people, would have known. An examination of their correspondence reveals the improbability of the rumor. In 1858, following Kane's peacemaking efforts in Utah, President Young wrote to him, "My Dear and Tried Friend:"

Though our acquaintance from its commencement, which now dates from many years past, has ever been marked by that frank interchange of views and feelings which should ever characterize the communications of those who have the welfare of mankind at heart, irrespective of sect or party, as I am well assured by a long and intimate acquaintance, is a feeling signally shared by yourself in common with your best friends; yet, so far as I can call to mind I do not remember to have ever, either in correspondence, or in familiar conversation, except, perhaps, by a casual and unpursued remark, alluded to matters of religious belief, as entertained by myself and others who are commonly called "Mormons," nor do I remember that you have ever overstepped the most guarded reserve on this subject in all your communications with me. So invariably and persistently has this peculiarity marked our friendly and free interchanges of views, upon policy and general topics, that I have at times imagined, and still am prone to imagine, that you are more or less inclined to scepticism even upon many points commonly received by the religious world.

Young went on to invite Kane to have a frank discussion of Mormon religious beliefs, hardly an invitation to someone who had been secretly baptized twelve years earlier.[30] Young was even more direct in 1864, "You are doubtless aware that, as heretofore, we should be much pleased to have you embrace the Gospel we profess and are striving to obey, and doubt not but what you will do so in the Spirit world, if you do not in this time."[31]

Major Themes of the Letters

A major topic of the Young and Kane correspondence was politics—especially affairs in Utah, the Mormon quest for statehood, and the growing national sentiment against the Mormons. Thus, their letters contain reports and concerns as well as strategies for dealing with these matters. Because Kane personally knew several U.S. presidents (especially Polk, Fillmore, Buchannan, and Grant), various cabinet members, and other important public figures, like Horace Greeley, Kane's relationships were vital to keeping the Mormons informed of the national mood. Ulysses S. Grant even stayed with the Kanes in 1869 while he was president. (Elizabeth left a manuscript account of that visit, which the BYU Library now owns.)

Before Utah became a state, its colony-like status meant that most of its key leaders would be appointed in Washington rather than elected locally, and that most of these officials would be strangers, if not enemies, to the Latter-day Saints. Thus, a key theme of the correspondence was discussion of federally appointed officials: who they were and how they behaved once they arrived in Utah.[32] Kane also advised the Mormons as they strove to attain statehood status, although this did not come until 1896, after both Young and Kane were gone from the scene.[33] The Mormons, in turn, kept Kane apprised of the great possibilities of investment and the potential for the development of lands in the West, a topic that had been on Kane's mind from the very beginning of his association with the Mormons.[34]

By July 1850, Kane thought he was finished in the battle for the Mormon reputation, that "there is nothing more left to do than scatter here or there a routed squad or two, and bury the dead upon the field." He continued:

> I believe that Providence brings about these crises for all of us, by events in our lives which are the evangelists to us of preparation and admonition. Such an event, I believe to, was my visit to you. I had had many disregarded hints and warnings before, but it was the spectacle of your noble self denial and suffering for conscience sake, first made a truly Serious and abiding impression upon my mind, commanding me to note that there was something higher and better than the pursuit of the interests of earthly life for the spirit made after the image of Deity.[35]

Renouncing all interest in politics at the time, Kane told Young that he had prepared a manuscript history of his official connection with the Mormons. In it, Kane said, he "told all," implying that there had been a conspiracy of certain government officials to do harm to the Latter-day Saints. While no copy of this history has yet been found, Kane promised he would keep it in his possession, but should an accident happen to him, the history would become the property of Young.[36]

It was a measure of the Mormon's trust in Kane that Governor Young invited him to serve as Utah's territorial delegate to Congress in 1855, an offer Kane turned down because he felt he could be of better service to the Latter-day Saints by remaining an outsider.[37]

Some Key Episodes

To read and study the extensive correspondence between Young and other Church leaders with Kane is to feel the great love and respect each side had for the other. Space limitations allow us to address only a few topics of their correspondence here.

Kane and the Mormon Practice of Plural Marriage. In 1851, the eastern press attacked Young's character and that of President Millard Fillmore for knowingly appointing such a supposedly bad character to the office of territorial governor. Kane previously had defended Young and Fillmore both in newspapers and in private correspondence.[38] In 1852, various charges by the first set of federally appointed officials to Utah were made public and published in the *New York Herald* on January 10, 1852.[39] Kane and Jedediah M. Grant met together at Kane's home in Philadelphia to prepare a response. This response eventually took the form of three letters, but initially only the first was printed in the *New York Herald*, with a fuller response subsequently published in pamphlet form (fig. 9). The federal officials charged the Mormons with a number of violations of the law, but the only charge that attracted public attention and that would increasingly become the major criticism was that the Mormons were practicing plural marriage.

The official public acknowledgement of the Mormon practice of plural marriage came in August 1852, probably in response to the growing public awareness of their marital arrangements. In a letter to Young, Grant describes how he first informed Kane of the practice.[40] Kane strongly opposed this marriage system, but he wrote to Young in October 1852:

> I wish to thank you for making my old friend Grant the bearer to me of his tidings. I ought not to conceal from you that they gave me great pain. Independent of every other consideration, my Pride in you depends so

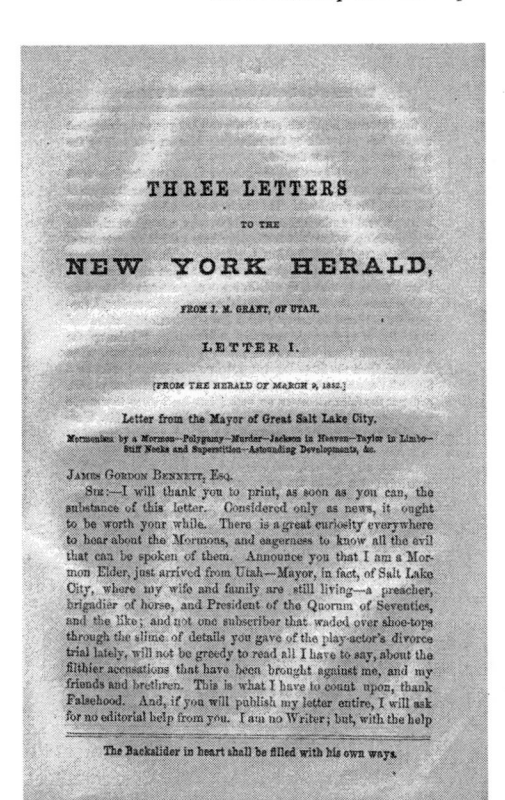

FIG. 9. Title page from *Three Letters to the New York Herald*. In May 1852, a sixty-four page pamphlet was published in New York City bearing the title *Three Letters to the New York Herald, from J. M. Grant, of Utah*. These letters and four appendixes were published in response to the charges made against the Church and its leaders by federal territorial appointees to Utah who had abandoned their assignments and returned to the East Coast in December 1851. Charging disloyalty and irregularities in the governing of Utah, Justices Lemuel G. Brandebury and Perry E. Brocchus also charged the Mormons with practicing polygamy. Thomas Kane assisted Grant in preparing these responses. L. Tom Perry Special Collections, Harold B. Lee Library, Brigham Young University.

much on your holding your position in the van of Human Progress, that I have to grieve over your favor to a custom which belongs essentially, I think, to communities in other respects behind your own.

. . . I think it my duty to give you thus distinctly my opinion that you err: I can now discharge you and myself from further notice of the subject.[41]

Young responded on May 20, 1853:

Permit me to thank you most cordially for the open, frank, and candid expression of your views and feelings, on one important truth connected with my history, and the history of friends and worlds with which I associate. Your brief, explicit, and plain expression of fear and feeling, endears you to me, more than all the Rhetoric of ages could have done. . . .

Permit me to repeat, your plainness strengthens our bonds of endearment, for my soul delights in plainness.[42]

After receiving Young's letter, Kane responded on July 18, 1853:

> I must honestly tell you how glad I have been to get [your last letter]. I was discomforted by your not answering my letter of October last. . . .
>
> It cost me a great deal. Not for nothing, old friend, do men stand by one another through good and evil report for years. Their attachment strikes so deep in time that to get it down you must tear up the earth with its roots. I could not believe I had not rightly known you; it was harder still to believe you changed, And now your letter explains [to] me everything as I would have it, and its internal evidence more than its words of text satisfies me my heartfull that you are as you say: "a lover of truth, and an undeviating friend." I never have changed, and therefore know you will understand my pledging you in your own offer. Long may we truly know each other, for so long we shall be friends![43]

Thus, in spite of the deep, personal challenge that the reality of plural marriage presented to Kane, truth between him and Young strengthened their friendship.[44]

Young and the Mountain Meadows Massacre. In 1859, U.S. Attorney General Jeremiah Black, a friend of Kane, requested through Kane a written statement from Young regarding his knowledge, as the territorial governor, of the infamous Mountain Meadows massacre, a September 1857 tragedy that occurred in southern Utah when Mormons with the assistance of a few Paiutes attacked and murdered about one hundred twenty unarmed men, women, and children.[45] Young responded to this request on December 15, 1859, with a long letter that contained one of his few expressions regarding this terrible episode:

> Neither yourself, nor any one acquainted with me, will require my assurance that, had I been apprized of the intended onslaught at the Meadows, I should have used such efforts for its prevention as the time, distance, and my influence and facilities, would have permitted. The horrifying event transpired without my knowledge, except from after report, and the recurring thought of it ever causes a shudder in my feelings.
>
> It is a subject exclusively within the province of judicial proceedings, and I have known and still prefer to know nothing touching the affair, until I in common with the people, learn the facts as they may be developed before those whose right it is to investigate and adjudicate thereupon. Colonel, you may think this a singular statement, but the facts of the massacre of men, women, and children are so shocking and crucifying to my feelings, that I have not suffered myself to hear anymore about them than the circumstances of conversation compelled.[46]

The letter also outlined what Governor Young's course had been during this critical period, suggesting why he did not pursue any specific course of action. Again, Kane was a trusted confidant to whom Young could convey his deepest feelings.

The Kanes' Visit to Utah in 1872–73. Throughout their correspondence, Young had regularly invited Kane and his family to visit Utah.[47] The Kanes finally came in 1872 and journeyed south with Brigham Young to St. George, where the group spent the winter. Both Elizabeth's journal and her later published accounts are remarkable documents of Mormon social history. Her *Twelve Mormon Homes*, published in 1874, was a compilation of letters she had sent to her family during her visit to Utah, with a focus on the Mormon communities they visited while traveling south from Salt Lake City. Elizabeth came to see the Brigham Young that her husband had known for years. Her own prejudices against plural marriage and Mormon religion ran deep, but this visit among the Mormons softened her perceptions. She was a great observer, giving us this account of their evening at the home of Bishop William Dame in Parowan in December 1872:

> When we reached the end of the day's journey, after taking off our outer garments and washing off the dust, it was the custom of our party to assemble before the fire in the sitting-room, and the leading "brothers and sisters" of the settlement would come in to pay their respects. The front door generally opened directly from the piazza into the parlor, and was always on the latch, and the circle round the fire varied constantly as the neighbors dropped in or went away. At these informal audiences, reports, complaints, and petitions were made; and I think I gathered more of the actual working of Mormonism by listening to them than from any other source. They talked away to Brigham Young about every conceivable matter, from the fluxing of an ore to the advantages of a Navajo bit, and expected him to remember every child in every cotter's family. And he really seemed to do so, and to be at home, and be rightfully deemed infallible on every subject. I think he must make fewer mistakes than most popes, from his being in such constant intercourse with his people. I noticed that he never seems uninterested, but gave an unforced attention to the person addressing him, which suggested a mind free from care. I used to fancy that he wasted a great deal of power in this way; but I soon saw that he was accumulating it. Power, I mean, at least as the driving-wheel of his people's industry.[48]

During their stay in St. George, Thomas took ill. One day, when Elizabeth had returned to their residence after a walk, she found Young in her husband's room, praying over him. She was deeply moved by this private act and told her children that she wished she could tone down her earlier harsher remarks about Young in her journals and letters home.[49]

Kane and Young discussed a variety of things during their time together in southern Utah.[50] Based on their activities and correspondence thereafter, they discussed economics, education, colonization, and the need for Young to prepare a will. These are all topics beyond our detailed concern here, but a brief examination will reveal a better understanding of their deep friendship.

Kane had an intense interest in education, and no doubt the two discussed this topic at length. After returning home, Kane wrote to Young, recalling their discussions on education:

> The most cheering, probably the most important feature of the tidings brought by Mr. Cannon is your resolve to found an Educational Institution worthy to bear your name. It is impossible to deprecate too seriously the growing practice of sending your bright youths abroad to lay the basis of the opinions of their lives on the crumbling foundations of modern Unfaith and Specialism. Why should you not inaugurate a System of education informed by your own experience of the world, embodying your own dearly earned wisdom, and calculated peradventure to endure for ages with the stamp of your originality upon it?[51]

Another important topic of conversation was the possible expansion of Mormon colonization and settlement southward, first into Arizona and then into Mexico. Kane strongly advocated both plans before they were seriously considered by the Mormons. Again, the correspondence of Young and Kane reveals this interest for both. Kane actually traveled into Mexico after his meetings with Young, hoping to establish a plantation in Coahulia,[52] and Young (fig. 10) sent Mormon settlers into Arizona initially in 1873, but more extensively along the Little Colorado River in 1876 under Lot Smith and others.[53] The Mormons first ventured into Mexico in 1875 in search of places to settle, but serious colonization did not begin until 1885.[54]

Kane had earlier counseled Young about the need to prepare a will, including the need to carefully separate his personal properties from those belonging to the Church, and the men discussed these matters in more detail in St. George. As further testimony of Young's trust in Kane, Young's son John prepared a detailed family listing containing all of Young's plural wives and children to be used as part of Young's "Last Will and Testament."[55] Young wanted Kane to prepare the will, but Kane referred him to Eli K. Price, a Philadelphia lawyer and friend of the Kane family. That such personal and private matters were discussed between them is another measure of the trust and high regard each had for the other.[56] Young wrote to Kane after their time together in Utah: "We often think of yourself, Mrs. Kane and Evan and Willie and the many pleasant hours we spent together. Your visit made impressions that will never be forgotten."[57]

FIG. 10. Brigham Young on his seventy-fifth birthday, June 1, 1876. As was common among friends separated by geographical distance, they shared photographic likenesses of themselves. The Kane Collection at BYU has a number of Brigham Young photographs given to Kane, including this one. L. Tom Perry Special Collections, Harold B. Lee Library, Brigham Young University.

Conclusion

When Thomas Kane was informed of Brigham Young's death in August 1877, he immediately made plans to journey to Utah, in part to assist with the settlement of the Brigham Young Estate. Once there, Kane assured the remaining Mormon leaders of his continued friendship and support, and he was invited by John Taylor to journey to Logan for the groundbreaking of the temple there.[58]

Young remained a consistent friend of Kane throughout his lifetime. Running throughout their correspondence are strong expressions of respect and brotherly love. Kane had planned to visit Utah as early as 1855 "and brighten up again the links of the brave chain of trusting friendship with which time has so long held us."[59] He managed to visit during the Utah War and later in 1872–73. In 1851, Kane wrote:

> It is my hope, and I am ready to say, God willing, my intention, to correspond with you freely, about your interests in this quarter of the world. . . . But now my second nights candles are burning low, on one of them sputtering over one of my ink smeared pages, suggests to me to avoid tiring you as much as myself with this long worldly letter. Write

to me in answer to this; for, even with the best intentions, I have found there is no keeping up a correspondence without some degree of mutuality. Your writings shall continue to be regarded confidential, of course . . . command me freely as of old when I can render you or yours any service. Nothing will better keep fresh my feeling in your favor.[60]

Throughout their correspondence are expressions of friendship and trust, as well as an eagerness to hear from a distant friend. In May 1852, Young expressed his thoughts: "Relying upon your generosity to excuse the tedium of this sparseness of past correspondence I bid you adieu invoking the choicest of heavens blessings in your behalf that from henceforth your health may be preserved and truth as hitherto abide with you"[61] In 1871, Young again wrote, "For my part, you have my undeviating friendship which has never abated one particle, not lessened in the measure one grain since we first became acquainted; and I can assure you that I have no more doubt of your faithfulness and integrity of heart that I have of my own."[62] A year later, in March 1872, Young penned, "Your past labors of love for us, your meditations in our interest, and your counsels to me are sweet and precious, and let me say, that when I perused your late letters, I felt in my heart, the spirit of the Gods is with the General."[63] In June 1854, Young wrote:

> I endeavor to answer in truth and friendship, even as I ever cherish you in my memory: in this spirit I formed your acquaintance, which I found you a ready sympathizer with the distressed, since when you have given ample assurances by <u>acts</u> more than words, of the deep impression then received. You then for the first time learned us as we were, and found a people, few in number, it is true, yet a people full of faith, of good works, struggling for an existence upon this earth, of whom you previously had comparatively little knowledge.[64]

When offering Kane the position of Utah territorial delegate in 1854, Young referred to the feelings of openness and honesty they had shared in their communications:

> I take it for granted that you are sufficiently acquainted with me and my course, to know that when I speak, or write, I do so in all frankness and candor, for the best interests of the people of Utah, and their friends, and the lovers of truth in all the world, and I think I am not mistaken in your feelings when I presume that you will candidly receive, weigh, and act upon my business views in this letter as proceeding from one truly your <u>friend</u>.[65]

And in 1871, following a break in their letter writing, Young again reflected on their relationship: "For my part, you have my undeviating friendship which has never abated one particle, nor lessened in the measure one grain since we first became acquainted; and I can assure you I have no more doubt of your faithfulness and integrity of heart than I have of my own."[66]

It is not always possible to understand what draws people into a circle of friendship: shared values tested in the furnace of real life, a sense of integrity felt and known between individuals, honesty and consistency in their relationship, a serious level of tolerance between them, and specific actions that gave public life to the friendship are surely at the core.[67] It was said that Young was a shrewd judge of character; the fact that Kane was one of his closest non-Mormon friends speaks strongly of this gift. Kane appeared at a critical time in Mormon history, and he remained a consistent supporter of Young and the Latter-day Saints throughout the remainder of his life. At the center of this relationship was his connection with Young. It was a friendship that only deepened with time and circumstance. Their correspondence serves as a window into a comradeship that had significant impact on both Mormon and American history.

Wilford Woodruff, who served as a clerk for Kane's 1846 patriarchal blessing, had written to Kane in 1858, providing what remains a truism in Mormon culture: "Your name will of necessity stand associated with the history of this people for years to come, whatever may be their destiny."[68] Brigham Young himself, during a personal conversation in 1858, told Kane, "Brother Thomas the Lord sent you here and he will not let you die. No you Cannot die till your work is done. I want to have your name live with the Saints to all Eternity."[69] Kane's good friend Jedediah Grant had written to him in 1852: "We can never in this world, cancel the Debt we owe you. . . . The poor Mormons will never forget Col. Kane."[70] In a quiet moment of introspection, probably feeling the weight of public opinion judging him harshly for even associating with the Mormons, Kane wrote in a journal: "Others may respect me less for being alone in the defence of a dispised and injured people—but I respect myself more."[71] These were the reflections of a true friend. On Kane's deathbed in 1883, some of his last thoughts were recorded by his wife, Elizabeth: "My mind is too heavy, but do send the sweetest message you can make up to my Mormon friends—to all, my dear, Mormon friends."[72] Had Brigham Young been alive, Thomas Kane would have no doubt directed these thoughts specifically to him.

David J. Whittaker (who can be reached by email via byustudies@byu.edu) is curator of nineteenth-century Western and Mormon manuscripts in the L. Tom Perry Special Collections at Harold B. Lee Library and is an Associate Professor of history at Brigham Young University. He was the curator of the Thomas L. Kane exhibition in the Lee Library and served as the guest editor of this publication containing the lectures that were presented as part of the exhibit.

1. Thomas Jefferson to Robert Walsh, April 5, 1823, in Dumas Malone, *Jefferson the Virginian* (Boston: Little, Brown, and Co., 1948), 127.

2. William W. Phelps to Sally Phelps, January 1836, in Bruce A. Van Orden, ed., "Writing to Zion: The William W. Phelps Kirtland Letters (1835–1836)," *BYU Studies* 33, no. 3 (1993): 578.

3. Dean C. Jessee, ed., *Letters of Brigham Young to His Sons* (Salt Lake City: Deseret Book in collaboration with the Historical Department of the Church of Jesus Christ of Latter-day Saints, 1974).

4. See Leonard J. Arrington, *Brigham Young: American Moses* (New York: Knopf, 1985).

5. See Matthew J. Grow, *"Liberty to the Downtrodden": Thomas L. Kane, Romantic Reformer* (New Haven: Yale University Press, 2009).

6. For a listing, see Arrington, *Brigham Young: American Moses*, 121. See also Jeffrey O. Johnson, "Determining and Defining 'Wife': The Brigham Young Households," *Dialogue: A Journal of Mormon Thought* 20 (Autumn 1987): 57–70. Kane would not learn of the Mormon practice of plural marriage until 1851, but in 1847, he asked Young for the details of a well-reported Boston divorce case relating to Augusta Cobb (she had become one of Young's plural wives in 1843). See Kane to Young, December 9, 1847, Brigham Young Papers, Church History Library, Church History Department, The Church of Jesus Christ of Latter-day Saints, Salt Lake City (hereafter cited as Young Papers, Church History Library). The best account of Young's family during this period is Dean C. Jessee, "Brigham Young's Family: The Wilderness Years," *BYU Studies* 19, no. 4 (1979): 474–500.

7. Grow's biography treats Kane's health issues in some detail; for Brigham Young, see Lester E. Bush Jr., "Brigham Young in Life and Death: A Medical Overview," *Journal of Mormon History* 5 (1978): 79–103.

8. One thinks of the friendships of Oliver Wendell Holmes and Harold Laski, and Samuel Johnson and James Boswell; both were relationships between older and younger men, and like Boswell, Kane wanted to interview Young and write his biography. It is interesting to speculate, given his Boswell-like relationship and interest in Young, just what kind of biography Kane would have produced had he fulfilled his wish. See further, Jeffrey O'Connell and Thomas E. O'Connell, *Friendships across Ages: Johnson and Boswell; Holmes and Laski* (Lanham, MD: Lexington Books, 2008). Writing Young's biography was a subject that was addressed in several of the letters; for example, in Kane to Young, October 12, 1871 (Young Papers, Church History Library), Kane spoke of his plans of coming out to Utah to compile materials "for the Life of Brigham Young," and in Kane to Young, October 16, 1872 (Young Papers, Church History Library), Kane announced he was coming to Utah for "daily literary work," recording Young's thoughts for the anticipated biography. Young sent Kane typescript drafts of chapters from Edward Tullidge's forthcoming *Life of Brigham Young*; this probably ended Kane's plans for such a work by himself. It is not known when Young sent this material to Kane; the biography was published in New York in 1876. The typescript of six chapters in seventy-five pages is in the Thomas L. Kane and Elizabeth W. Kane Collection, L. Tom Perry Special Collections, Harold B. Lee Library, Brigham Young University, Provo, Utah (hereafter cited as Kane Collection, Perry Special Collections).

9. The main location of these letters is the Brigham Young Papers, Church History Library, supplemented by those in the Kane Collection, Perry Special Collections. Especially useful are the typescripts of the Young-Kane correspondence prepared by Edyth J. Romney and Debbie Lilenquist in the Church History Library. Photocopies of these typescripts were made available to me by the staff of the Church History Library. There are other Kane letters located in various repositories throughout the United States, although some still remain in private hands. Much of the original Thomas L. Kane archive was gathered and organized by his wife Elizabeth, who had served as his scribe; various family descendants inherited portions of the extensive collection through the years, and they have disposed of the materials as they saw fit. The bulk of John K. Kane's papers are in possession of the American Philosophical Society in Philadelphia. Some of the Thomas Kane manuscripts and the papers of his brother Elisha Kent Kane remain in private hands.

10. For more on Brigham Young's rise to leadership, see Ronald K. Esplin, "The Emergence of Brigham Young and the Twelve to Mormon Leadership" (PhD diss., Brigham Young University, 1981; BYU Studies, 2006).

11. Henry G. Boyle, "A True Friend," *Juvenile Instructor* 17, no. 5 (March 1, 1882): 74–75.

12. Kane to First Presidency, July 11, 1850, Young Papers, Church History Library.

13. Brigham Young to Babbitt, Heywood, and Fulmer, September 7, 1846, Cutlers Park, Willard Richards, Clerk, Draft Letterbook, Church History Library, vol. 1. Some punctuation added for readability.

14. Thomas L. Kane, Patriarchal Blessing, September 7, 1846, Kane Collection, Perry Special Collections. The earliest handwritten copy is dated September 7, but others were dated September 8. In April 1853, when he was thirty-one, he married his sixteen-year-old second cousin Elizabeth Wood. The couple eventually had one daughter and three sons; see also Kane to Young, July 18, 1853, Young Papers, Church History Library. See Darcee D. Barnes, "A Biographical Study of Elizabeth D. Kane" (master's thesis, Brigham Young University, 2002).

15. Kane to Young, Fall 1850, Kane Collection, Perry Special Collections.

16. Kane to Young, February 19, 1851, Young Papers, Church History Library. In the same letter, Kane referred to 4 Nephi in the Book of Mormon, actually citing page 555 (4 Nephi 1:15 in modern editions), which refers to there being "no contention in the land," and he also referred to the "honey bee in the valley of Nimrod" from the Book of Ether (chapter 2:3 in modern editions). These lines clearly suggest Young had presented Kane with a copy of the Book of Mormon and Kane had read it carefully.

17. Young to Kane, September 15, 1851, Kane Collection, Perry Special Collections.

18. Young to Kane, January 31, 1854, Kane Collection, Perry Special Collections.

19. Kane to Young, July 10, 1855, Young Papers, Church History Library.

20. Elizabeth Kane, St. George Journal, February 11, 1873, Kane Collection, Perry Special Collections.

21. Kane to First Presidency, July 11, 1850, Young Papers, Church History Library. This personal sense of honor runs through much of Kane's life; for more

detail, see Matthew J. Grow, "'I Have Given Myself to the Devil': Thomas L. Kane and the Culture of Honor," *Utah Historical Quarterly* 73, no. 4 (2005): 346–64.

22. Kane to First Presidency, July 11, 1850, Young Papers, Church History Library; and "Last Will and Testament of Thomas L. Kane," n.d. [1850], Kane Collection, Perry Special Collections. This ought to be seen as a symbolic expression of love, reflecting the contemporary view that where one's heart is, there are his deepest feelings. In this same will, he donated his body to science. However, when Kane died in December 1883, he was buried in Kane, Pennsylvania.

23. Kane to "My Dear Friends," February 19, 1851, Young Papers, Church History Library.

24. Kane to Young, September 22, 1846, Young Papers, Church History Library. Kane was still suffering from a "disease shattered frame" when he wrote Young and included copies of John K. Kane's correspondence, presumably to keep Young informed of national concerns.

25. Kane to Young, December 2, 1846, Young Papers, Church History Library. In his December 6, 1847, letter to Kane (Young Papers, Church History Library), According to Webster's 1828 dictionary, *thereout* was an adjective, meaning "out of that or this." Kane was an educated man who rarely misspelled words. Young hoped that the Mormons could be the recipients of the same kind of assistance Americans were then offering to victims of the Irish famine, mentioning specifically that the Mormons were "a fit subject for an appeal to the American people," as Kane himself had suggested. The Kane Collection at BYU has a copy of an 1846 broadside that was just such an appeal for help, signed by a number of people in Philadelphia, including Kane.

26. For a detailed account of Kane's preparation and delivery of this address when he was very ill, see his letter to Young, Fall 1850, Kane Collection, Perry Special Collections. Young received a copy of the work in 1851 and conveyed his positive comments about it to Kane in a letter dated September 15, 1851.

27. See, for example, Kane to Young, April 28, 1854, Young Papers, Church History Library.

28. Elizabeth D. Kane, draft of letter to Rev. Dr. [James Monroe?] Buckley, March 6, 1906, Daytona, Fla., Kane Collection, Perry Special Collections, 6–7.

29. For more information as well as the sources, see David J. Whittaker, "New Sources on Old Friends: The Thomas L. Kane and Elizabeth W. Kane Collections," *Journal of Mormon History* 27, no. 1 (Spring 2000): 92–93.

30. Young to Kane, May 8, 1858, Young Papers, Church History Library. On Kane's religious views, which tended, much to Elizabeth's consternation, toward an anti-Evangelical Christianity, see Whittaker, "New Light on Old Friends," 90–94, and various comments throughout Matthew Grow's recent biography, "Liberty to the Downtrodden."

31. Young to Kane, April 29, 1864, Young Papers, Church History Library. Kane did not join the Church during his lifetime. His good Mormon friend George Q. Cannon had the vicarious ordinance work done for Kane after he died.

32. See two letters: Kane to Young, April 7, 1851, Young Papers, Church History Library (Kane's introduction of Perry E. Brocchus and Lemuel Brandeberry, newly appointed justices of the Utah Territorial Court whom Kane did not know personally); and Kane to First Presidency, July 29, 1851, Kane Collection, Perry Special Collections (Kane's defense of attacks on President Fillmore).

33. For the full story, see Ronald W. Walker, "Thomas L. Kane and Utah's Quest for Self-Government, 1846–51," *Utah Historical Quarterly* 69, no. 2 (Spring 2001): 100–119.

34. Kane's papers at BYU reveal his support for the purchase of Alaska and the development of plantations in northern Mexico (he publicly supported both subjects), as well as his own interest in the governorships of California and later Washington. Early on he encouraged the Mormons to move into Arizona and Mexico during Brigham Young's lifetime; after their meeting in St. George in 1873, Young did begin sending Mormon settlers into Arizona, but the movement of Latter-day Saints into northern Mexico came under the direction of John Taylor in the mid-1880s.

35. Kane to First Presidency, July 11, 1850, Young Papers, Church History Library. When Young responded on September 15, 1851, more realistically to this letter (which had only reached him much later), he wrote: "We rejoice, with you, that Providence spared [you], until you could rightfully 'esteem the <u>battle</u> for the Mormon reputation ended,' i.e. for the then time being, but to suppose for a moment that the General War, on 'Mormon reputation,' or Saint's Salvation, ended, or at its meridian: would be as absurd and false, as to suppose that all that shines is pure Gold. When the earth is purified by fire, it will be known whose works have been like Gold, Silver, and Precious Stone; and whose will be like wood, hay, and stubble; and until that day, the war between the Kingdom of God and the Kingdoms of the world (of Satan) will wax hotter and hotter, with occasional slight intervals of rest, in appearance only, as you have seen, but as yet there is no time for burying the dead. We drop this hint to a friend that he may not be found with his armor off, while spies attack him when asleep or he be ambushed in the rear."

36. Kane to First Presidency, July 11, 1850, Young Papers, Church History Library. There are a number of such references relating to Kane's work with the Mormons that have never surfaced, suggesting that there are additional Kane manuscripts yet to be discovered. Another aspect of Kane's own sense of paranoia was his telling Mormon leaders of high-level government conspiracies against them—opinions that undoubtedly fostered a deeper sense of mistrust of the federal government by the Latter-day Saints.

37. Young to Kane, October 30, 1854, Kane Collection, Perry Special Collections; Kane declined in a letter to Young January 5, 1855, Kane Collection, Perry Special Collections.

38. See Grow, *"Liberty to the Downtrodden,"* 86–89. Kane's letter of July 11, 1851, to President Fillmore is reprinted in B. H. Roberts, *A Comprehensive History of the Church of Jesus Christ of Latter-day Saints, Century One* (Salt Lake City: Deseret News Press, 1930), 3:538.

39. Lemuel G. Brandebury, Perry E. Brocchus, and Broughton D. Harris were the officials. Their report was republished as a twelve-page pamphlet in Liverpool [*Polygamy Revived in the West: Report of the Judges of Utah Territory to the President of the United States, on the Conduct of the Mormonites* (Liverpool: T. Brakell, 1852)], and it created a further stir in England, where the Church was having great missionary success at the time. See also Roberts, *Comprehensive History of the Church*, 3:516–44.

40. See Jedediah M. Grant to Brigham Young, December 30, 1851, in Young Papers, Church History Library. For the context of the 1852 public announcement,

see David J. Whittaker, "The Bone in the Throat: Orson Pratt and the Public Announcement of Plural Marriage," *Western Historical Quarterly* 18, no. 3 (July 1987): 293–314. The pamphlet came out under the name of Jedediah M. Grant, but the contemporary documents, especially Grant's letters to Young, reveal Kane's involvement. The publication was *Three Letters to the New York Herald, from J. M. Grant, of Utah* [New York, 1852]. The first letter appeared in the *New York Herald*, March 9, 1852. See further, Gene A. Sessions, *Mormon Thunder: A Documentary History of Jedediah Morgan Grant* (Urbana: University of Illinois Press, 1982), 100, 109–10, 264–65, with the entire pamphlet reprinted on 319–68.

41. See Kane to Young, October 17, 1852, Young Papers, Church History Library. More privately, Kane's notebooks reveal that he was deeply hurt by this knowledge, suggesting he felt as if he had just learned of a wife's infidelity. See the comments in Thomas L. Kane, November 1851–September 1852 Notebook, December 27 and 28, 1851, Kane Collection, Perry Special Collections. While in his October 17, 1852, letter Kane told Young that "you err" in this matter, Kane also reflected that the recent death of his brother seemed to draw his thoughts closer to his Mormon friends: "It seems to me that as the ties grow fewer which attach me to the world here my thought turns more frequently toward happy Deseret and my many cherished friends there."

42. Young to Kane, May 20, 1853, Kane Collection, Perry Special Collections. In this same letter, Young defended the Mormon marriage practice as protected by the U.S. Constitution under its guarantee of religious freedom. Young called the Constitution our great "Magna Charta" and declared that he would defend it "while God gives me breath, if I have to flee to Africa's Deserts for doing it."

43. Kane to Young, July 18, 1853, Young Papers, Church History Library. In this same letter, Kane informed Young of his recent marriage to Elizabeth Dennistoun Wood, writing he was "married as if on purpose to fulfill my old Patriarch friend's seemingly long ago lost prediction." Young responded with great enthusiasm on January 31, 1854 (Kane Collection, Perry Special Collections). Kane reported the birth of his first daughter in a letter of July 10, 1855 (Young Papers, Church History Library). Young responded to the news on September 30, 1855 (Kane Collection, Perry Special Collections), conveying his "warmest wishes that Heaven's choice blessings may attend your daughter during her sojourn in this time, . . . for you are more or less aware of the high estimation in which I hold children as a blessing."

44. In the same letter of July 18, 1853, Kane discussed the growing national attention to the construction of a railroad across the country. Kane asked Young if he would consider it "your policy to have the Road conducted through your Valley"? This would become another thread in their correspondence: the transcontinental railroad and western development. In Young to Kane, January 31, 1854, Kane Collection, Perry Special Collections, Young commented that both the railroad and the telegraph would be a "most natural highway" for trade and commerce.

45. The request of Jeremiah Black is mentioned in Kane to Young, July 24, 1859, Young Papers, Church History Library.

46. Young to Kane, December 15, 1859. Young included in this letter a copy of George A. Smith's letter to Young regarding the massacre, dated August 17, 1858. Both letters are in Thomas L. Kane Correspondence, Perry Special Collections.

For the full story, see Ronald W. Walker, Richard E. Turley Jr., and Glen M. Leonard, *Massacre at Mountain Meadows* (New York: Oxford University Press, 2008). As this study reveals, few Paiute Indians were involved in the planning or killing, but Mormons did try to cover their own involvement by telling others that the Indians were the guilty murderers.

47. See, for example, the following letters from Young to Kane: December 6, 1847, Young Papers, Church History Library; May 20, 1853, Kane Collection, Perry Special Collections; January 5, 1855, Kane Collection, Perry Special Collections; September 30, 1855, Kane Collection, Perry Special Collections; June 29, 1857, Young Papers, Church History Library; September 27, 1860, Kane Collection, Perry Special Collections; September 21, 1861, Young Papers, Church History Library; October 15, 1869, Young Papers, Church History Library; April 16, 1871, Kane Collection, Perry Special Collections. See also, Kane to Young, October 16, 1872, Young Papers, Church History Library (Kane writes that he is coming to Utah); and October 31, 1872, Kane Collection, Perry Special Collections (Young writes that he is glad Kane is coming to Utah, and he hopes Kane's wife and children will come, too).

48. Elizabeth Wood Kane, *Twelve Mormon Homes Visited in Succession on a Journey through Utah to Arizona*, ed. Everett L. Cooley (1874; Salt Lake City: University of Utah Library Tanner Trust Fund, 1974), 101.

49. Elizabeth Wood Kane, *A Gentile Account of Life in Utah's Dixie, 1872–73: Elizabeth Kane's St. George Journal*, ed. Norman R. Bowen (Salt Lake City: University of Utah Library Tanner Trust Fund, 1995), 167–70. The original journal is in the Kane Collection, Perry Special Collections. Elizabeth's account of a dinner in Brigham Young's home in Salt Lake City remains a wonderful description of domestic life seldom mentioned in Mormon sources. See Elizabeth Kane's letters to her daughter Harriet Kane, December 7 and 11, 1872, originals in Kane Collection, BYU.

50. George Q. Cannon was summoned to St. George by Brigham Young during this time. Cannon recorded in his journal that Kane dispensed "much valuable advice which his familiarity with public affairs and the public men of the country enabled him to do." Cannon, Journal, January 8, 1873, as cited in Matthew J. Grow, "'Liberty to the Downtrodden': Thomas L. Kane, Romantic Reformer" (PhD diss., University of Notre Dame, 2006), 623 n. 60.

51. See Kane to Young, December 4, 1873, Young Papers, Church History Library, in which Kane actually calls this school "Brigham Young University." President Young would found a number of academies throughout Mormon settlements; Brigham Young Academy in Provo was founded in 1875 and was renamed Brigham Young University in 1903.

52. See Thomas L. Kane, "Coahulia," *Proceedings of the American Philosophical Society* 16 (January 19, 1877): 561–567. Kane's trip to Mexico is detailed in his Notebook, July 31, 1873–December 1876, Kane Collection, Perry Special Collections. See also Kane to Young, May 28, 1876, Young Papers, Church History Library, in which Kane reports his contacts with Mexican officials and his plans to establish a colony in the "rich unpeopled lands of Northern Mexico." In Kane to Young, March 2, 1877, Young Papers, Church History Library, Kane discusses his project in more detail and seems to be inviting the Mormons to assist him. See also John Taylor to Kane, May 14, 1878, Kane Collection, Perry Special

Collections, in which President Taylor reveals his "complete sympathy" with the earlier plans of Brigham Young. The only question, Taylor wrote, was the matter of timing for the Mormons to establish colonies in Mexico.

53. Young to Kane, July 31, 1873, Kane Collection, Perry Special Collections, reported that the initial movement into Arizona was not successful, and that Young planned to personally lead the next group in the Mormon exploration of Arizona. In his November 16, 1873, letter (Kane Collection, Perry Special Collections), Young told Kane, "I have forgotten nothing connected with Arizona; my eye is constantly on the mark." See further, Charles S. Peterson, *Take Up Your Mission: Mormon Colonizing along the Little Colorado River, 1870–1900* (Tucson: University of Arizona Press, 1973). Peterson first called my attention to the Kane-Young plans for exploration and settlement into Arizona and then in the Sonora Valley of Mexico (5–6, 15, 17). The plans called for railroad development as well. For Kane's positive account of the plans for Mexican settlement, see Kane to Young, March 2, 1877, Young Papers, Church History Library.

54. For the larger story, see F. LaMond Tullis, *Mormons in Mexico: The Dynamics of Faith and Culture* (Logan: Utah State University Press, 1987).

55. This listing, or "Family Record," received by Kane on May 20, 1873, is in the Kane Collection, Perry Special Collections. Kane had written to Young on April 4, 1873 (Kane Collection, Perry Special Collections), that Young's estate was so complex a legal issue that its settlement would take much time: "There is scarcely a feature of your case that is not bristling with law points," he wrote. In spite of Young's efforts to address this matter, the settlement of his estate following his death in 1877 took several years. See Leonard J. Arrington, "The Settlement of the Brigham Young Estate, 1877–1879," *Pacific Historical Review* 21, no. 1 (February 1952): 1–20. Young expressed his gratitude to Kane for his advice on these matters in letters to him on May 7, 1873, and November 16, 1873 (both in Kane Collection, Perry Special Collections).

56. Drafts of Brigham Young's will and related materials are in the Kane Collection, Perry Special Collections.

57. Young to Kane, July 31, 1873, Kane Collection, Perry Special Collections.

58. The telegram to Kane informing him of Brigham Young's death, from John W. Young, George Q. Cannon, Daniel H. Wells, and Brigham Young Jr., dated August 29, 1877, is in the Kane Collection, Perry Special Collections. A note at the bottom says Kane left for Salt Lake City on September 6, 1877. Kane's account of his 1877 visit to Utah is in the Kane Collection, Perry Special Collections.

59. Kane to Young, January 5, 1855, Kane Collection, Perry Special Collections.

60. Kane to "My Dear Friends" [Brigham Young, Willard Richards, and Heber C. Kimball], February 19, 1851.

61. Young to Kane, May 29, 1852, draft letterbook, volume 1, May 27, 1852–February 27, 1853, Young Papers, Church History Library. In the same letter, Young described his recent tours of the Mormon settlements. Such local information was a regular part of Young's communications with Kane. Kane's growing interest in the plight of Native Americans was also informed by Young's occasional reports of his own interactions with the native peoples of Utah.

62. Young to Kane, April 16, 1871, Brigham Young letterbook, volume 12, September 9, 1870–May 31, 1871, Young Papers, Church History Library.

63. Young to Kane, March 5, 1872, Kane Collection, Perry Special Collections.

64. Young to Kane, June 29, 1854, draft letterbook, volume 3, November 30, 1853–August 26, 1854, Young Papers, Church History Library. Underlining in original.

65. Young to Kane, October 30, 1854, Kane Collection, Perry Special Collections. Underlining in original. Toward the end of the letter, Young thanked Kane for the kindness he had shown to the missionaries who had passed through Philadelphia, especially since such treatment was a "rare occurrence" from those "not of our faith, but as evidencing that high toned fellow feeling so indicative of upright, sympathetic magnanimity."

66. Young to Kane, April 16, 1871, Kane Collection, Perry Special Collections.

67. It was Cicero who suggested that "only those are to be judged friendships in which the characters have been strengthened and matured by age." Cited in Michel de Montaigne, "Of Friendship," in Montaigne, *The Complete Works: Essays, Travel Journal, Letters*, trans. Donald M. Frame (Stanford: Stanford University Press, 1957), 139.

68. Wilford Woodruff to Thomas L. Kane, March 4, 1858, Young Papers, Church History Library.

69. Wilford Woodruff, *Wilford Woodruff's Journal, 1833–1898, Typescript*, ed. Scott G. Kenney, 9 vols. (Midvale, Utah: Signature Books, 1984), 5:171, February 25, 1858. This had been seen in more tangible ways in Mormon history: they named their main settlement in western Iowa "Kanesville" (name later changed to Council Bluffs); in 1864 a southern Utah county was named after him; and a bronze statue of Thomas L. Kane remains on the grounds of the Utah State Capitol in Salt Lake City.

70. Jedediah M. Grant to Thomas L. Kane, May 5, 1852, Kane Collection, Perry Special Collections.

71. Undated entry, Thomas L. Kane Diary, 1858, Perry Special Collections, [5]. Underlining in original.

72. Elizabeth W. Kane to George Q. Cannon, December 30, 1883, Church History Library as cited in Leonard J. Arrington, "'In Honorable Remembrance': Thomas L. Kane's Services to the Mormons," *BYU Studies* 21, no. 4 (1981): 400–1. For details of Thomas Kane's last weeks of life, see the diary of Harriet A. Kane, December 13–27, 1883, Kane Collection, Perry Special Collections.

Matthew J. Grow. *"Liberty to the Downtrodden": Thomas L. Kane, Romantic Reformer.*
New Haven: Yale University Press, 2009

Reviewed by Charles S. Peterson

In this heartening book, Matthew J. Grow examines the life of Mormon friend Thomas L. Kane in terms of the reform impulses that propelled America during the antebellum and succeeding decades of the nineteenth century. Born to a well-situated Pennsylvania family early in the Jacksonian era, Kane reached maturity before the economic and social opportunities of the "gilded age" opened the modern era of industrial urbanism and professional specialization. Like many of his contemporaries, he was almost forced to become a reformer, a career he later integrated with the development of an upstate Pennsylvania area where his family had long-standing land interests.

Responding to shifting times as well as to contradictory aspects in his own nature, Kane was loyal to the Democratic Party until the Civil War but then became a Republican and thereafter tended in the direction of Progressive impulses without abandoning many of his earlier commitments. Throughout his life, he manifested a penchant for iconoclasm and a distaste for the moral and doctrinal limitations imposed by the country's evangelical Protestant majority. These characteristics were combined with a dated romantic idealism—including an affinity for dueling and related chivalrous and gentlemanly attitudes commonly connected with the Old South. Thus inclined, he became an avid foe of slavery and the nation's foremost defender of the Mormons. "At critical junctures, . . . notably during the Utah War and the Civil War," as Grow tells us, Kane's efforts "changed history" while his life also cast light on the world "of mid-nineteenth century reform" (xx).

Although not widely recognized, Kane occupies an important "place both in scholarship on Mormonism and in the Mormon cultural memory."

However, even the Mormon understanding of his role is lacking, owing in part to the Latter-day Saints' limited interest in "Kane's other activities and the broader world of reform culture" to which he belonged. Plumbing Kane's personal story fully for the first time, Matthew J. Grow opens a door into a broadened national context from which, to a degree, Latter-day Saints sought originally to escape and until now have not been at particular pains to work entirely into either their scholarship or folk culture (xx).

My own case may be instructive. I first became aware of Kane in 1947 when I read Joseph Fielding Smith's *Essentials in Church History* while an LDS missionary. Ten years later my master's thesis focused on Alfred Cumming's role in the Utah War of 1857–1858. Kane's efforts in the Mormon cause struck me as perplexing but of passing importance. Grow suggests that he may have been, after all, the key to the conflict's peaceable outcome. Another decade down the pike I found Kane again, this time enlarging Brigham Young's already expansive plans for colonizing Arizona. After another ten years I was part of a Bureau of Outdoor Recreation study of the Mormon Battalion Trail, where I again found the ubiquitous Kane. Yet I remained unmoved and failed to study him further.

Educated at Brigham Young University and more recently at Notre Dame University, Matthew Grow now teaches at the University of Southern Indiana, where he also directs the Center for Communal Studies. Essential to the invitation Grow offers Mormon studies is a wealth of Kane-related material, including papers long held by Kane's descendants, which—in another manifestation of the continuing Mormon interest in Kane—became available at BYU in 2000. Included are "thousands of letters, manuscripts of published and unpublished writings, legal and business records," and the extensive journals of his wife, Elizabeth, who survived him by twenty-six years (xx). Other important Kane collections are at the American Philosophical Society, Yale University, Stanford University, the University of Michigan, the Historical Society of Pennsylvania, the Library of Congress, as well as in the LDS Church History Library and in the historical files of many newspapers.

The introduction and the first two chapters, "Raising Kane" and "Europe," give historical background and focus readers' attention on Kane as a reformer. Family, politics, and religion loom large in shaping Kane, as does Philadelphia society, its borderland locale between north and south, and its pride in its own culture and past. Kane's comment that he was "born with the gold spoon in my mouth, to station and influence and responsibility" bears on the entire the book (1). His mother was a member of a powerful political family, his brother an Arctic explorer, and his father was a confidant of presidents, a Philadelphia U.S. Court judge, and an ardent Democrat. All enjoyed access to America's social, political, and business elites. Although he frequently disagreed with Thomas, the elder Kane was also an inveterate supporter of his children, who sometimes lived in his Philadelphia homes and enjoyed all the perquisites of the era's no-holds-barred nepotism. Always of delicate health, Thomas still managed to make two youthful tours of England and France. There his tendency toward religious heterodoxy hardened, and he mingled with all the right Americans, adding depth to his personal connections.

The book's remaining eleven chapters progress by means of reform development, subject matter, and chronology. Chapter 3, "Beginnings of Reform," Chapter 8, "Reforming Marriage," and Chapter 12, "Developing Kane," describe how reform culture unfolded generally and influenced Kane and his family and brings to focus his marriage to Elizabeth Kane, who features largely in the book thereafter. Chapter 6, "Free Soil and Young America," Chapter 7, "Fugitive Slaves," and Chapter 11, "Honor, Reform, and War," pertain chiefly to antislavery issues, one of Kane's two great passions. Finally, Chapter 4, "Meeting the Mormons," Chapter 5, "The Suffering Saints," Chapter 9, "The Utah War, Act I," Chapter 10, "The Utah War, Act II," and Chapter 13 "Anti-Anti-Polygamy," trace his rescue work among the Saints.

Grow avoids most of the pitfalls of revisionism and writes in moderate but confident terms that enable him to distance himself from outmoded concepts without abandoning their essential meaning; an example is "Manifest Destiny," a widely-known concept he addresses as the "extension of liberty" (40–41 and 102–3). He also makes difficult judgments on a wide variety of themes and issues with fairness and civility.

A weakness of the book is its failure to include a bibliographic statement. One hopes the publishing trend is not to cast serious readers adrift in a heavily annotated sea of drifting footnotes. Readers may also wonder about conclusions that are largely drawn from the record of one man and his family. They may even wonder if historian Bernard De Voto's view of Kane as "neurotic" does not have its place when considering Kane's activities and viewpoints (30).

But in the main, *"Liberty"* opens new doors of understanding about the Civil War, Jacksonian Democracy, and Sectionalism's impact on the West. In terms of Mormon studies, it is refreshing partly because it helps bring Brigham Young back into the forefront of Mormon history after two decades of emphasis on Joseph Smith and his era.

As a reformer, Kane turned naturally to writing and publishing. His life was a "convergence of politics, reform, and print culture." He was adept at "using the press, staging events, and creating images to promote sympathy for various oppressed groups" (xvii). His influence upon some of the finest writers of Western Mormon history seems clearly suggested; William Mulder, Howard Lamar, and Wallace Stegner, for instance, have written in what might be termed a "Kane voice." Yet Mormon history in general has been less successful in finding a voice. Indeed, as Richard L. Bushman often reflects in his introspective *On the Road with Joseph Smith: An Author's Diary* on selling *Joseph Smith: Rough Stone Rolling,* Mormon historians have found it difficult to bring a fully appropriate voice to bear on both the Church and the profession of history. It is in the tensions of this context that *"Liberty"* is heartening. The voice of cultural studies as reflected by Grow offers a promising approach. Here's to Thomas L. Kane, friend of the Mormons. May he "change history" once again.

Charles S. Peterson (who may be reached via email at byu_studies@byu.edu) has served as Professor of History at Utah State University, editor of the *Western Historical Quarterly,* director of the Utah State Historical Society, and president of the Mormon History Association.

Thomas L. Kane
A Guide to the Sources

David J. Whitaker

Thomas Leiper Kane was born in 1822 to John K. Kane and Jane Duval Leiper. John K. Kane was a personal friend of several U.S. presidents, including Andrew Jackson and James K. Polk, who appointed John to the federal bench in Philadelphia. Until his death in 1858, John remained well connected to the power brokers in Washington, D.C. His son Thomas, also trained in the law, first learned of the Latter-day Saints through Philadelphia newspaper accounts that described the forced migration of the Mormons from their homes in Illinois in early 1846. Using connections through his father, Thomas began what would be a lifetime role as a friend, mediator, and peacemaker for the Mormons as they dealt with sometimes hostile government officials and tried to combat a negative public image. Thomas traveled west to the Mormon encampments along the Missouri River valley and assisted in the call of the Mormon Battalion in 1846; he publicized their plight in an influential lecture called *The Mormons*, published in 1850; and he was a major factor in the peaceful resolution of the Utah War in 1857–58. Thomas continued throughout his life to counsel, defend, and actively seek the welfare of the Latter-day Saints. He worked to soften anti-Mormon legislation while mentoring Latter-day Saint leaders like George Q. Cannon in the tasks of working with Congress and the public media to present a more positive and accurate view of the Latter-day Saints. Thomas's extensive correspondence with Brigham Young shows a deep friendship and trust developed between them. In 1872–73 Thomas and his wife, Elizabeth, journeyed to Utah and traveled with Brigham Young to his winter home in southern Utah. Elizabeth's *Twelve Mormon Homes* (1874) remains a classic account of Mormon social history.

Thomas Kane was also involved in a number of other causes during his lifetime, including the antislavery movement and educational and health reform. He was close to his brother Elisha Kent Kane, the famous arctic explorer, whose accounts Thomas helped edit for publication and whose accomplishments Thomas helped publicize. Thomas was a complex individual, never joining a church but living a deeply Christian life of selfless service. He suffered with poor health throughout his life but managed to accomplish much in spite of it. He died in 1883.

Thomas L. Kane (1822–1883)

I. Manuscript Sources

The L. Tom Perry Special Collections in the Harold B. Lee Library at Brigham Young University owns the largest collection of Thomas L. and Elizabeth W. Kane manuscripts in the world. Vault Manuscript 792 contains seventy-nine archival boxes of material, available to researchers on forty reels of microfilm. An eleven-hundred-page guide to this collection is available and includes a listing of important Kane material in other repositories as well as a biographical register of Kane family members and of people mentioned in the Kane papers. This extensive collection is described in David J. Whittaker, "New Sources on Old Friends: The Thomas L. Kane and Elizabeth W. Kane Collection," *Journal of Mormon History* 27 (Spring 2001): 67–94. The collection includes military material (Kane fought in the American Civil War, including in the Battle of Gettysburg); Kane's extensive correspondence with Mormon leaders; family correspondence; information on the development of Kane, Pennsylvania; and an extensive collection of Elizabeth's journals, miscellaneous writings, and scrapbooks. For both American and Mormon history, this collection is a treasure trove of material for the serious researcher. Very useful is Jana Darrington, "Ancestors and Descendents of Thomas L. Kane and Elizabeth W. Kane" (a professional genealogical compilation of two hundred pages relating to the extended Kane family), MSS 2212, L. Tom Perry Special Collections, BYU, 1999.

The BYU library has subsequently acquired additional Thomas L. Kane and Kane family manuscripts: Vault MSS 3190 was obtained in 2003 and contains an additional fourteen archival boxes. A guide (eighty-five pages) has also been prepared for these materials. The BYU library has been acquiring Kane manuscripts since about 1978, and additional collections are described in the guides mentioned above. A sampling includes the 1852 pocket diary of Thomas L. Kane (VMSS 796) and the 1858 pocket diary of Thomas L. Kane (VMSS 807). BYU also owns an extensive collection of Kane family photographs.

II. Published Sources

Thomas Leiper Kane (1822–1883)

A. Biographies

Grow, Matthew J. "'I Have Given Myself to the Devil': Thomas L. Kane and the Culture of Honor." *Utah Historical Quarterly* 73, no. 4 (Fall 2005): 346–64.

———. "'*Liberty to the Downtrodden*': Thomas L. Kane, Romantic Reformer." PhD diss., University of Notre Dame, 2006. Published by Yale University Press, 2009.

Zobell, Albert L., Jr. *Sentinel in the East: A Biography of Thomas L. Kane.* Salt Lake City: N. G. Morgan, 1965. Book based on his master's thesis (University of Utah, 1944), but without all the documentation in the thesis.

B. Civil War

Brandt, Dennis W. "The Bucktail Regiment." *Potter County Historical Society Historical Bulletin* 127 (January 1998): 1–4.

Imhof, John D. "Two Roads to Gettysburg: Thomas Leiper Kane and the 13th Pennsylvania Reserves." *Gettysburg* 9 (July 1993): 53–60.

Schroeder, Patrick A. *Pennsylvania Bucktails: A Photographic Album of the 42nd, 149th & 150th Pennsylvania Regiments.* Daleville, Va.: Schroeder Publications, 2001.

Thomson, O. R. Howard, and William H. Ranch. *History of the "Bucktails": Kane Rifle Regiment of the Pennsylvania Reserve Corps.* Philadelphia: Electric Printing Co., 1906.

C. Thomas Kane and the Mormons

Arrington, Leonard J. "'In Honorable Remembrance': Thomas L. Kane's Services to the Mormons." *Task Papers in LDS History*, No. 22. Salt Lake City: Historical Department, The Church of Jesus Christ of Latter-day Saints, 1978. Reprinted in *BYU Studies* 21, no. 4 (Fall 1981): 389–402.

Arrington, Leonard J., and Davis Bitton. *Saints without Halos: The Human Side of Mormon History.* Salt Lake City: Signature Books, 1981, 31–38.

Ashton, Wendell J. *Theirs Is the Kingdom.* Salt Lake City: Deseret Book, 1970, 167–205.

———. "Defender of Zion: Pioneer Benefactor Thomas L. Kane." *The Pioneer* 41 (September/October 1994): 4–7, 30.

Bitton, Davis. "American Philanthropy and Mormon Refugees, 1846–1849." *Journal of Mormon History* 7 (1980): 63–81.

Bowen, Norman R. "General Thomas L. Kane: How He Came to Write 'The Mormons.'" *Times and Seasons* 7 (December 1971): 2–5.

Bowen, Norman R., and Albert L. Zobell Jr. "General Thomas L. Kane: The Pioneer." *Ensign* 1 (October 1971): 2–5.

———. "General Thomas L. Kane: The Soldier." *Ensign* 1 (June 1971): 22–27.

Cannon, Donald Q. "Thomas L. Kane Meets the Mormons." *BYU Studies* 18, no. 1 (Fall 1977): 126–28. [Letter of Thomas Kane to George Bancroft, July 11, 1846.]

"Colonel Thomas L. Kane and the Mormons." In *Treasures of Pioneer History,* edited by Kate B. Carter, 6:69–128. Salt Lake City: The Daughters of Utah Pioneers, 1957.

Crocheron, Augusta Joyce. "Reminiscence of General Kane." *Contributor* 6 (September 1885): 475–77.

Fleek, Sherman L. "Thomas L. Kane, Friend of the Saints." *Mormon Heritage* 2 (May/June 1994): 36–42.

"Friends of the Pioneers." In *Heart Throbs of the West,* 2:27–41. Salt Lake City: The Daughters of Utah Pioneers, 1940.

Hartley, William G. "Fair-Minded Gentiles." *New Era* 10 (September 1980): 40–46.

Holzapfel, Richard N., and Jeffrey J. Cottle. "A Visit to Nauvoo: September 1846." *Nauvoo Journal* 7 (Spring 1995): 3–12.

Melville, J. Keith. "Colonel Thomas L. Kane on Mormon Politics." *BYU Studies* 12 (Autumn 1971): 123–25. [Letter of Thomas Kane to Church Leaders, September 24, 1850.]

Morgan, Nicholas G., Sr. "Thomas L. Kane: Peacemaker." *Instructor* 96 (July 1961): 246–47.

"The Mormons and Thomas Leiper Kane." *Collector* 58 (December 1944/January 1945): 1–10.

Poll, Richard D. *Quixotic Mediator: Thomas L. Kane and the Utah War.* Dello G. Dayton, Memorial Lecture, 1984. Ogden, Utah: Weber State College Press, 1984.

———. "Thomas L. Kane and the Utah War." *Utah Historical Quarterly* 61 (Spring 1993): 112–35.

Sawin, Mark Metzler. "A Sentinel for the Saints: Thomas Leiper Kane and the Mormon Migration." *Nauvoo Journal* 10 (Spring 1998): 12–27.
Walker, Ronald W. "Thomas L. Kane and Utah's Quest for Self-Government." *Utah Historical Quarterly* 69 (Spring 2001): 100–119.
Whittaker, David J. "New Sources on Old Friends: The Thomas L. Kane and Elizabeth W. Kane Collection." *Journal of Mormon History* 27 (Spring 2000): 67–94.
———. "Thomas Leiper Kane." In *American National Biography,* edited by John A. Garraty and Mark C. Carnes, 12:370–72. New York: Oxford University Press, 1998.
Winther, Oscar O. "Thomas L. Kane: Unofficial Emissary to the Mormons." *Indiana Historical Bulletin* 15 (February 1938): 83–90.
Young, Richard W. "Major General Thomas L. Kane." *Latter-day Saints' Millennial Star* 72 (February 24, 1910–March 3, 1910): 2-part series.
Zobell, Albert L., Jr. "Thomas L. Kane, Ambassador to the Mormons." *Utah Humanities Review* 1 (October 1847): 320–46.

D. Obituaries

Boyle, H. G. "A True Friend." *Juvenile Instructor* 17 (March 1, 1882): 74–75.
Cannon, George Q. "Editorial Thoughts." *Juvenile Instructor* 19 (January 15, 1884): 24–25.
Cannon, John Q. "The Spouting Well at Kane." *Contributor* 2 (February 1881): 151–53.
"Death of General Thos. L. Kane." *Deseret News* (January 2, 1884): 790–91.
Obituary, *The Press* [Philadelphia] (December 27, 1883).
Wells, Junius F., ed. "General Thomas L. Kane." *Contributor* 5 (March 1884): 234–39.

E. Published Writings of Thomas L. Kane

Kane, Thomas L. *Alaska and the Polar Regions.* New York: Journeymen Printer's Cooperative Association, 1868. [Lecture of Kane before the American Geographical Society, New York City, May 7, 1868.]
———. "Coahulia." *Proceedings of the American Philosophical Society Held at Philadelphia for Promoting Useful Knowledge* 16 (January 19, 1877): 561–67.
———. *The Mormons: A Discourse Delivered before the Historical Society of Pennsylvania, March 26, 1850.* Philadelphia: King & Baird, Printers, 1850. [A 2nd edition, expanded, also appeared in 1850.]
Winther, Oscar O., ed. *The Private Papers and Diary of Thomas Leiper Kane, A Friend of the Mormons.* San Francisco: Gelber-Lilienthal, 1937. [Printed at Grabhorn Press, limited to 500 copies.]

Elizabeth Dennistoun Wood Kane (1836–1909)

A. Biographies

Barnes, Darcee D. "A Biographical Study of Elizabeth D. Kane." Master's thesis, Brigham Young University, 2002.

B. Published Writings of Elizabeth Kane

Kane, Elizabeth Wood. *A Gentile Account of Life in Utah's Dixie, 1872–73: Elizabeth Kane's St. George Journal.* Edited by Norman R. Bowen. Salt Lake City: Tanner Trust Fund, University of Utah Library, 1995.

———. *Twelve Mormon Homes Visited in Succession on a Journey through Utah to Arizona.* Edited by Everett L. Cooley. Salt Lake City: Tanner Trust Fund, University of Utah Press, 1974. [This volume was first published in 1874 in Philadelphia by J. P. Lippincott.]

C. Articles

Bushman, Claudia L. *Mormon Domestic Life in the 1870s: Pandemonium or Arcadia?* Leonard J. Arrington Mormon History Lecture, Utah State University, October 7, 1999. Logan: Special Collections and Archives, Utah State University, 2000.

Solomon, Mary Karen Bowen, and Donna Jenkins Bowen. "Elizabeth Dennistoun Kane: 'Publicans, Sinners and Mormons.'" In *Women in the Covenant of Grace*, edited by Dawn Hall Anderton and Susette Fletcher Green, 212–30. Salt Lake City: Deseret Book, 1994.

Elisha Kent Kane (1820–1857)

Chapin, David. *Exploring Other Worlds: Margaret Fox, Elisha Kent Kane, and the Antebellum Culture of Curiosity.* Amherst and Boston: University of Massachusetts Press, 2004.

McGoogan, Ken. *Race to the Polar Sea: The Heroic Adventures and Romantic Obsessions of Elisha Kent Kane.* Toronto: Harper Collins, 2008.

Mirsky, Jeannette. *Elisha Kent Kane and the Seafaring Frontier.* Boston: Little, Brown and Company, 1954.

Sawin, Mark Metzler. *Raising Kane: Elisha Kent Kane and the Culture of Fame in Antebellum America.* Philadelphia: American Philosophical Society, 2008.

Index

Allen, James (captain) 43, 197
American Society for the Abolition of Capital Punishment 19–20
Anderson, Christian 160
Appleby, William I. 202, 203

Babbitt, Almon Whiting 57, 60–61, 63
Baskin, Robert N. 74, 75, 77
Bates, George C. 75, 76
Beehive House 145, 170
Bellevue, Utah 179, 180
Benton, Thomas Hart 42
Bernhisel, John M. 56–57, 57, 60–61, 63, 68, 70, 95–96, 102
Bigler, Jacob G. 170, 172
Black, Jeremiah 208
Blair, Seth M. 62, 63
Boreman, Jacob S. 74
Bowen, Norman 13
Bowman, Isabella 76
Boyle, Henry G. 194
Brandebury, Lemuel G. 64, 68–69
Brocchus, Perry E. 64–65, 65, 66, 68–69, 71
Brown, Canute 177
Brown, Homer 177
Browne, Joseph D. 48
Buchanan, James 24, 88, 89, 89, 94–95, 101, 102–104, 105, 106
Bucktail Regiment 27, 135, 192
Buffington, Joseph 63
Bunyan, John 137
Burton, Robert T. 75

Cain, Joseph 165
Cameron, Simon 78, 181
Camp Floyd, Utah 91
Cannon, George Q. 76, 124, 124, 146, 181
Carey, William 74
Cazier, John 177
Christensen, C. C. A. 34

Civil War 27, 135
Clinton v. Engelbrecht 78
Comté, Auguste 18, 119
Cope, Thomas P. 48
Council Bluffs, Iowa 125
Cumming, Alfred 105, 105, 110–111, 135
Cuyler, Cornelius C. 18–19

Dallas, George M. 20, 57, 58, 119
Dame, William 168, 209
Day, Henry R. 63, 65
Douglas, Stephen A. 59, 59, 61
Douglass, William 168
Drummond, W. W. 94

Edwards, John C. 42
Egan, Howard 72–73
Emerson, Philip H. 75
Emerson, Ralph Waldo 16, 16, 24, 25
Evans, David 175
Evans, Frank 13
Evarts, William M. 77

Female Medical College of Pennsylvania 22, 132, 133
Ferris, Benjamin G. 73
Fillmore, Millard 58, 61, 63–64, 65–66, 73, 206
Fillmore, Utah 179
Fish, Hamilton 78
Fitch, Thomas 76
Floyd, John B. 92, 92
Forney, John W. 103
Free Soilers 20–21, 55

Geary, John W. 25
Goldsbrough, Amelia Hallam 173
Goldsbrough, Ellen Jackson 173
Goldsbrough, Henry 165, 173–174
Goldsbrough, Sarah Ann. *See* Pitchforth, Sarah Ann Goldsbrough

Goldsbrough, Susannah Spencer 173–174
Grant, Jedediah M. 70–73, *71*, 127, 206, 213
  Three Letters to the New York Herald 206, *207*
Grant, Ulysses S. 74, 78, 205
Greeley, Horace 20, *20*
Grier, Robert C. 21
Grow, Matthew J. 101, 123

Hallam, Amelia 173
Hamilton, Madison 72
Harley, Edwin 179
Harley, Margaret 179
Harley, Mary Emily 179
Harris, Broughton D. 64, 65, 67, 68–69
Harvey, Elizabeth 172–173
Hawley, Cyrus M. 74
Heywood, Joseph L. 62
Hickman, William Adams 77
Hinckley, Ira N. 168, 179
Hooper, William H. 77
Howard, Sumner 75
Hughlings, Ann 163, 165
Huntington, William 43
Hyde, Orson 11, *12*

Indians 104, 165

Jackson, Andrew 119
Jackson, Ellen 173
Jefferson, Thomas 189
Jenkins, Mercy Pitchforth 172
Jenkins, Richard 172
Johnston, Albert Sidney *91*
Johnston's Army. *See* Utah War
Jones, William 75
Judd, John W. 173

Kane collection at Brigham Young University 48, 87, 106–107, 110–111, 223
Kane, E. Kent (Thomas's grandson) 13
Kane, Elisha (Thomas's grandfather) 118
Kane, Elisha Kent (Thomas's brother) 17, *17*, 40, 97, 147
  sources for 231
Kane, Elisha Kent (Thomas's son) 132, 136

Kane, Elizabeth Dennistoun Wood
  attitude of, toward Mormons 134, 136, 137–144, 209
  character of 117, 136
  courtship and marriage of 128–133
  diary of 99, 107
  family background of 120, 129
  family tree of 147
  hope of, for Kane to be a Christian 98, 101–102, 133–134
  humanitarian activities of 22
  opinion of Brigham Young 139–140, 209
  pictures of *116*, *130*, *131*, *136*, *154*
  received blessing 197
  sacrifices of, during mediation of Utah War 96, 133–134
  sources for 231
  studied medicine 22, 132, 136
  Twelve Mormon Homes 13, 137–138, 140, 155, 159, 181, 209
  view of plural marriage 140–142, 157, 159, 172, 180–181
  visited Mormons in Utah in 1872–73 136–144, 155–181, 156, 209–210
Kane, Harriet Amelia (Elizabeth's mother). *See* Wood, Harriet Amelia Kane
Kane, Harriet Amelia (Thomas's daughter) 132
Kane, Jane Duval Leiper 17, 119, 147
Kane, John (Elizabeth's grandfather) 118
Kane, John Kent (Thomas's brother) 98, 147
Kane, John Kintzing (Thomas's father)
  against Evangelical reform 18
  aided son 45
  background of 118–119
  descendents of 147
  donated money to Mormons 48
  and Fugitive Slave Act 21
  picture of *118*
  political influence of 17, 119
  sympathetic to Mormons 42
  wrote to President Buchannan about son's meeting 110
Kane, John (Thomas's great-grandfather) 118

Kane, Robert Patterson (Pat) 101, 103, 147
Kanesville, Iowa 48
Kane, Sybil Kent 13
Kane, Thomas Leiper
   accompanied Cumming to Salt Lake City 105
   advised Brigham Young 77, 209–210
   as agent for President Polk 42, 43, 45, 122
   alleged baptism of 13, 99, 99–102, 146, 202–205
   character of 14, 18, 25–27, 39–40, 117, 222
   correspondence of, with Brigham Young 193–194
   courtship and marriage of 128–133
   defended Mormons' religious liberty 22–24
   defended territorial government 70–73
   family background of 118–119, 223–224
   family tree of 147
   first account of Mormons in Iowa 49
   friendship of, with Brigham Young 95, 128, 136, 190, 191, 193–194, 206–213
   gave advice on early statehood quest 57, 59–61
   gave advice on territorial appointees 65–66
   health of 50, 59, 61, 119, 135, 143–144, 155, 197, 202, 204, 209
   helped Jesse Little 41
   helped recruit Mormon Battalion 43, 45, 197
   honesty of, in relationship with Brigham Young 206–208
   humanitarian activities of 14, 19–24, 40, 50–51, 191
   influenced by Comté 18, 119–120
   interactions of, with President Buchannan 93–94, 98, 103, 105
   interceded for Mormons in national politics 55–80, 92–96
   interest in education 210
   invited to investigate Mormonism 99–101, *100*, 204–205
   invited to serve as Utah's territorial delegate 206, 212
   journeyed to England and France 17–18
   learned Mormons practiced plural marriage 70, 127, 206–207
   lectured in New York 110
   lectured in Philadelphia 48–50, 61, 124–125
   marriage of 22
   mediated for Brigham Young 77–78, 92–96
   mediated Utah War 24, 102–106
   mediated with Indian agents 45, 46
   met Bessie 120–121
   military career of 27, 74, 135
   The Mormons 23–24, 125–126, 201, 202, 203
   obituary of 198–200
   patriarchal blessing for 11, 123, *196*, 196–197
   persuasive writings of 20, 23, 68, 70–73, 125–126, 134–135, 224
   pictures of *10, 116, 191, 199*
   poem to, by Eliza R. Snow 108–109
   political aspirations of 96, 206
   reasons of, to help and identify with Mormons 50–51, 96–99, 121–124
   as reformer 14, 19–22, 25
   religiosity of 19, 98, 119–120
   retold miracle of seagulls 201–202, 203
   sentenced to prison 21
   sketches by 45, *47*
   sources for 226–230
   statue of 13
   tombstone of *200*
   visited Mormons in Council Bluffs in 1846 43, 50, 122, 190, 194–197
   visited Mormons in Salt Lake City in 1858 24, 102
   visited Mormons in Utah in 1872–73 135–144, 155, 156, 157, 209–210
   visited Nauvoo, Illinois, in 1846 125, 201
   visited Utah in 1877 211
Kane, William Leiper (Willie) 128, 147
Kane, Pennsylvania 13, 25, 135, 191, *193*
Kane Memorial Chapel 13–14, *15, 192*

Kearney, Stephen W. 122
Kempis, Thomas à 120
Kendall, Amos 42
Kienke, Elizabeth Harvey 172–173
Kienke, John 172–173, *173*
Kienke, Sarah Barbara Pitchforth 172, *173*
Kimball, Heber C. 63, *64*
Kimberly, Amos E. 73
Kinney, John Fitch 75, *75*
Kniffen, Fred 168

Lawrence, Henry W. 76
Leiper, Jane Duval. *See* Kane, Jane Duval Leiper
Leiper, Thomas 119
Lion House 144, *145*, 166
Little, Jesse Carter 40–41, *41*, 43, 44, 121, 190
Livingston, Charles 67

Macfarlane, John M. 142
Mann, Samuel A. 75
maps
    of Mormon Camps on trail west 36
    of Nephi, Utah *163*, *178*
    of Utah towns visited by Kanes *156*
May, Mary Amelia Pitchforth 172
May, Sarah Alice Pitchforth 172
May, William Robert 172
McKean, James B. *74*, 74–79
Medill, William 42
Milton, John 137
Mitchell, Mary. *See* Pitchforth, Mary Mitchell
Mitchell, R. B. 46
Monroe, James 72
Morgan, Nicholas 13
Mormon Battalion 43–45, 47
The Mormons by Thomas L. Kane 23–24, 124–126, 201, *202*, 203
Morris, Joseph 75
Morrison, Archibald 121
Mount Nebo *175*
Mountain Meadows massacre 92, 208
Muir, John 175

Nauvoo, Illinois 125

Nephi, Utah 162, 163, *164*, 165–166, 177, 178, 179, 180, 182
New York Herald 70, 206

O'Kane, John. *See* Kane, John (Thomas's great-grandfather)

Paradise Lost by John Milton 137
Pennsylvania Bucktails 27, 135, *192*
Pennsylvania Free Soil Committee. *See* Free Soilers
Perkins, William G. 197
Phelps, Sally 190
Phelps, William W. 190
Phillips, Wendell 24
Pilgrim's Progress by John Bunyan 137
Pintura, Utah. *See* Bellevue, Utah
Pitchforth, Ann Hughlings 163, 165
Pitchforth, Annie 170
Pitchforth, Mary Amelia 172
Pitchforth, Mary Mitchell 163, 165, *166*, 172
Pitchforth, Mercy 172
Pitchforth, Samuel 162–163, 165, *166*, 173
Pitchforth, Sarah Alice 172
Pitchforth, Sarah Ann Goldsbrough 163, 165, 170, 172
Pitchforth, Sarah Barbara 172, 173
Pitchforth, Solomon 163, 165
Plitt, George 103
Poland Act of 1874 79
Polk, James K. *40*, *41*, 42–43, 57, 119
Poll, Richard D. 91
Pratt, Eleanor McComb 12, *13*
Pratt, Parley P. 165
Price, Eli K. 210

Quincy, Josiah 49, *49*

Reed, Lazarus H. 73
Richards, Willard 11, *62*, 63
Rose, Stephen B. 65

Scipio, Utah 180
Scott, Winfield 95, *95*
Sentinel in the East by Albert L. Zobell Jr. 10, 13
Shaver, Leonidas 73
Smith, George A. 102–103, 110

Smith, George Albert 13
Smith, John 11, 12, 123, 196, 196–197
Smith, Truman 60, 60, 61
Snow, Artemisia Beaman 143
Snow, Eliza R. 109
Snow, Erastus 168, 170
Snow, Zerubbabel 62, 63, 64, 65
Sparks, Edward 179
Spencer, Susannah 173–174
St. George, Utah 179
Staines, William C. 138, 138–139, 142
Stout, Hosea 77
Strickland, Obed F. 74
Stuart, Alexander H. H. 65
Sumner, Charles 24

Taylor, John 94, 165, 211
Taylor, Zachary 58, 60–61
Thomas L. Kane Memorial Chapel 13–14, 15, 192
Thompson, Daniel 168
Three Letters to the New York Herald by J. M. Grant 206, 207
Twelve Mormon Homes by Elizabeth W. Kane 13, 137–138, 140, 155, 159, 181, 209

Utah, statehood quest for 56–61, 89
Utah War
    Kane's mediation of peace in 24
    reasons for 88–89
    results of 102–106
    terminology of 89, 91–92
Ute Indians 165

Van Dyke, James C. 87, 97–98, 102
Vaughn, John M. 72, 73

Warren, Fitz Henry 60
Warwood, William 179
Washington, D.C., Union 101, 103
Webster, Daniel 63, 63
Wells, Daniel H. 76, 77, 111
Whitney, Newel K. 48, 63, 64
Winter Quarters, Nebraska 34, 48
Wood, Harriet Amelia Kane 120, 147

Wood, William 120, 120–121, 127, 132, 147
Woodruff, Wilford 57, 58, 59, 213

Young, Ann Eliza Webb Dee 78, 79
Young, Brigham
    correspondence of, with Kane 193–194
    described by Bessie Kane 139
    divorced by Ann Eliza Young 78–79
    efforts to replace, as territorial governor 88
    feelings on Mountain Meadows massacre 208
    friendship of, with Kane 95, 128, 136, 190, 191, 193–194, 206–213
    honesty of, in relationship with Kane 207, 212
    ideology of, as governor 89
    indicted on cohabitation 76
    influenced by Kane during Utah War 104–105
    invited Kane to investigate Mormonism 99–101, 100, 204–205
    letters of, to sons 190
    Mormon Battalion and 45
    nominated territorial governor of Utah 63, 65–66
    offered Kane territorial delegate position 206, 212
    pictures of 37, 211
    plans of, for westward trek 36–39, 45
    prayed over Kane 144, 209
    proclaimed martial law, 90
    promised Kane he would do great work 12
    wrote to Kane for help with gubernatorial appointment 92–93
    wrote to Kane for help with McKean 76, 76–77
    wrote to President Fillmore 67–68
Young, Eliza B. 141
Young, John W. 76, 210
Young, Joseph 202, 203
Young, Lucy 141

Zobell, Albert L., Jr. 10, 13